SHADOW WALK™

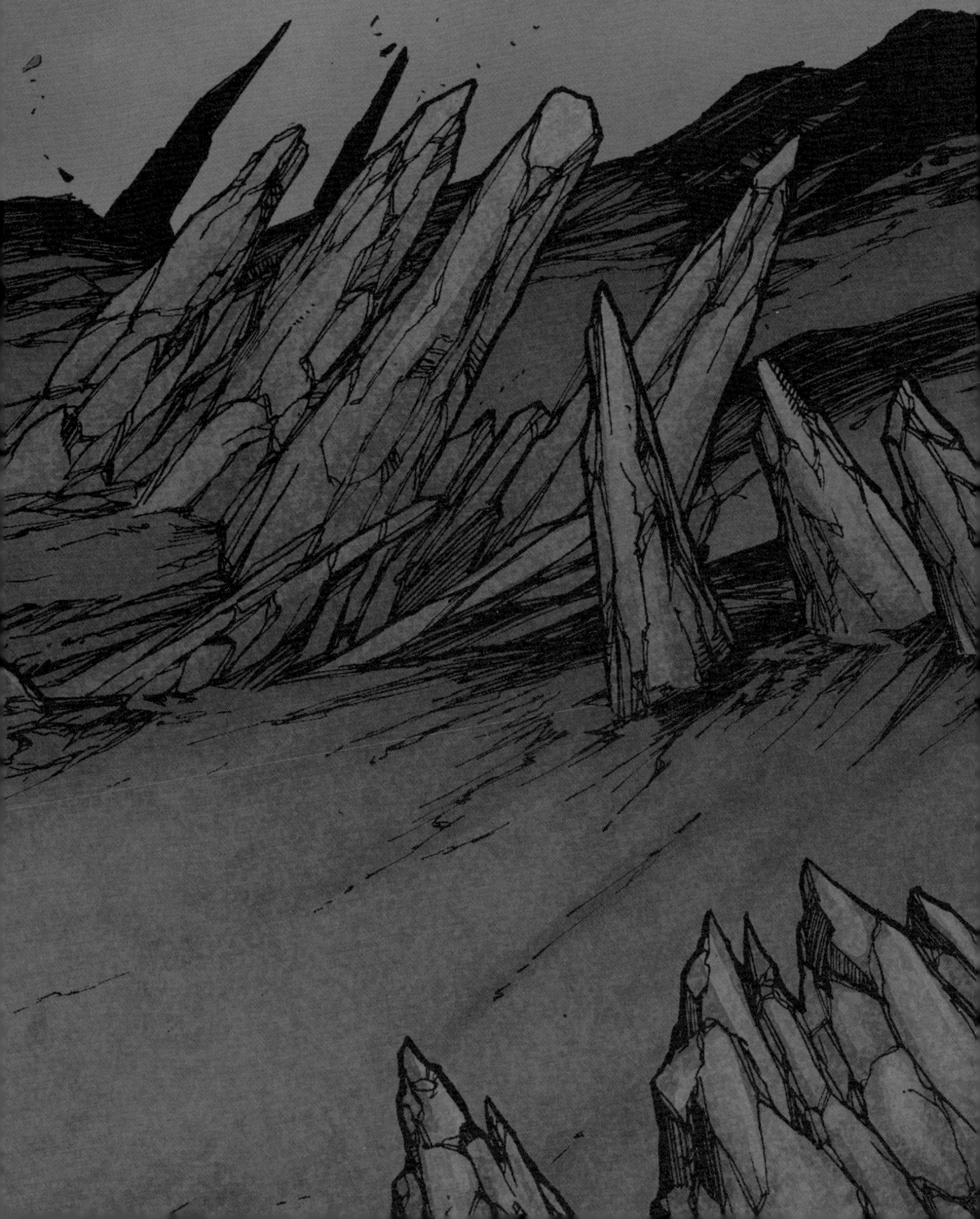

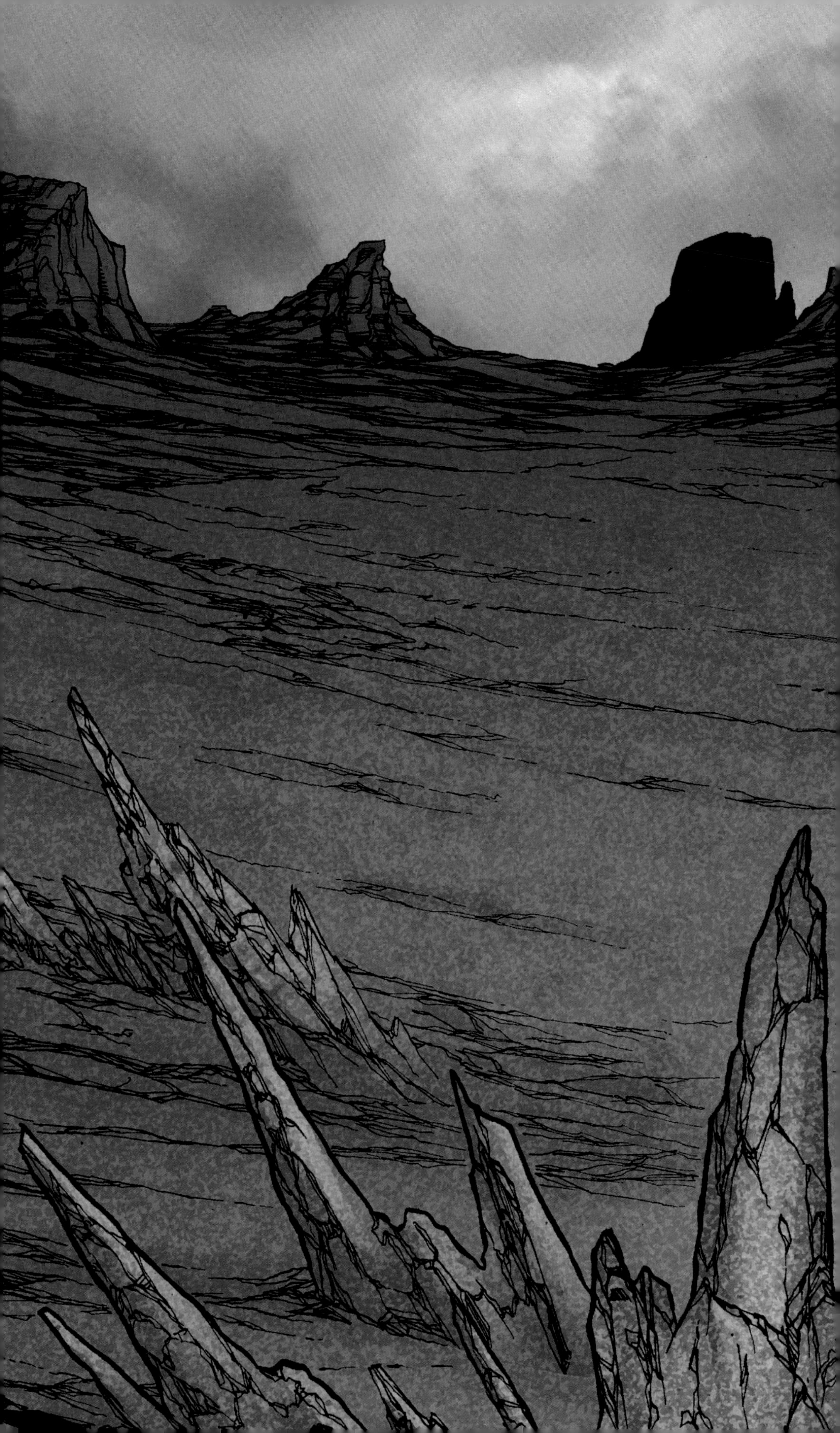

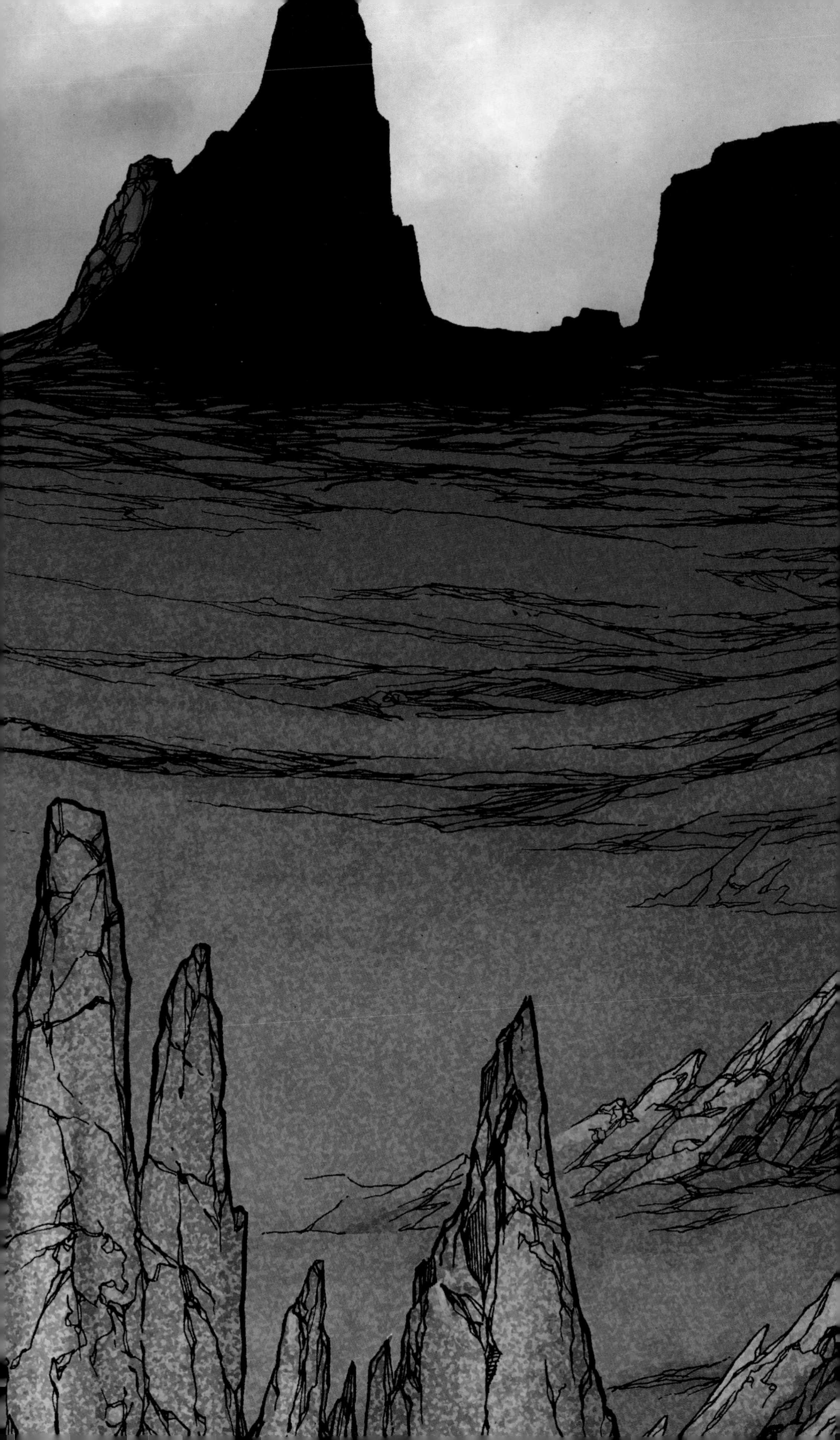

LEGENDARY™

Legendary Comics
4000 Warner Blvd. Bldg. 76
Burbank, CA 91522

THOMAS TULL Chairman & Chief Executive Officer
JON JASHNI President & Chief Creative Officer
J. MARTIN WILLHITE Chief Operating Officer & General Counsel
BOB SCHRECK Editor-In-Chief
EMILY CASTEL EVP, Marketing & Transmedia
CHRIS ERB EVP, Consumer Marketing
JOEL CHIODI EVP, Theatrical Marketing
BARNABY LEGG Director, Transmedia Strategy
JESSICA KANTOR Vice President, Business & Legal Affairs
NATALIE LEVECK Legal Counsel
GREG TUMBARELLO Associate Editor
DAVID SADOVE Publishing Operations Coordinator
DANIEL BARBER Copywriter
AUGIE CHUN Director, Digital
LUKE BESHAR Social Community Coordinator
DANIEL BRITTON Digital Coordinator

First Printing: November 2013
10 9 8 7 6 5 4 3 2 1

ISBN-10: 0-7851-5397-7
ISBN-13: 978-0-7851-5397-9

Printed in the United States
Manufactured between 9/27/2013 and 11/11/2013
by R.R. DONNELLEY, INC., SALEM, VA, USA.

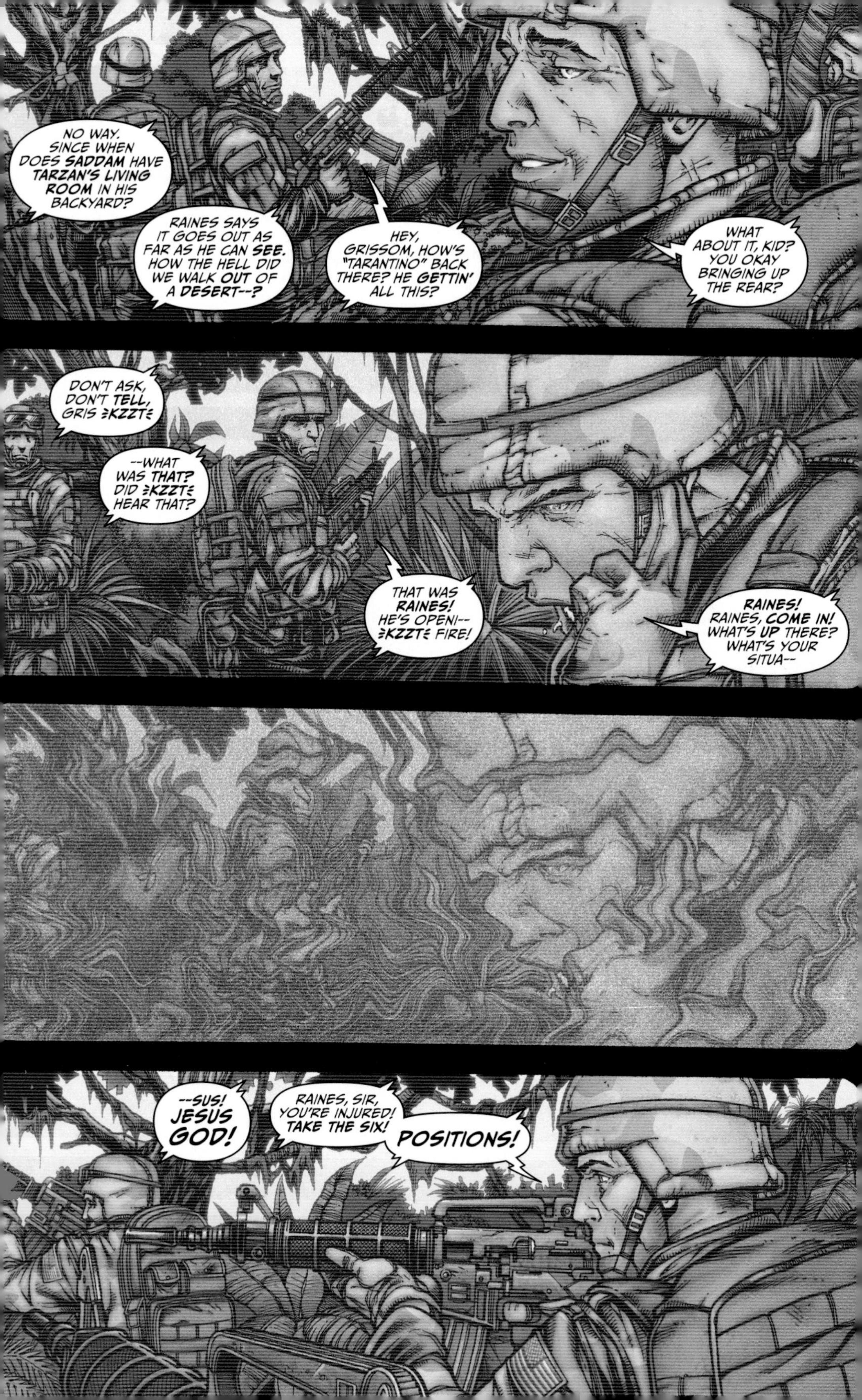
NO WAY. SINCE WHEN DOES SADDAM HAVE TARZAN'S LIVING ROOM IN HIS BACKYARD?
RAINES SAYS IT GOES OUT AS FAR AS HE CAN SEE. HOW THE HELL DID WE WALK OUT OF A DESERT--?
HEY, GRISSOM, HOW'S "TARANTINO" BACK THERE? HE GETTIN' ALL THIS?
WHAT ABOUT IT, KID? YOU OKAY BRINGING UP THE REAR?
DON'T ASK, DON'T TELL, GRIS ≡KZZT≡
--WHAT WAS THAT? DID ≡KZZT≡ HEAR THAT?
THAT WAS RAINES! HE'S OPENI-- ≡KZZT≡ FIRE!
RAINES! RAINES, COME IN! WHAT'S UP THERE? WHAT'S YOUR SITUA--
--SUS! JESUS GOD!
RAINES, SIR, YOU'RE INJURED! TAKE THE SIX!
POSITIONS!

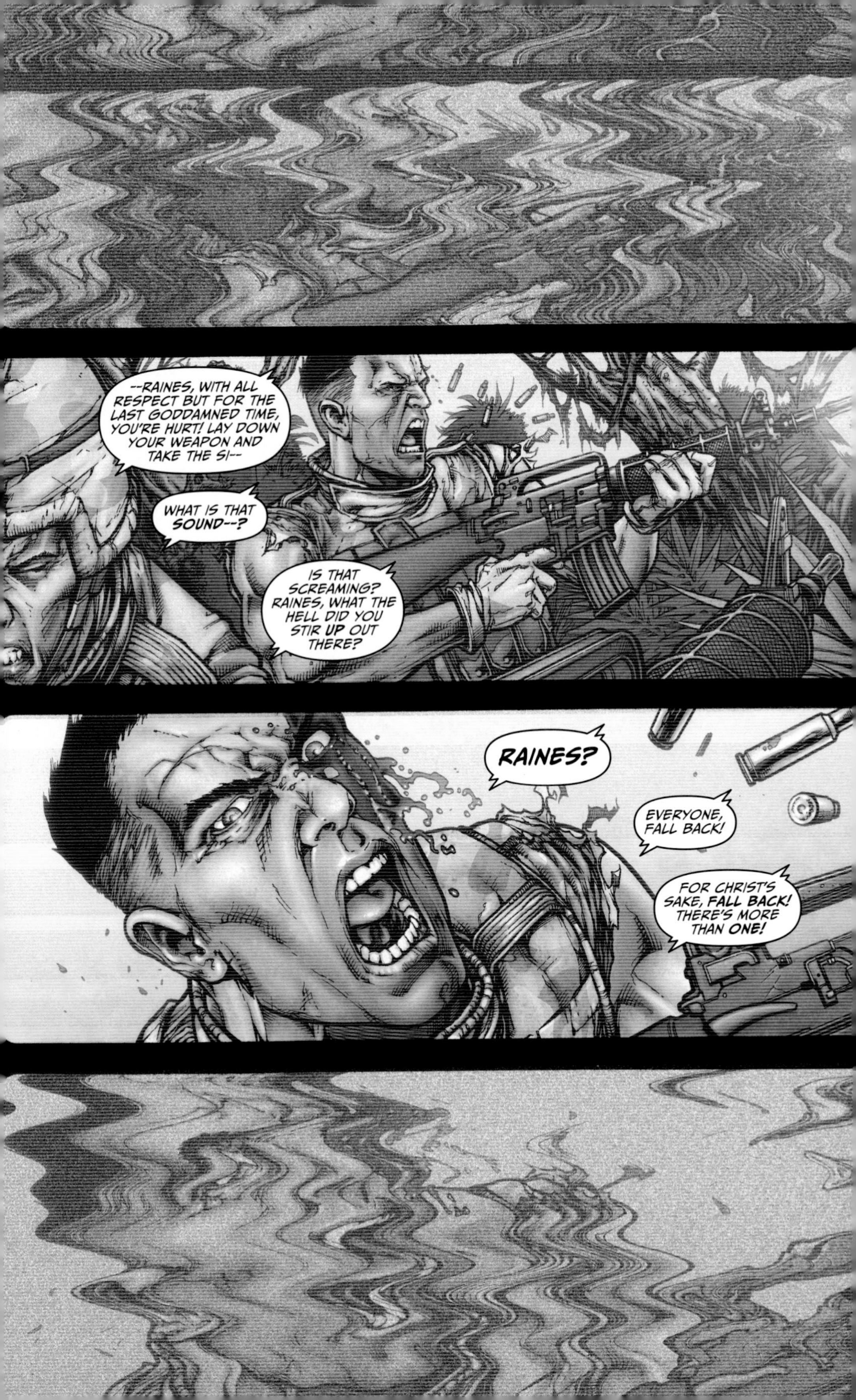
--RAINES, WITH ALL RESPECT BUT FOR THE LAST GODDAMNED TIME, YOU'RE HURT! LAY DOWN YOUR WEAPON AND TAKE THE SI--
WHAT IS THAT SOUND--?
IS THAT SCREAMING? RAINES, WHAT THE HELL DID YOU STIR UP OUT THERE?
RAINES?
EVERYONE, FALL BACK!
FOR CHRIST'S SAKE, FALL BACK! THERE'S MORE THAN ONE!

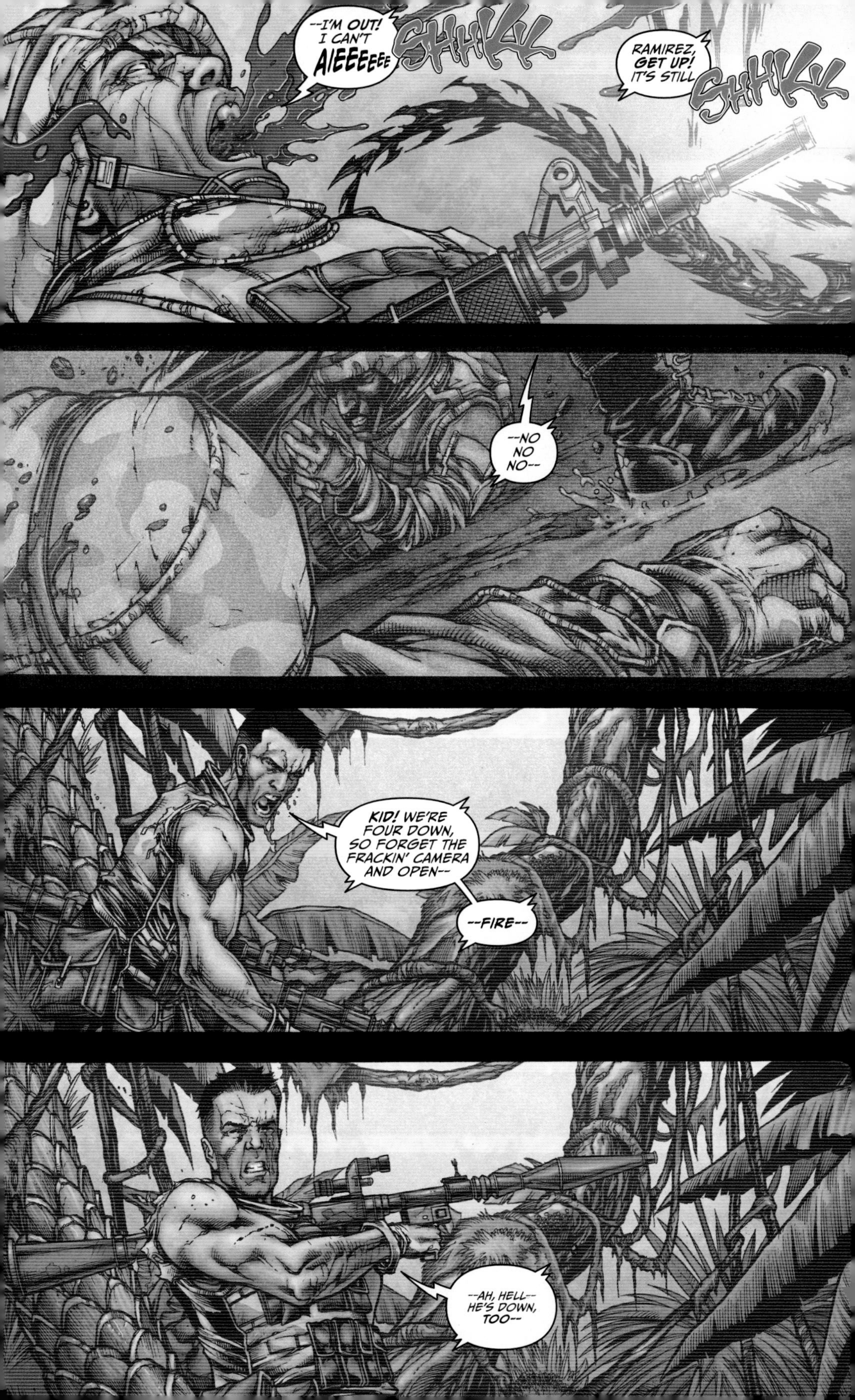
--I'M OUT! I CAN'T AIEEEEEE
SHHKKK
RAMIREZ, GET UP! IT'S STILL
SHHKKK
--NO NO NO--
KID! WE'RE FOUR DOWN, SO FORGET THE FRACKIN' CAMERA AND OPEN--
--FIRE--
--AH, HELL-- HE'S DOWN, TOO--

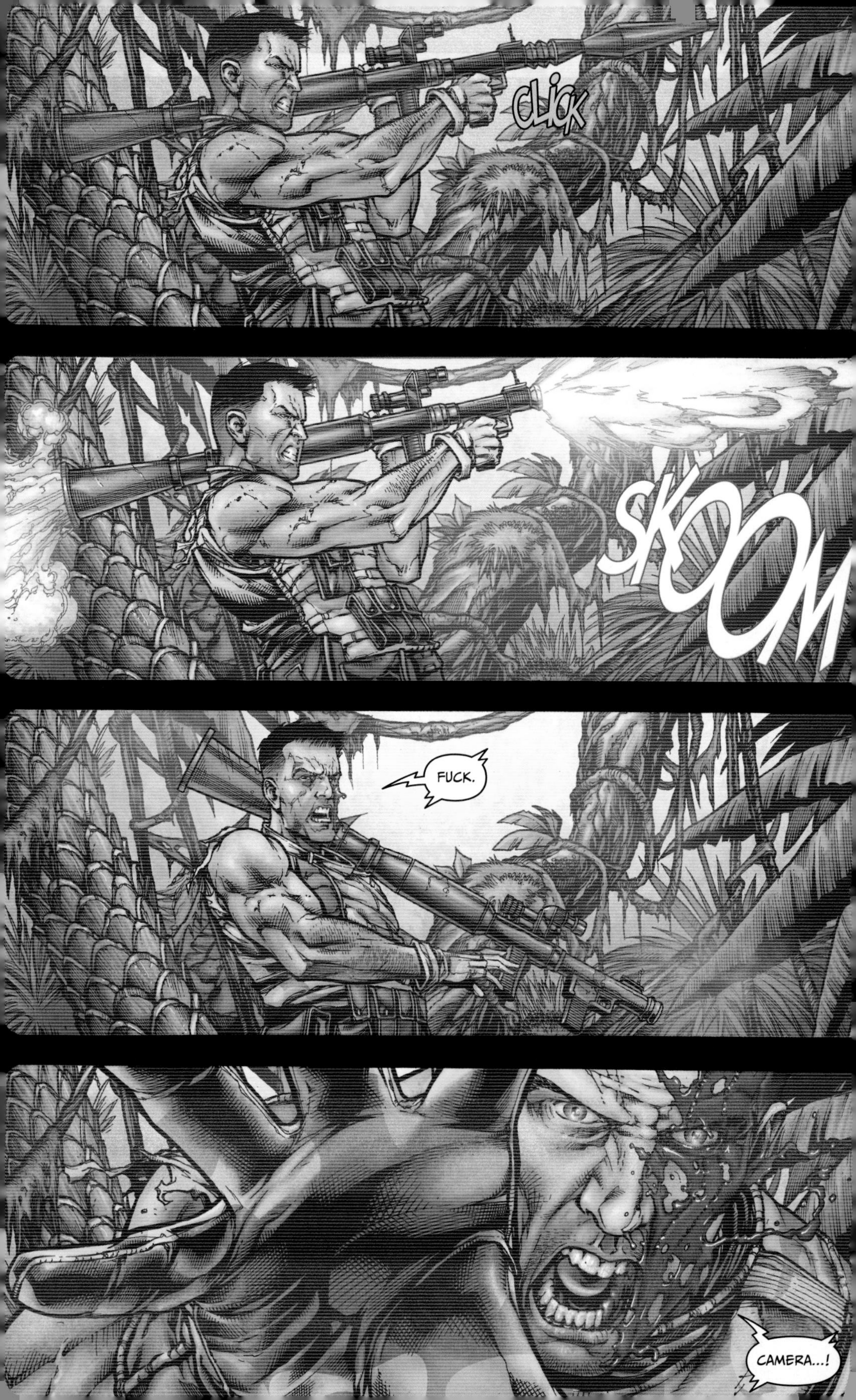
CLICK
SKOOM
FUCK.
CAMERA...!

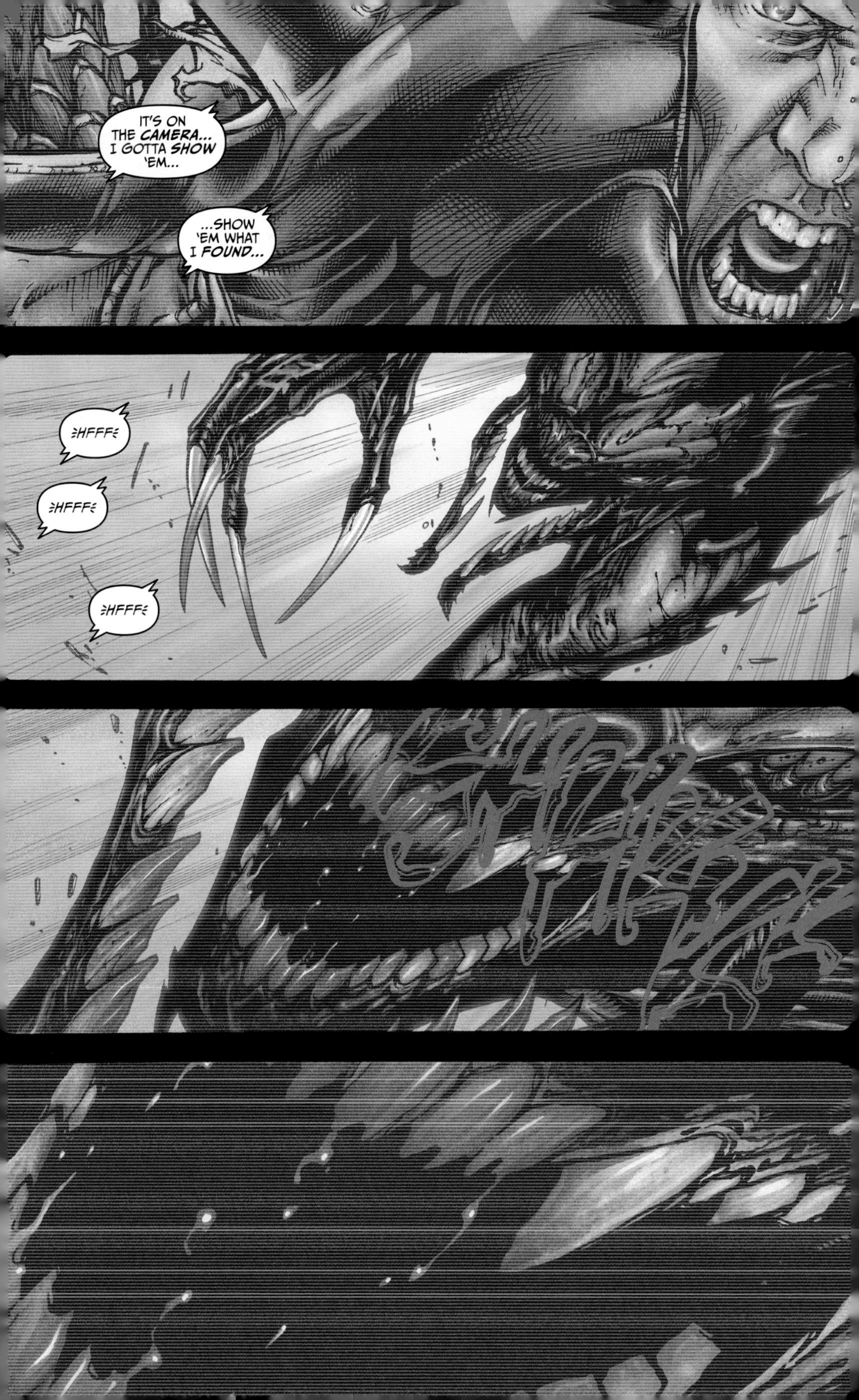
IT'S ON THE CAMERA... I GOTTA SHOW 'EM...
...SHOW 'EM WHAT I FOUND...
HFFF
HFFF
HFFF

SHADOW WALK

Writer
MARK WAID

Penciler
SHANE DAVIS

Inker
MARK MORALES

Colorist
MORRY HOLLOWELL

Letterer
JARED K. FLETCHER

Pre-Press/Production
NICOLAS SIENTY

Book Design/Production
STEVEN BIRCH

Associate Editor
GREG TUMBARELLO

Editor
BOB SCHRECK

Story Created by
THOMAS TULL
MAX BROOKS
MARK WAID

Artwork Created & Designed by
SHANE DAVIS

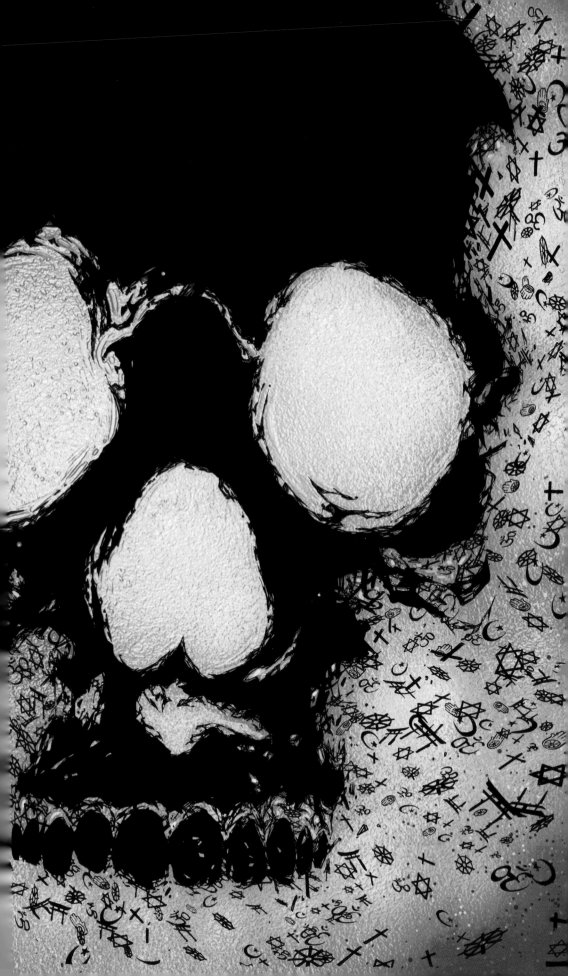

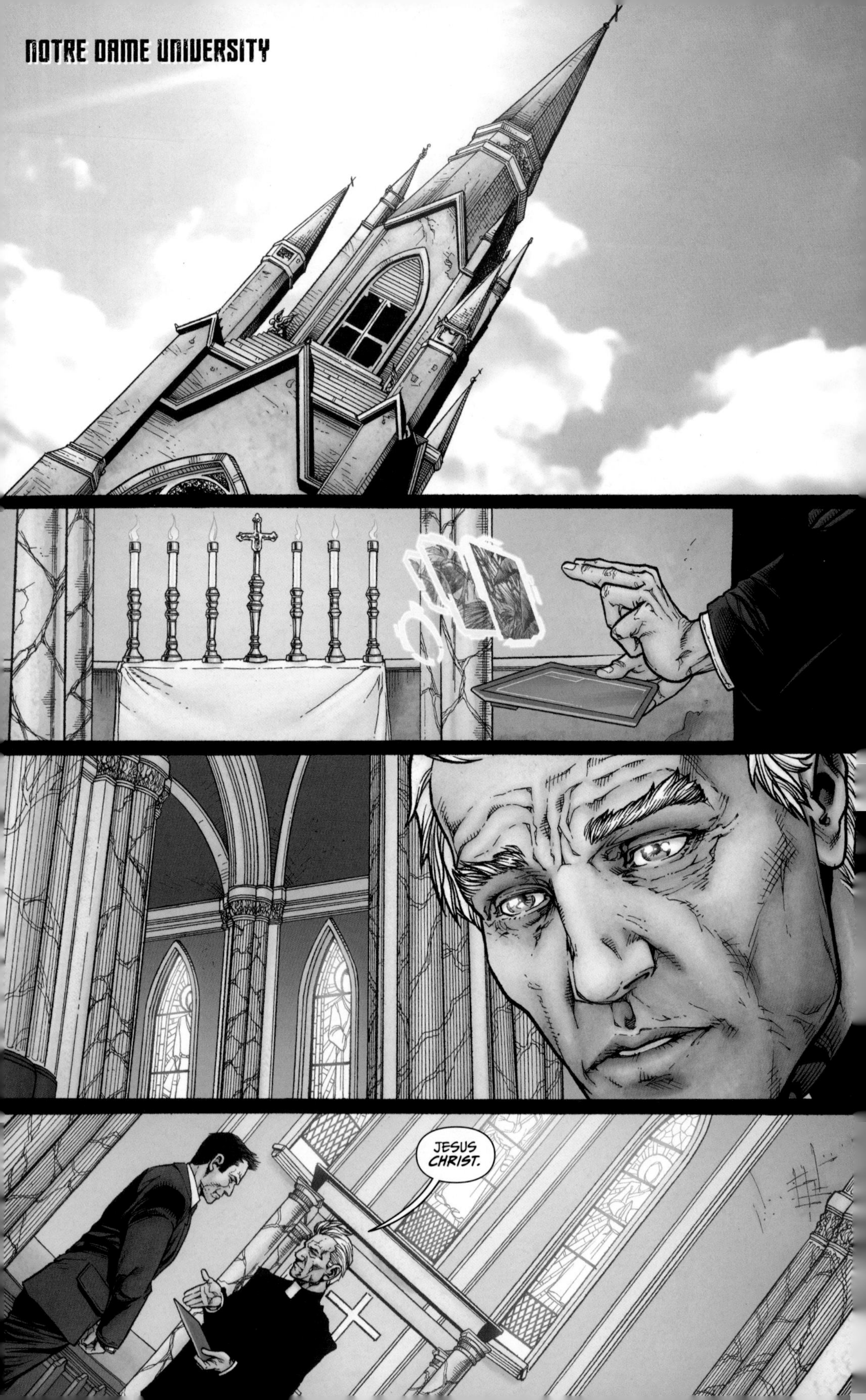
NOTRE DAME UNIVERSITY
JESUS CHRIST.

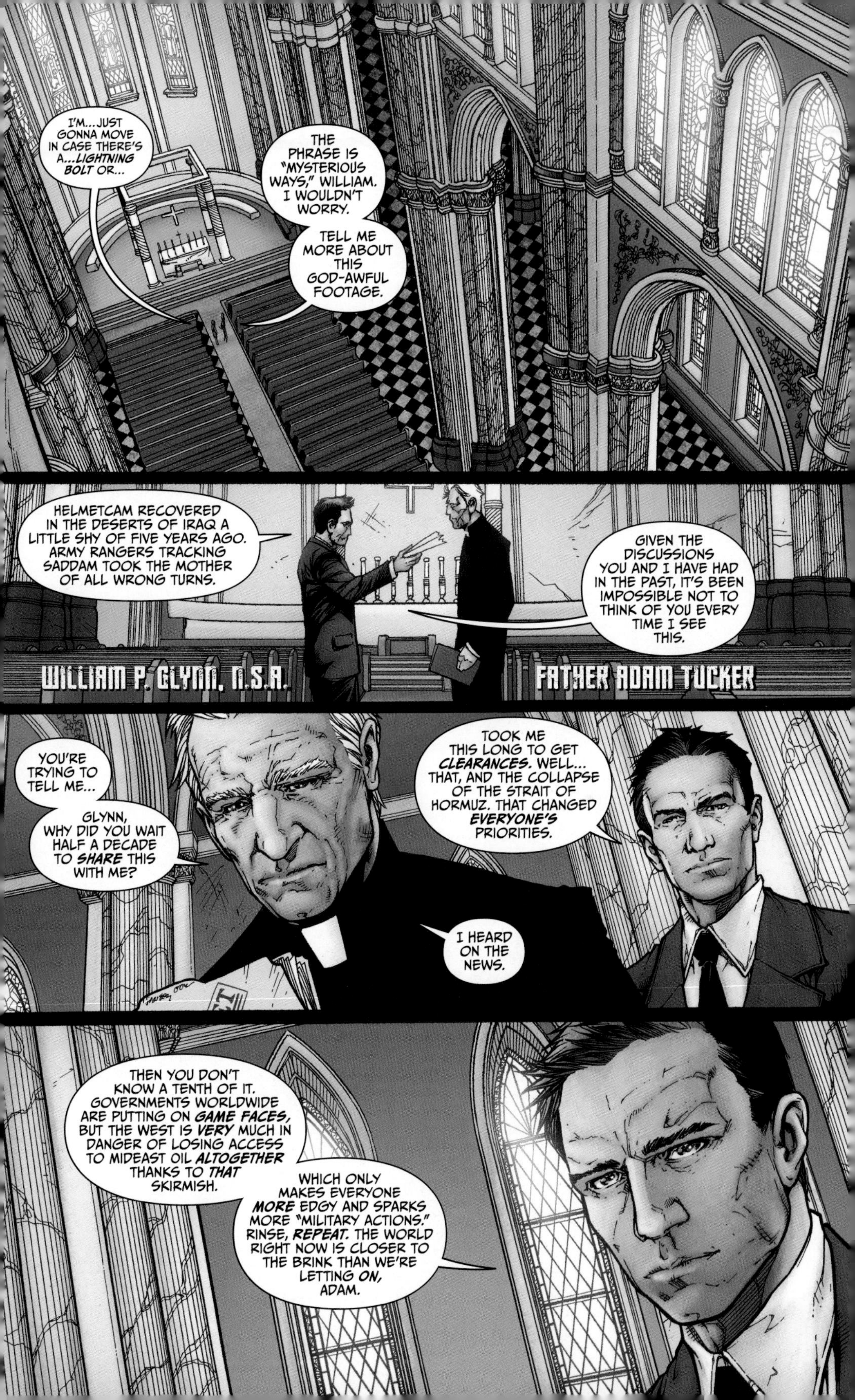

I'M...JUST GONNA MOVE IN CASE THERE'S A...LIGHTNING BOLT OR...
THE PHRASE IS "MYSTERIOUS WAYS," WILLIAM. I WOULDN'T WORRY.
TELL ME MORE ABOUT THIS GOD-AWFUL FOOTAGE.
HELMETCAM RECOVERED IN THE DESERTS OF IRAQ A LITTLE SHY OF FIVE YEARS AGO. ARMY RANGERS TRACKING SADDAM TOOK THE MOTHER OF ALL WRONG TURNS.
GIVEN THE DISCUSSIONS YOU AND I HAVE HAD IN THE PAST, IT'S BEEN IMPOSSIBLE NOT TO THINK OF YOU EVERY TIME I SEE THIS.
WILLIAM P. GLYNN, N.S.A.
FATHER ADAM TUCKER
YOU'RE TRYING TO TELL ME...
GLYNN, WHY DID YOU WAIT HALF A DECADE TO SHARE THIS WITH ME?
TOOK ME THIS LONG TO GET CLEARANCES. WELL... THAT, AND THE COLLAPSE OF THE STRAIT OF HORMUZ. THAT CHANGED EVERYONE'S PRIORITIES.
I HEARD ON THE NEWS.
THEN YOU DON'T KNOW A TENTH OF IT. GOVERNMENTS WORLDWIDE ARE PUTTING ON GAME FACES, BUT THE WEST IS VERY MUCH IN DANGER OF LOSING ACCESS TO MIDEAST OIL ALTOGETHER THANKS TO THAT SKIRMISH.
WHICH ONLY MAKES EVERYONE MORE EDGY AND SPARKS MORE "MILITARY ACTIONS." RINSE, REPEAT. THE WORLD RIGHT NOW IS CLOSER TO THE BRINK THAN WE'RE LETTING ON, ADAM.

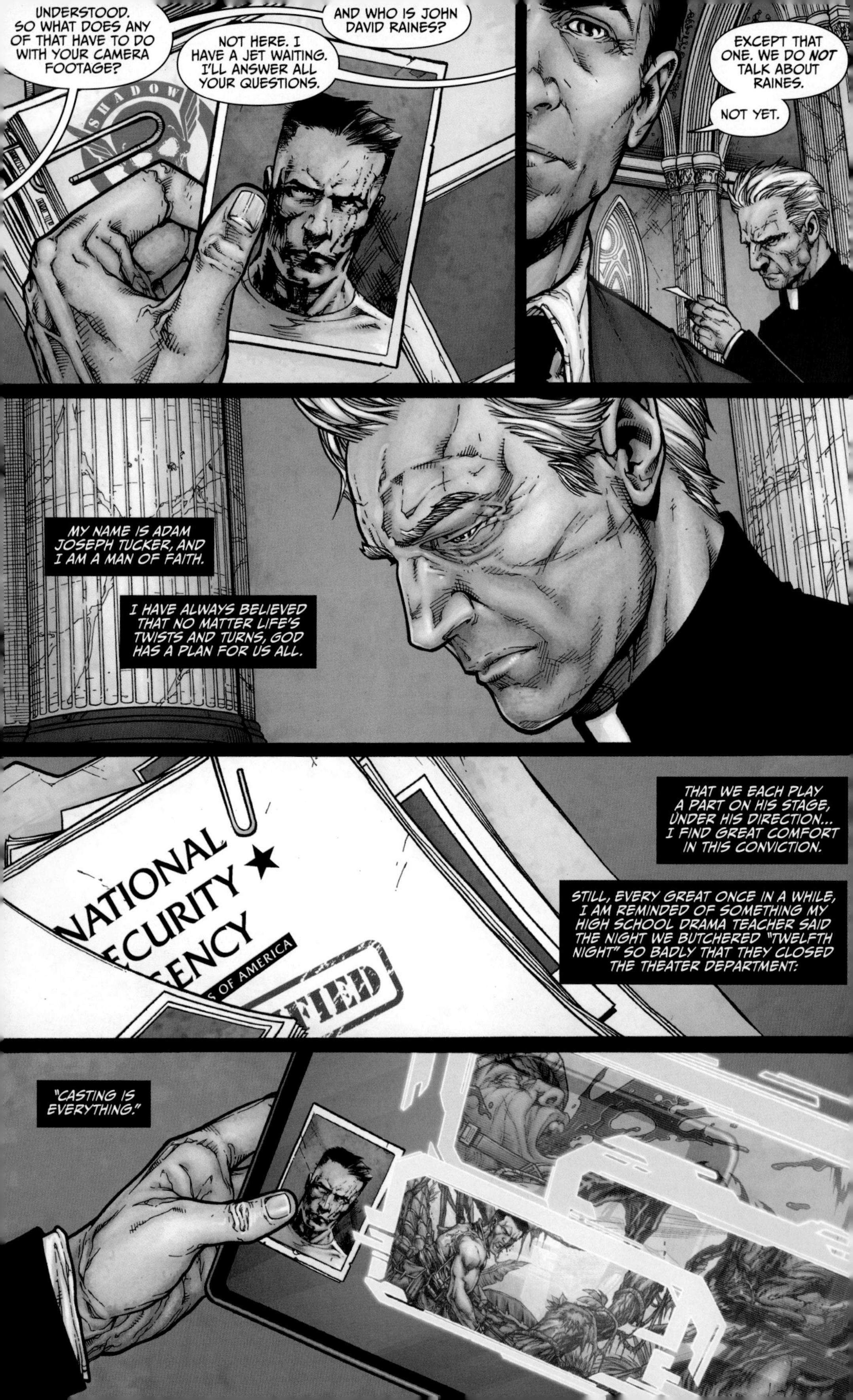
UNDERSTOOD. SO WHAT DOES ANY OF THAT HAVE TO DO WITH YOUR CAMERA FOOTAGE?
NOT HERE. I HAVE A JET WAITING. I'LL ANSWER ALL YOUR QUESTIONS.
AND WHO IS JOHN DAVID RAINES?
SHADOW
EXCEPT THAT ONE. WE DO *NOT* TALK ABOUT RAINES.
NOT YET.
MY NAME IS ADAM JOSEPH TUCKER, AND I AM A MAN OF FAITH.
I HAVE ALWAYS BELIEVED THAT NO MATTER LIFE'S TWISTS AND TURNS, GOD HAS A PLAN FOR US ALL.
NATIONAL SECURITY AGENCY
THAT WE EACH PLAY A PART ON HIS STAGE, UNDER HIS DIRECTION... I FIND GREAT COMFORT IN THIS CONVICTION.
STILL, EVERY GREAT ONCE IN A WHILE, I AM REMINDED OF SOMETHING MY HIGH SCHOOL DRAMA TEACHER SAID THE NIGHT WE BUTCHERED "TWELFTH NIGHT" SO BADLY THAT THEY CLOSED THE THEATER DEPARTMENT:
"CASTING IS EVERYTHING."

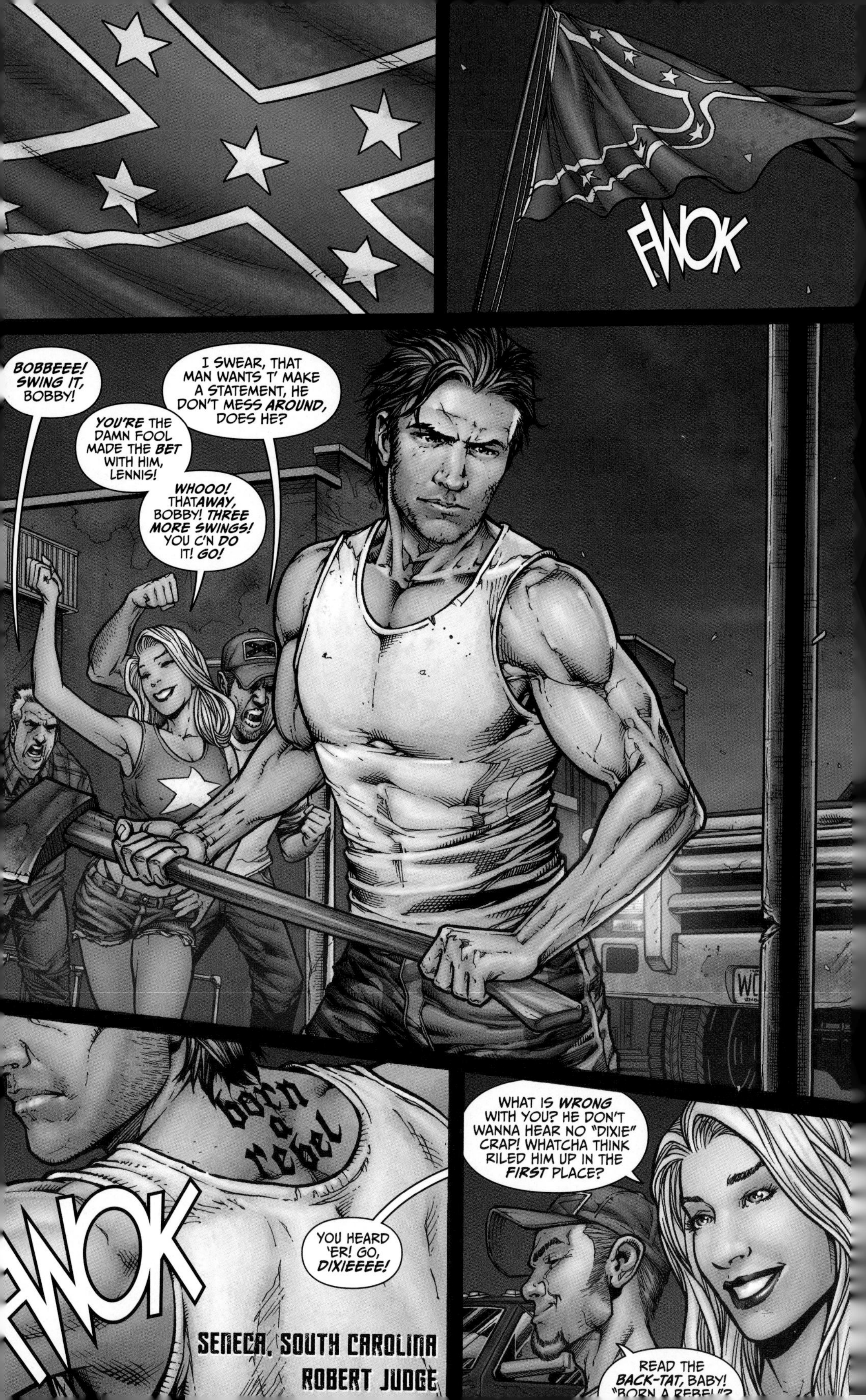
FWOK
BOBBEEE! SWING IT, BOBBY!
I SWEAR, THAT MAN WANTS T' MAKE A STATEMENT, HE DON'T MESS AROUND, DOES HE?
YOU'RE THE DAMN FOOL MADE THE BET WITH HIM, LENNIS!
WHOOO! THATAWAY, BOBBY! THREE MORE SWINGS! YOU C'N DO IT! GO!
born a rebel
FWOK
YOU HEARD 'ER! GO, DIXIEEEE!
SENECA, SOUTH CAROLINA
ROBERT JUDGE
WHAT IS WRONG WITH YOU? HE DON'T WANNA HEAR NO "DIXIE" CRAP! WHATCHA THINK RILED HIM UP IN THE FIRST PLACE?
READ THE BACK-TAT, BABY!

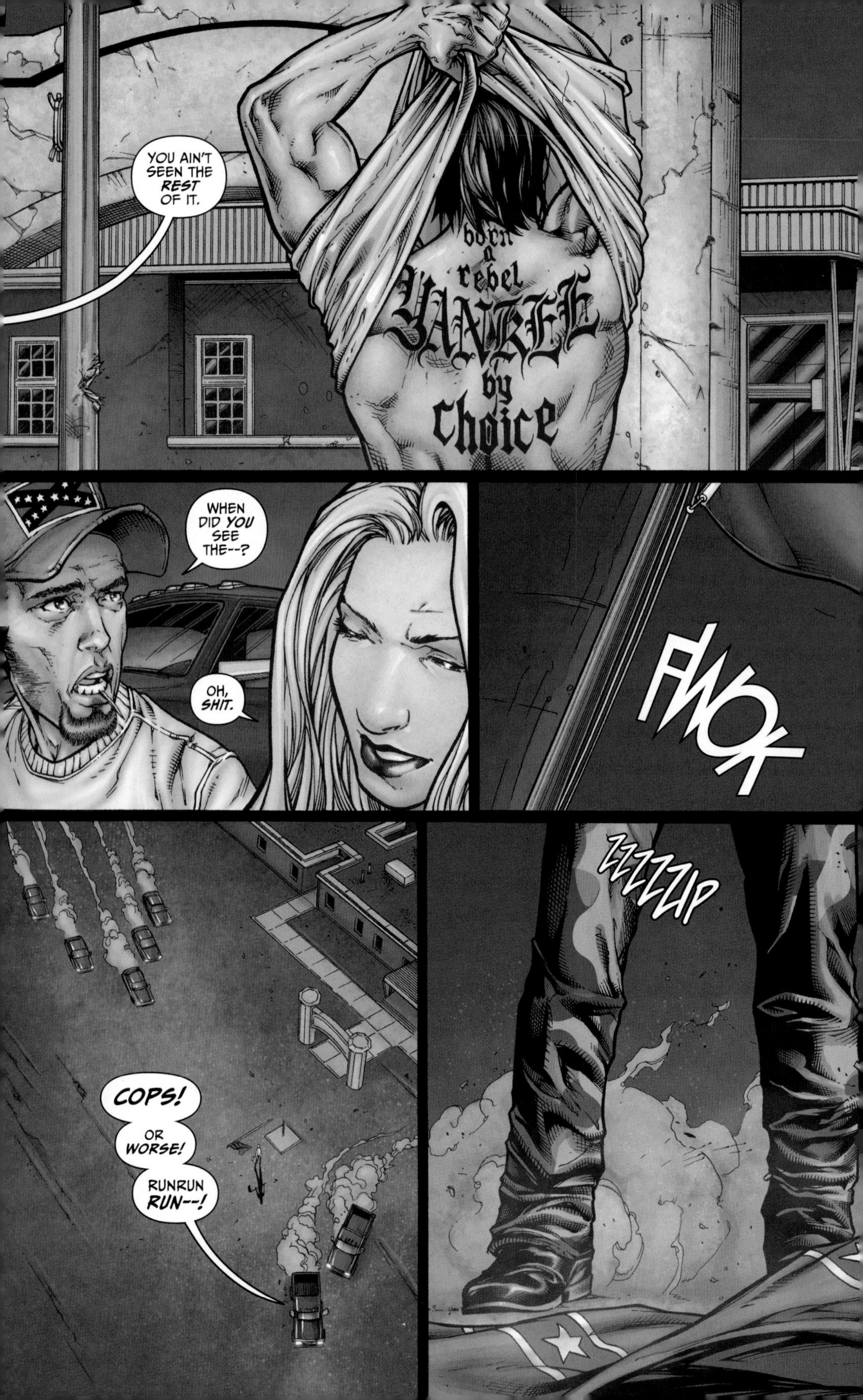
YOU AIN'T SEEN THE REST OF IT.
born a rebel YANKEE by Choice
WHEN DID YOU SEE THE--?
OH, SHIT.
FWOK
COPS!
OR WORSE!
RUNRUN RUN--!
ZZZZZIP

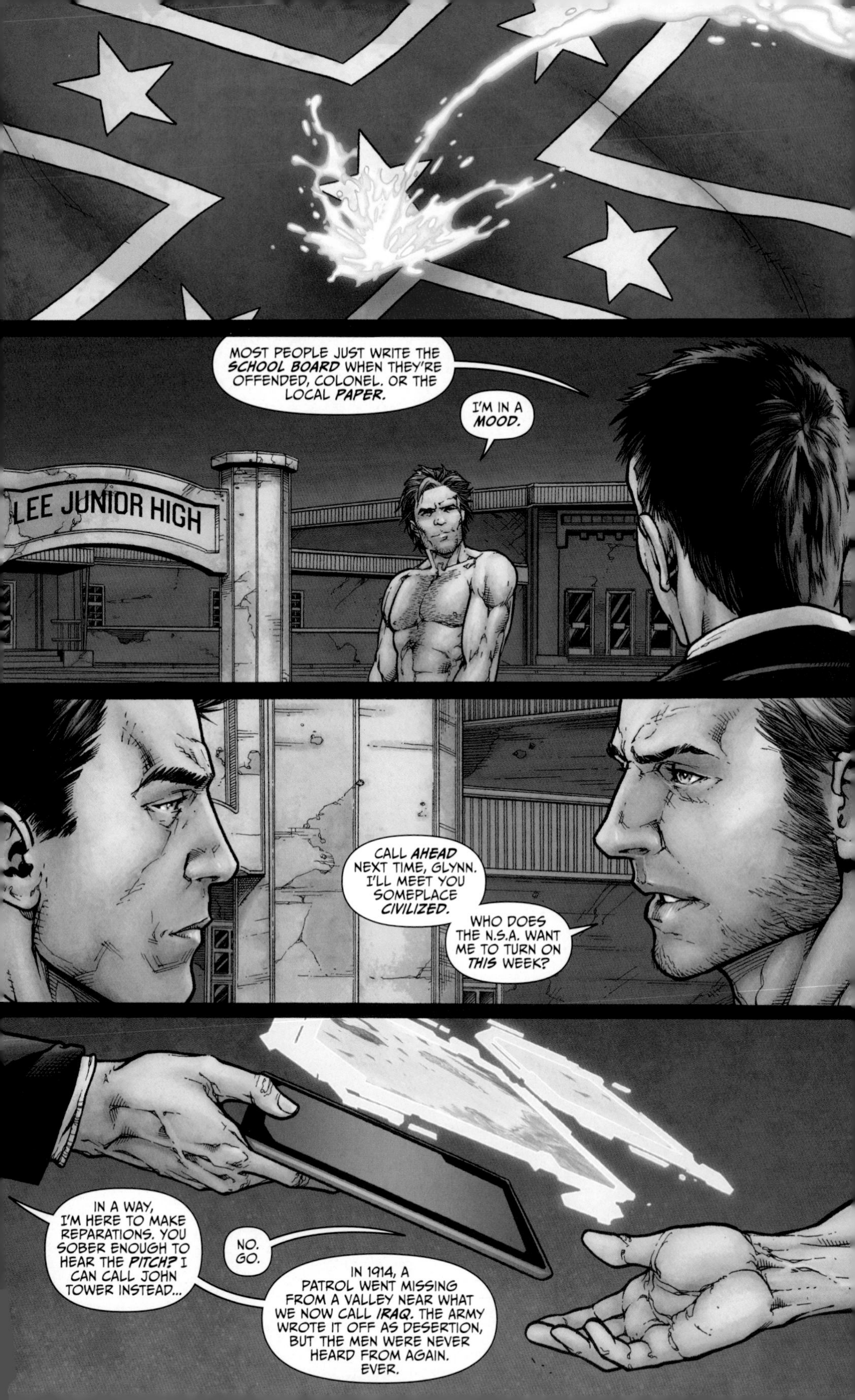
MOST PEOPLE JUST WRITE THE SCHOOL BOARD WHEN THEY'RE OFFENDED, COLONEL. OR THE LOCAL PAPER.
I'M IN A MOOD.
LEE JUNIOR HIGH
CALL AHEAD NEXT TIME, GLYNN. I'LL MEET YOU SOMEPLACE CIVILIZED.
WHO DOES THE N.S.A. WANT ME TO TURN ON THIS WEEK?
IN A WAY, I'M HERE TO MAKE REPARATIONS. YOU SOBER ENOUGH TO HEAR THE PITCH? I CAN CALL JOHN TOWER INSTEAD...
NO. GO.
IN 1914, A PATROL WENT MISSING FROM A VALLEY NEAR WHAT WE NOW CALL IRAQ. THE ARMY WROTE IT OFF AS DESERTION, BUT THE MEN WERE NEVER HEARD FROM AGAIN. EVER.

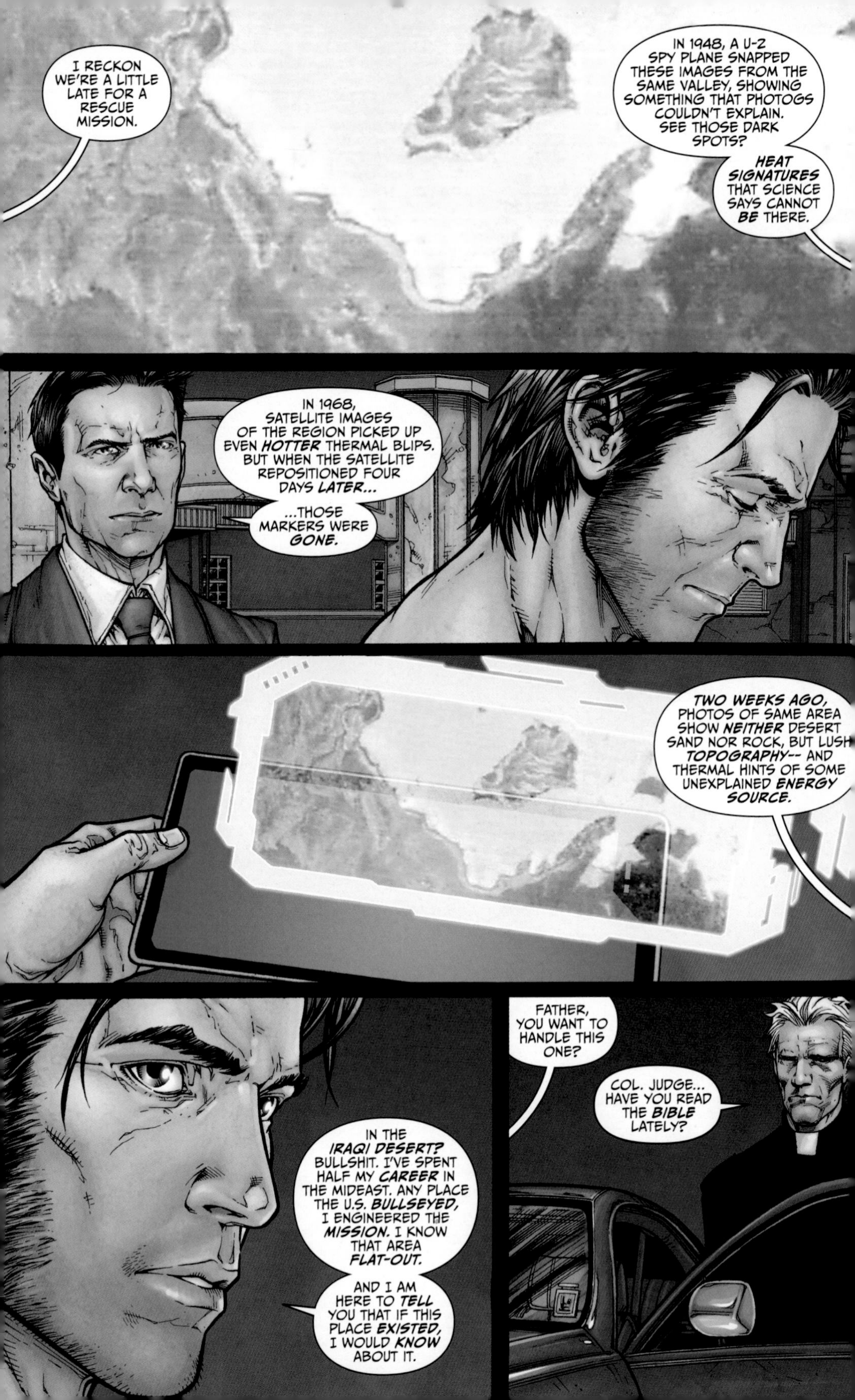
I RECKON WE'RE A LITTLE LATE FOR A RESCUE MISSION.
IN 1948, A U-2 SPY PLANE SNAPPED THESE IMAGES FROM THE SAME VALLEY, SHOWING SOMETHING THAT PHOTOGS COULDN'T EXPLAIN. SEE THOSE DARK SPOTS?
HEAT SIGNATURES THAT SCIENCE SAYS CANNOT BE THERE.
IN 1968, SATELLITE IMAGES OF THE REGION PICKED UP EVEN HOTTER THERMAL BLIPS. BUT WHEN THE SATELLITE REPOSITIONED FOUR DAYS LATER...
...THOSE MARKERS WERE GONE.
TWO WEEKS AGO, PHOTOS OF SAME AREA SHOW NEITHER DESERT SAND NOR ROCK, BUT LUSH TOPOGRAPHY-- AND THERMAL HINTS OF SOME UNEXPLAINED ENERGY SOURCE.
IN THE IRAQI DESERT? BULLSHIT. I'VE SPENT HALF MY CAREER IN THE MIDEAST. ANY PLACE THE U.S. BULLSEYED, I ENGINEERED THE MISSION. I KNOW THAT AREA FLAT-OUT.
AND I AM HERE TO TELL YOU THAT IF THIS PLACE EXISTED, I WOULD KNOW ABOUT IT.
FATHER, YOU WANT TO HANDLE THIS ONE?
COL. JUDGE... HAVE YOU READ THE BIBLE LATELY?

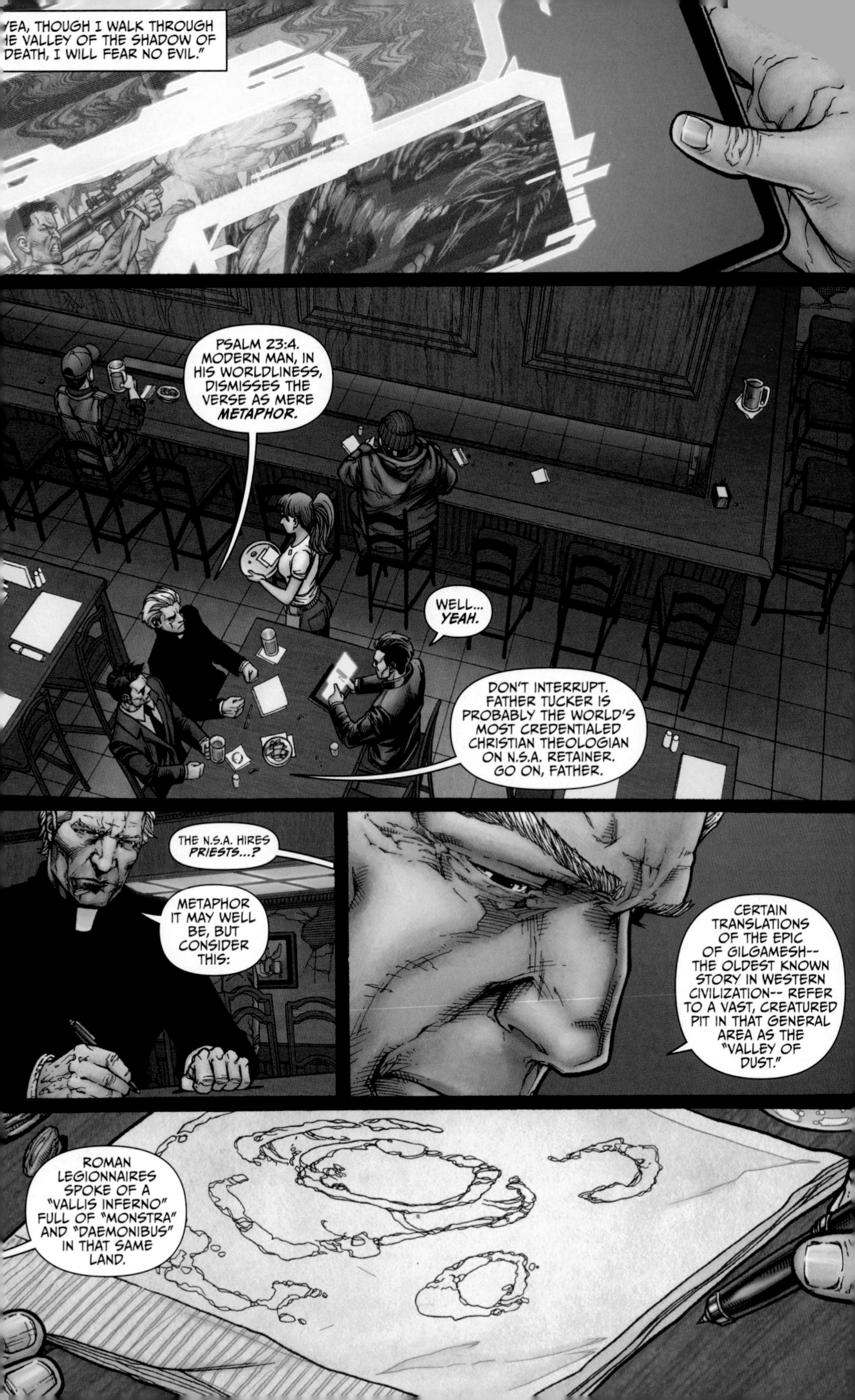
"YEA, THOUGH I WALK THROUGH THE VALLEY OF THE SHADOW OF DEATH, I WILL FEAR NO EVIL."
PSALM 23:4. MODERN MAN, IN HIS WORLDLINESS, DISMISSES THE VERSE AS MERE METAPHOR.
WELL... YEAH.
DON'T INTERRUPT. FATHER TUCKER IS PROBABLY THE WORLD'S MOST CREDENTIALED CHRISTIAN THEOLOGIAN ON N.S.A. RETAINER. GO ON, FATHER.
THE N.S.A. HIRES PRIESTS...?
METAPHOR IT MAY WELL BE, BUT CONSIDER THIS:
CERTAIN TRANSLATIONS OF THE EPIC OF GILGAMESH-- THE OLDEST KNOWN STORY IN WESTERN CIVILIZATION-- REFER TO A VAST, CREATURED PIT IN THAT GENERAL AREA AS THE "VALLEY OF DUST."
ROMAN LEGIONNAIRES SPOKE OF A "VALLIS INFERNO" FULL OF "MONSTRA" AND "DAEMONIBUS" IN THAT SAME LAND.

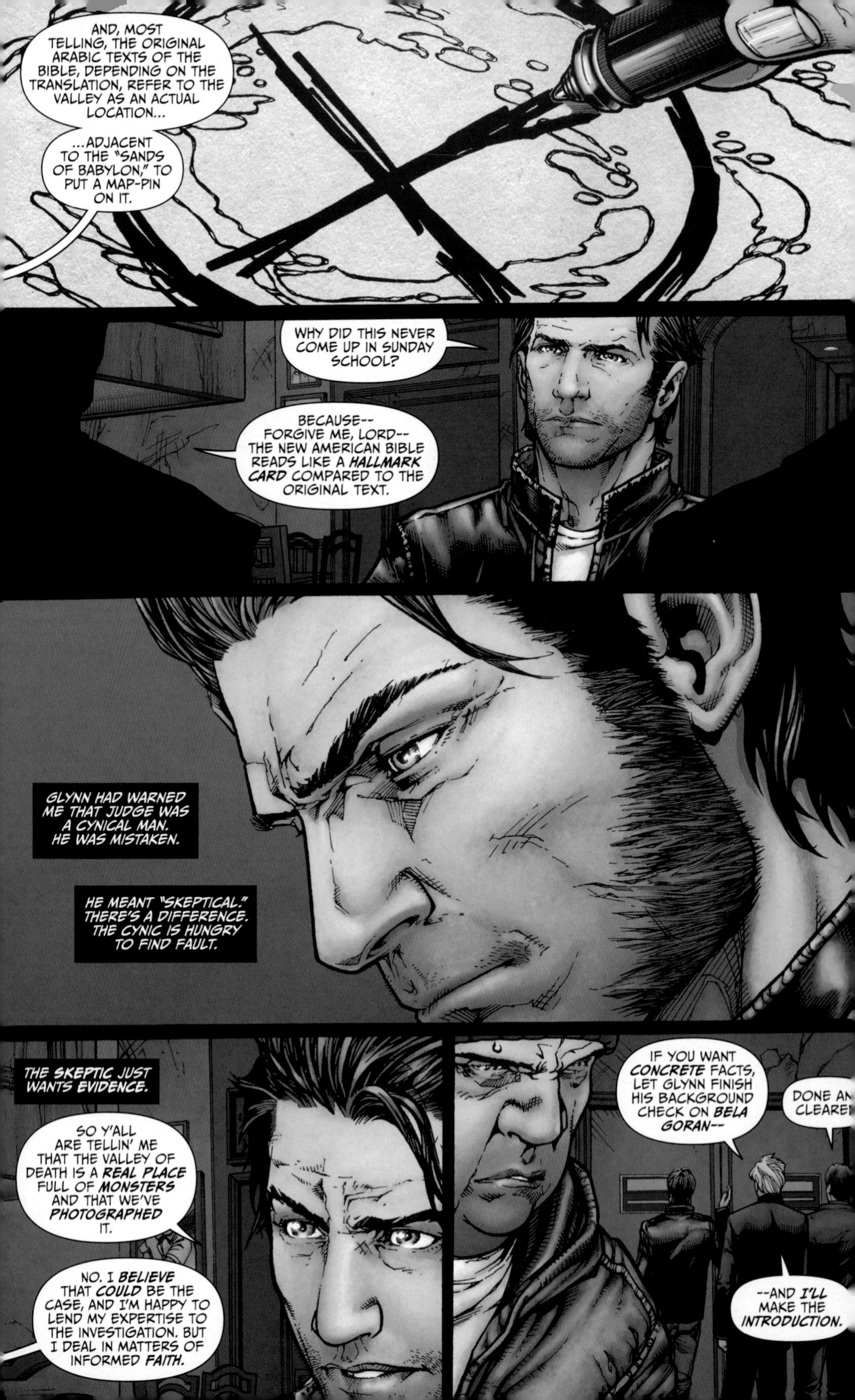
AND, MOST TELLING, THE ORIGINAL ARABIC TEXTS OF THE BIBLE, DEPENDING ON THE TRANSLATION, REFER TO THE VALLEY AS AN ACTUAL LOCATION...
...ADJACENT TO THE "SANDS OF BABYLON," TO PUT A MAP-PIN ON IT.
WHY DID THIS NEVER COME UP IN SUNDAY SCHOOL?
BECAUSE-- FORGIVE ME, LORD-- THE NEW AMERICAN BIBLE READS LIKE A *HALLMARK CARD* COMPARED TO THE ORIGINAL TEXT.
GLYNN HAD WARNED ME THAT JUDGE WAS A CYNICAL MAN. HE WAS MISTAKEN.
HE MEANT "SKEPTICAL." THERE'S A DIFFERENCE. THE CYNIC IS HUNGRY TO FIND FAULT.
THE *SKEPTIC* JUST WANTS *EVIDENCE*.
SO Y'ALL ARE TELLIN' ME THAT THE VALLEY OF DEATH IS A *REAL PLACE* FULL OF *MONSTERS* AND THAT WE'VE *PHOTOGRAPHED* IT.
NO. I *BELIEVE* THAT *COULD* BE THE CASE, AND I'M HAPPY TO LEND MY EXPERTISE TO THE INVESTIGATION. BUT I DEAL IN MATTERS OF INFORMED *FAITH*.
IF YOU WANT *CONCRETE* FACTS, LET GLYNN FINISH HIS BACKGROUND CHECK ON *BELA GORAN*--
--AND *I'LL* MAKE THE *INTRODUCTION*.

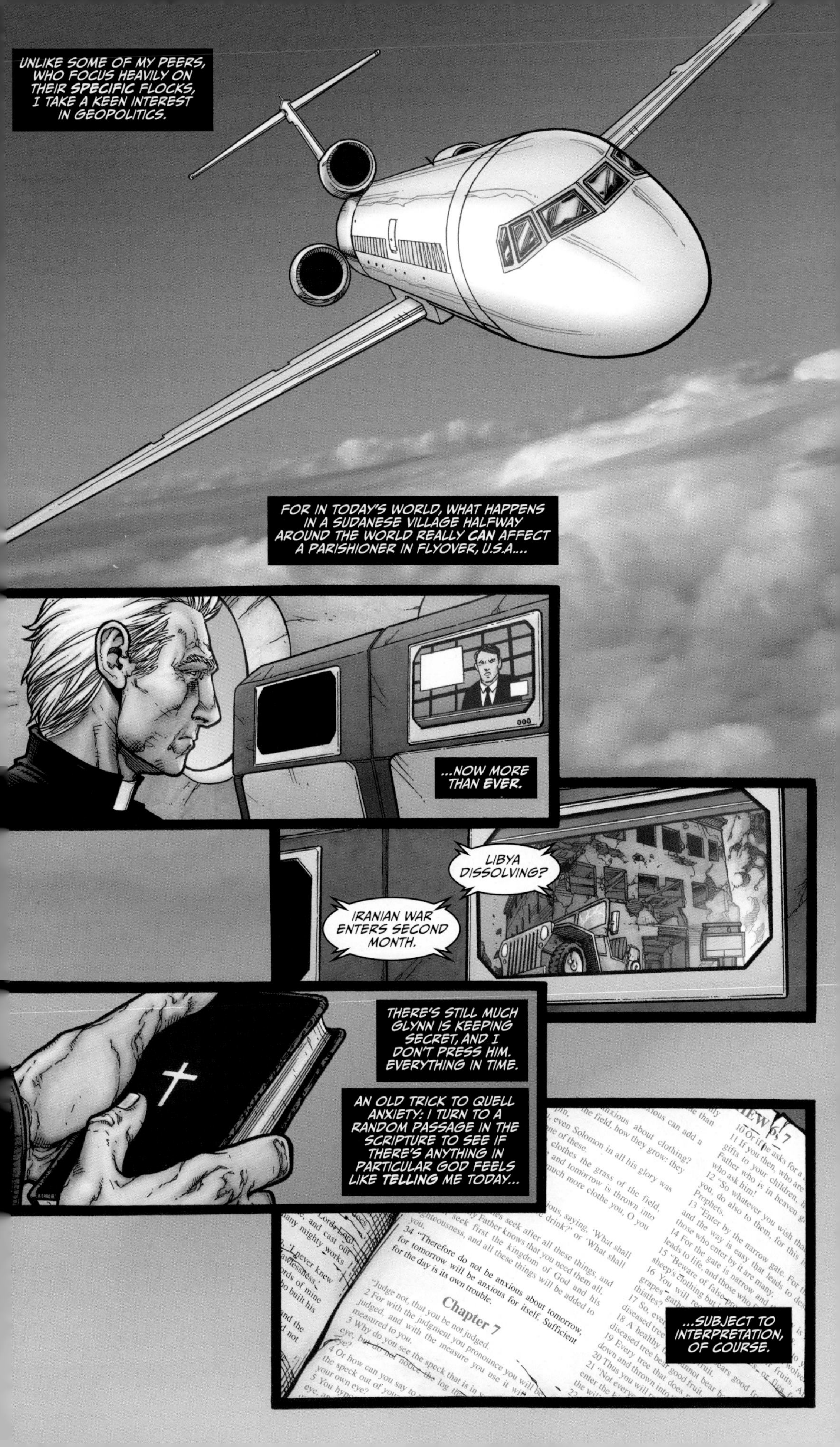
UNLIKE SOME OF MY PEERS, WHO FOCUS HEAVILY ON THEIR SPECIFIC FLOCKS, I TAKE A KEEN INTEREST IN GEOPOLITICS.
FOR IN TODAY'S WORLD, WHAT HAPPENS IN A SUDANESE VILLAGE HALFWAY AROUND THE WORLD REALLY CAN AFFECT A PARISHIONER IN FLYOVER, U.S.A....
...NOW MORE THAN EVER.
LIBYA DISSOLVING?
IRANIAN WAR ENTERS SECOND MONTH.
THERE'S STILL MUCH GLYNN IS KEEPING SECRET, AND I DON'T PRESS HIM. EVERYTHING IN TIME.
AN OLD TRICK TO QUELL ANXIETY: I TURN TO A RANDOM PASSAGE IN THE SCRIPTURE TO SEE IF THERE'S ANYTHING IN PARTICULAR GOD FEELS LIKE TELLING ME TODAY...
34 "Therefore do not be anxious about tomorrow, for tomorrow will be anxious for itself. Sufficient for the day is its own trouble.
Chapter 7
...SUBJECT TO INTERPRETATION, OF COURSE.

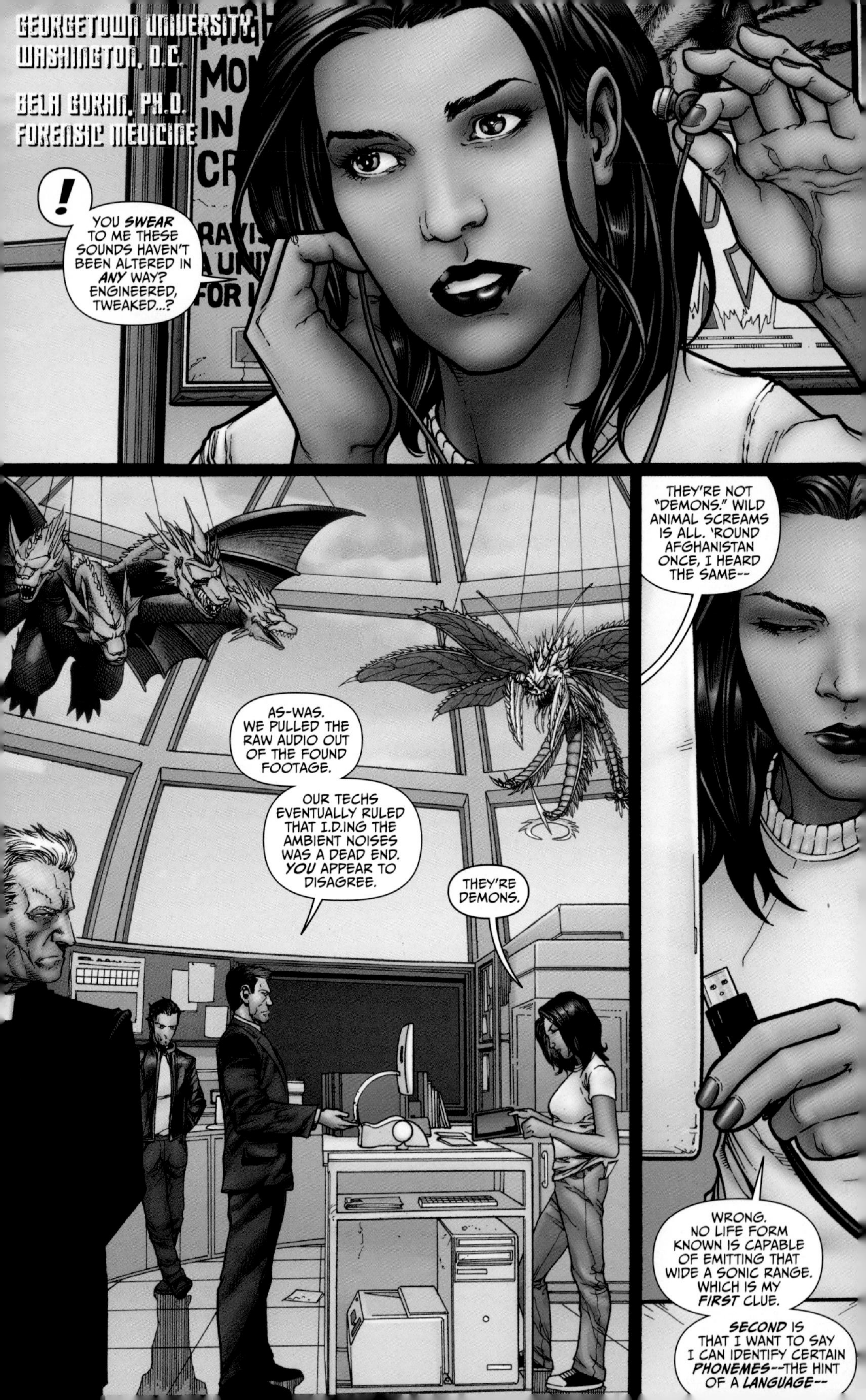
GEORGETOWN UNIVERSITY,
WASHINGTON, D.C.
BELA GORAN, PH.D.
FORENSIC MEDICINE
!
YOU SWEAR TO ME THESE SOUNDS HAVEN'T BEEN ALTERED IN ANY WAY? ENGINEERED, TWEAKED...?
AS-WAS. WE PULLED THE RAW AUDIO OUT OF THE FOUND FOOTAGE.
OUR TECHS EVENTUALLY RULED THAT I.D.ING THE AMBIENT NOISES WAS A DEAD END. YOU APPEAR TO DISAGREE.
THEY'RE DEMONS.
THEY'RE NOT "DEMONS." WILD ANIMAL SCREAMS IS ALL. 'ROUND AFGHANISTAN ONCE, I HEARD THE SAME--
WRONG. NO LIFE FORM KNOWN IS CAPABLE OF EMITTING THAT WIDE A SONIC RANGE. WHICH IS MY FIRST CLUE.
SECOND IS THAT I WANT TO SAY I CAN IDENTIFY CERTAIN PHONEMES--THE HINT OF A LANGUAGE--

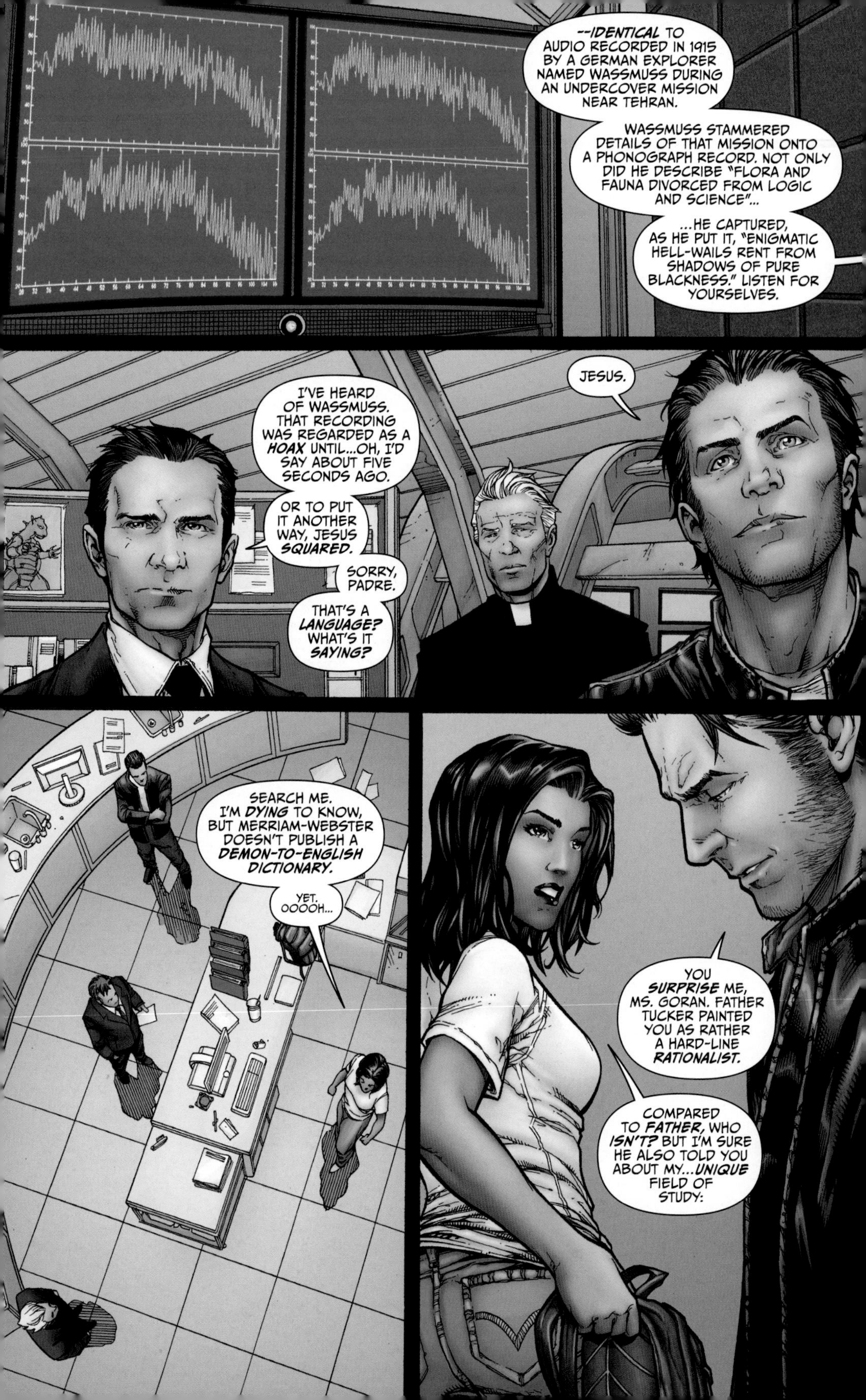

--IDENTICAL TO AUDIO RECORDED IN 1915 BY A GERMAN EXPLORER NAMED WASSMUSS DURING AN UNDERCOVER MISSION NEAR TEHRAN.
WASSMUSS STAMMERED DETAILS OF THAT MISSION ONTO A PHONOGRAPH RECORD. NOT ONLY DID HE DESCRIBE "FLORA AND FAUNA DIVORCED FROM LOGIC AND SCIENCE"...
...HE CAPTURED, AS HE PUT IT, "ENIGMATIC HELL-WAILS RENT FROM SHADOWS OF PURE BLACKNESS." LISTEN FOR YOURSELVES.
JESUS.
I'VE HEARD OF WASSMUSS. THAT RECORDING WAS REGARDED AS A HOAX UNTIL...OH, I'D SAY ABOUT FIVE SECONDS AGO.
OR TO PUT IT ANOTHER WAY, JESUS SQUARED.
SORRY, PADRE.
THAT'S A LANGUAGE? WHAT'S IT SAYING?
SEARCH ME. I'M DYING TO KNOW, BUT MERRIAM-WEBSTER DOESN'T PUBLISH A DEMON-TO-ENGLISH DICTIONARY.
YET. OOOOH...
YOU SURPRISE ME, MS. GORAN. FATHER TUCKER PAINTED YOU AS RATHER A HARD-LINE RATIONALIST.
COMPARED TO FATHER, WHO ISN'T? BUT I'M SURE HE ALSO TOLD YOU ABOUT MY...UNIQUE FIELD OF STUDY:

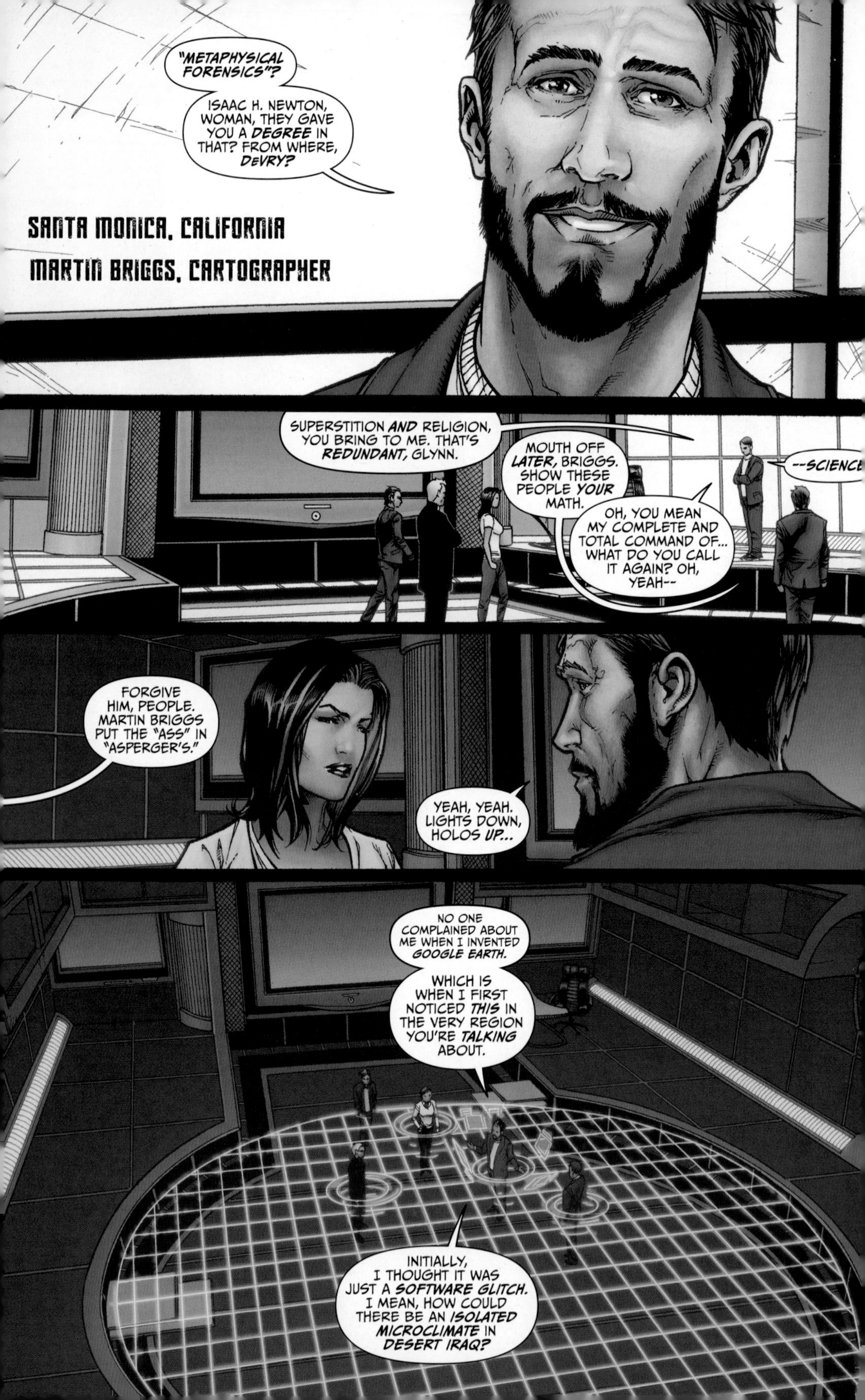
"METAPHYSICAL FORENSICS"?
ISAAC H. NEWTON, WOMAN, THEY GAVE YOU A DEGREE IN THAT? FROM WHERE, DEVRY?
SANTA MONICA, CALIFORNIA
MARTIN BRIGGS, CARTOGRAPHER
SUPERSTITION AND RELIGION, YOU BRING TO ME. THAT'S REDUNDANT, GLYNN.
MOUTH OFF LATER, BRIGGS. SHOW THESE PEOPLE YOUR MATH.
OH, YOU MEAN MY COMPLETE AND TOTAL COMMAND OF... WHAT DO YOU CALL IT AGAIN? OH, YEAH--
--SCIENCE
FORGIVE HIM, PEOPLE. MARTIN BRIGGS PUT THE "ASS" IN "ASPERGER'S."
YEAH, YEAH. LIGHTS DOWN, HOLOS UP...
NO ONE COMPLAINED ABOUT ME WHEN I INVENTED GOOGLE EARTH.
WHICH IS WHEN I FIRST NOTICED THIS IN THE VERY REGION YOU'RE TALKING ABOUT.
INITIALLY, I THOUGHT IT WAS JUST A SOFTWARE GLITCH. I MEAN, HOW COULD THERE BE AN ISOLATED MICROCLIMATE IN DESERT IRAQ?

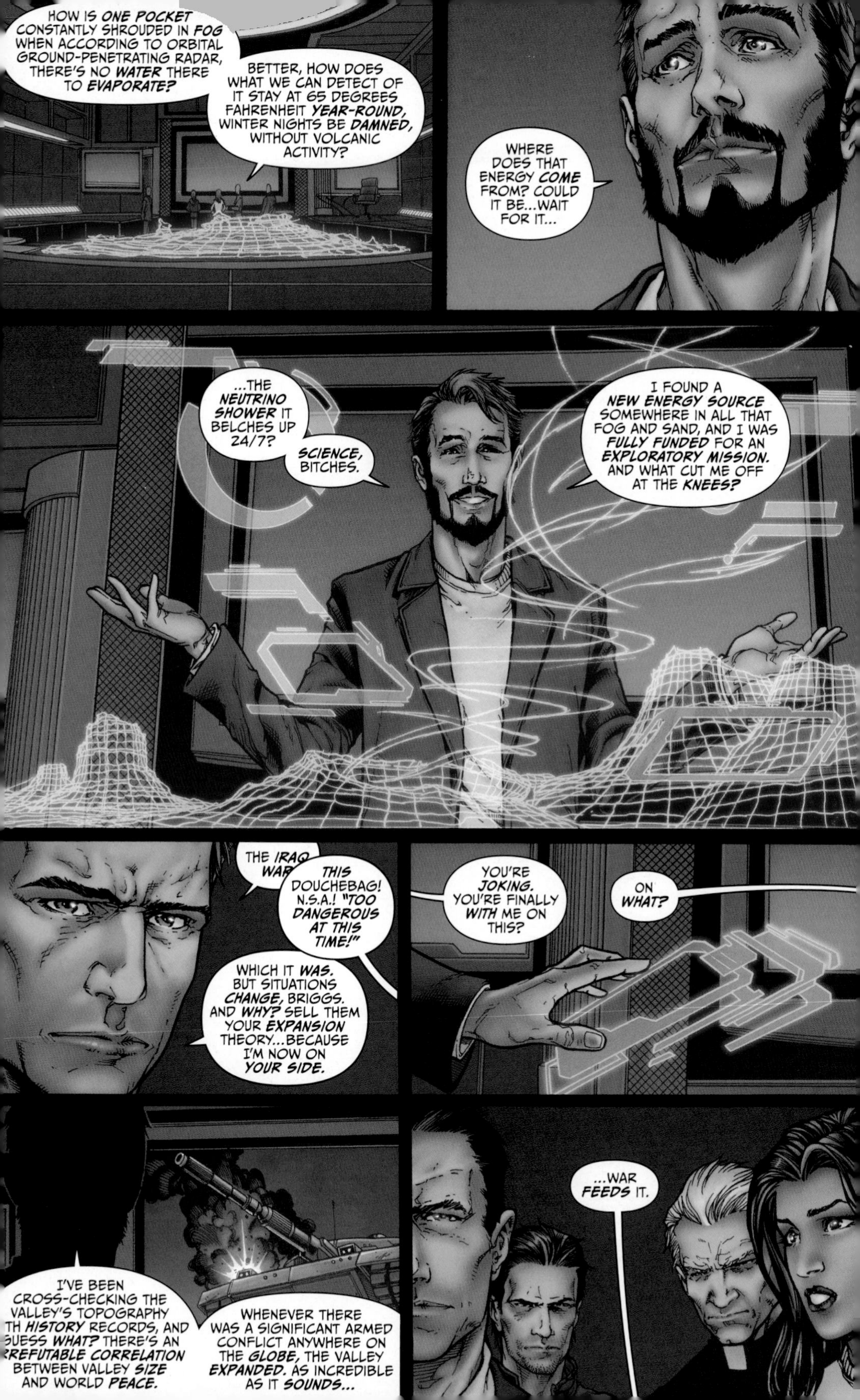

HOW IS ONE POCKET CONSTANTLY SHROUDED IN FOG WHEN ACCORDING TO ORBITAL GROUND-PENETRATING RADAR, THERE'S NO WATER THERE TO EVAPORATE?
BETTER, HOW DOES WHAT WE CAN DETECT OF IT STAY AT 65 DEGREES FAHRENHEIT YEAR-ROUND, WINTER NIGHTS BE DAMNED, WITHOUT VOLCANIC ACTIVITY?
WHERE DOES THAT ENERGY COME FROM? COULD IT BE...WAIT FOR IT...
...THE NEUTRINO SHOWER IT BELCHES UP 24/7?
SCIENCE, BITCHES.
I FOUND A NEW ENERGY SOURCE SOMEWHERE IN ALL THAT FOG AND SAND, AND I WAS FULLY FUNDED FOR AN EXPLORATORY MISSION. AND WHAT CUT ME OFF AT THE KNEES?
THE IRAQ WAR
THIS DOUCHEBAG! N.S.A.! "TOO DANGEROUS AT THIS TIME!"
WHICH IT WAS. BUT SITUATIONS CHANGE, BRIGGS. AND WHY? SELL THEM YOUR EXPANSION THEORY...BECAUSE I'M NOW ON YOUR SIDE.
YOU'RE JOKING. YOU'RE FINALLY WITH ME ON THIS?
ON WHAT?
I'VE BEEN CROSS-CHECKING THE VALLEY'S TOPOGRAPHY TH HISTORY RECORDS, AND UESS WHAT? THERE'S AN REFUTABLE CORRELATION BETWEEN VALLEY SIZE AND WORLD PEACE.
WHENEVER THERE WAS A SIGNIFICANT ARMED CONFLICT ANYWHERE ON THE GLOBE, THE VALLEY EXPANDED. AS INCREDIBLE AS IT SOUNDS...
...WAR FEEDS IT.

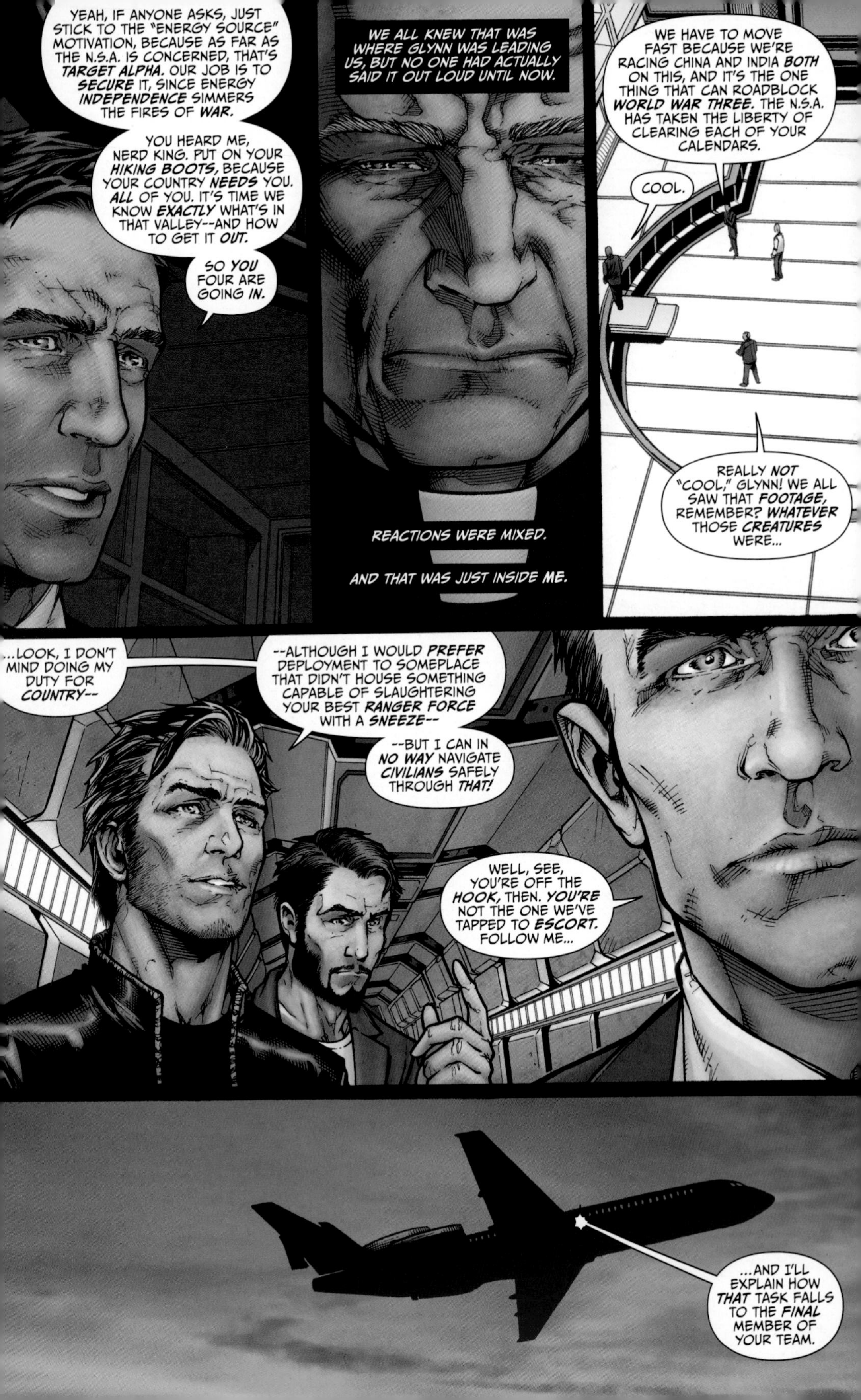

YEAH, IF ANYONE ASKS, JUST STICK TO THE "ENERGY SOURCE" MOTIVATION, BECAUSE AS FAR AS THE N.S.A. IS CONCERNED, THAT'S TARGET ALPHA. OUR JOB IS TO SECURE IT, SINCE ENERGY INDEPENDENCE SIMMERS THE FIRES OF WAR.
YOU HEARD ME, NERD KING. PUT ON YOUR HIKING BOOTS, BECAUSE YOUR COUNTRY NEEDS YOU. ALL OF YOU. IT'S TIME WE KNOW EXACTLY WHAT'S IN THAT VALLEY--AND HOW TO GET IT OUT.
SO YOU FOUR ARE GOING IN.
WE ALL KNEW THAT WAS WHERE GLYNN WAS LEADING US, BUT NO ONE HAD ACTUALLY SAID IT OUT LOUD UNTIL NOW.
REACTIONS WERE MIXED.
AND THAT WAS JUST INSIDE ME.
WE HAVE TO MOVE FAST BECAUSE WE'RE RACING CHINA AND INDIA BOTH ON THIS, AND IT'S THE ONE THING THAT CAN ROADBLOCK WORLD WAR THREE. THE N.S.A. HAS TAKEN THE LIBERTY OF CLEARING EACH OF YOUR CALENDARS.
COOL.
REALLY NOT "COOL," GLYNN! WE ALL SAW THAT FOOTAGE, REMEMBER? WHATEVER THOSE CREATURES WERE...
...LOOK, I DON'T MIND DOING MY DUTY FOR COUNTRY--
--ALTHOUGH I WOULD PREFER DEPLOYMENT TO SOMEPLACE THAT DIDN'T HOUSE SOMETHING CAPABLE OF SLAUGHTERING YOUR BEST RANGER FORCE WITH A SNEEZE--
--BUT I CAN IN NO WAY NAVIGATE CIVILIANS SAFELY THROUGH THAT!
WELL, SEE, YOU'RE OFF THE HOOK, THEN. YOU'RE NOT THE ONE WE'VE TAPPED TO ESCORT. FOLLOW ME...
...AND I'LL EXPLAIN HOW THAT TASK FALLS TO THE FINAL MEMBER OF YOUR TEAM.

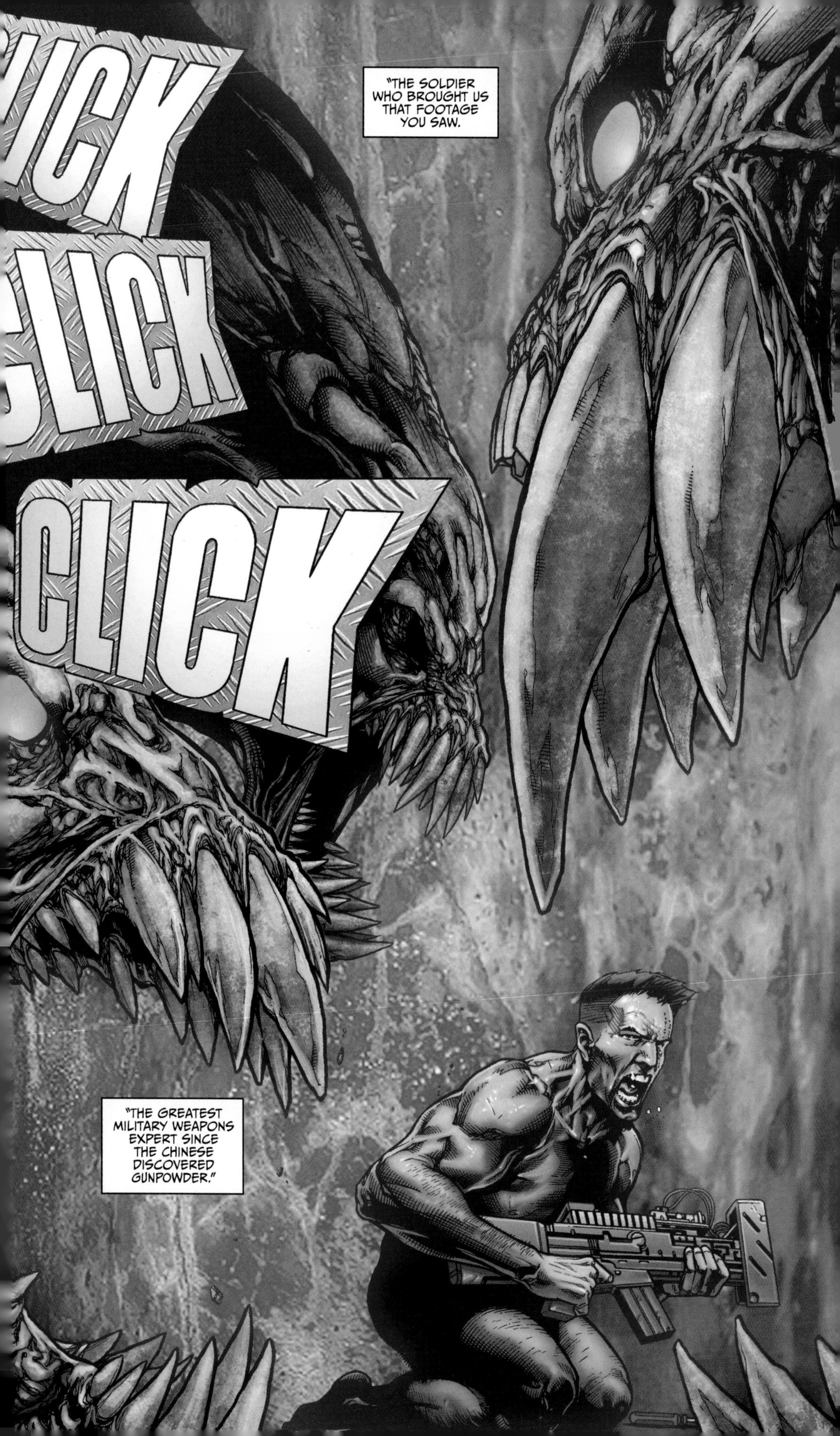
"THE SOLDIER WHO BROUGHT US THAT FOOTAGE YOU SAW.
CLICK
"THE GREATEST MILITARY WEAPONS EXPERT SINCE THE CHINESE DISCOVERED GUNPOWDER."

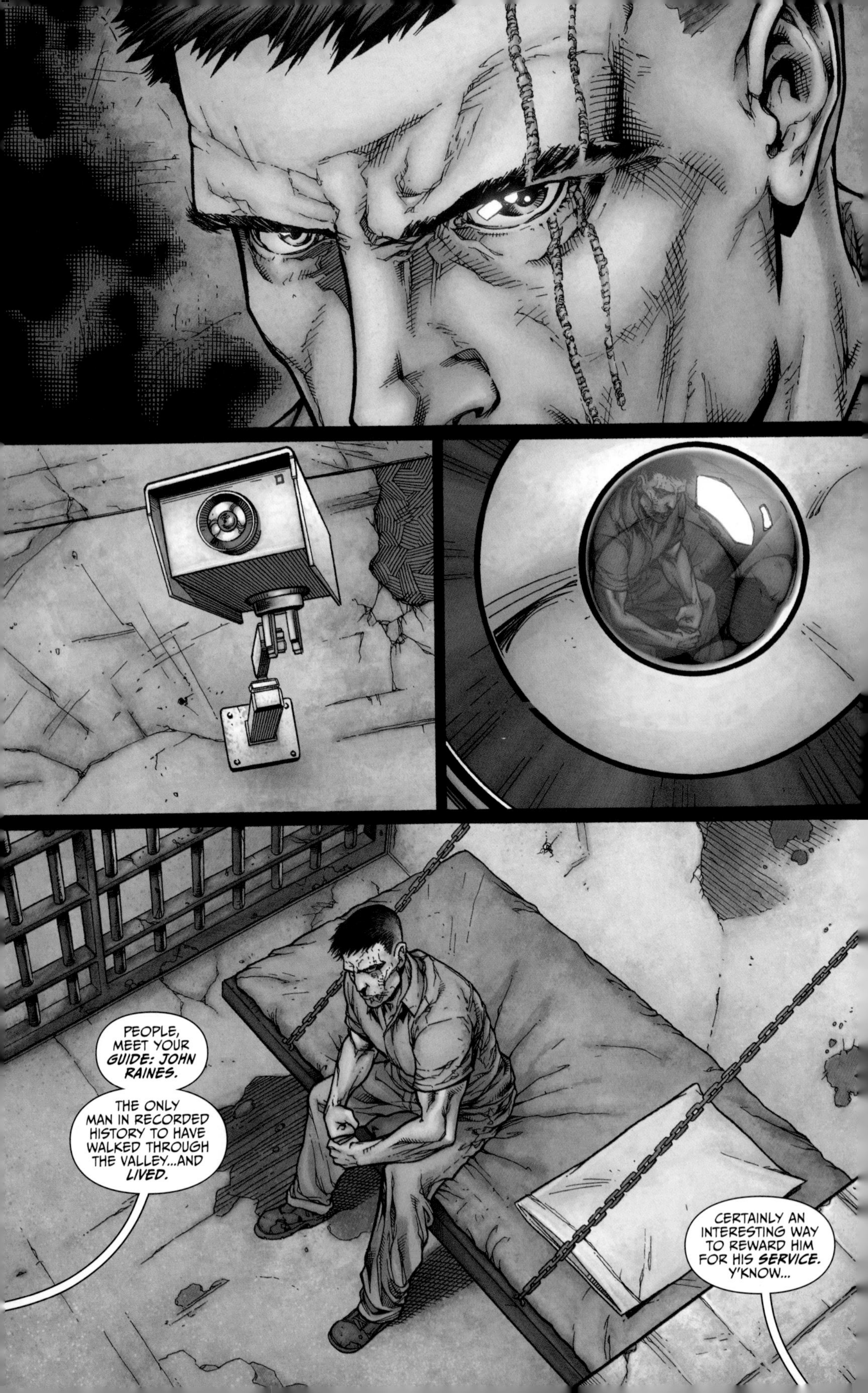
PEOPLE, MEET YOUR GUIDE: JOHN RAINES.
THE ONLY MAN IN RECORDED HISTORY TO HAVE WALKED THROUGH THE VALLEY...AND LIVED.
CERTAINLY AN INTERESTING WAY TO REWARD HIM FOR HIS SERVICE. Y'KNOW...

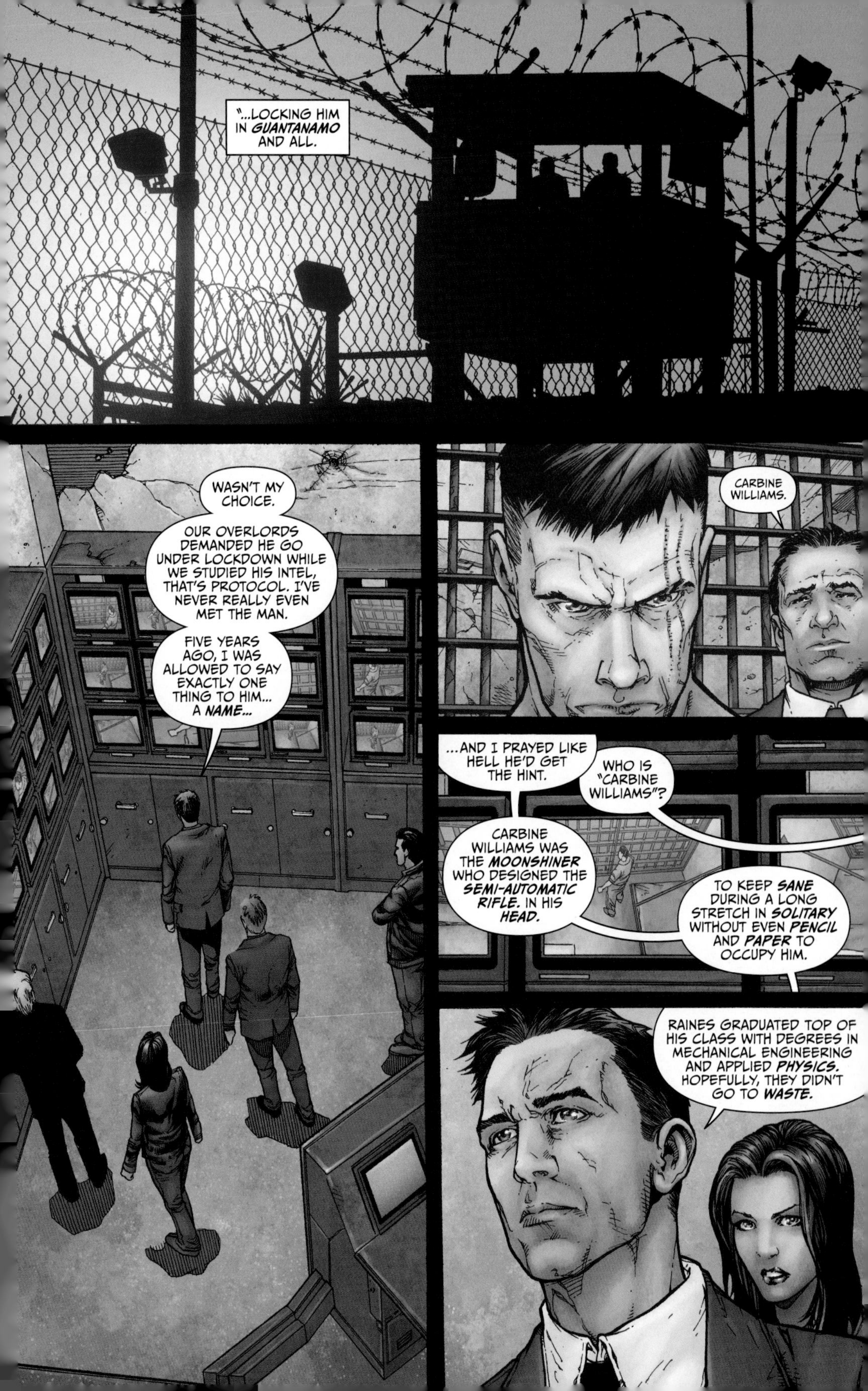
"...LOCKING HIM IN GUANTANAMO AND ALL.
WASN'T MY CHOICE.
OUR OVERLORDS DEMANDED HE GO UNDER LOCKDOWN WHILE WE STUDIED HIS INTEL, THAT'S PROTOCOL. I'VE NEVER REALLY EVEN MET THE MAN.
FIVE YEARS AGO, I WAS ALLOWED TO SAY EXACTLY ONE THING TO HIM... A NAME...
CARBINE WILLIAMS.
...AND I PRAYED LIKE HELL HE'D GET THE HINT.
WHO IS "CARBINE WILLIAMS"?
CARBINE WILLIAMS WAS THE MOONSHINER WHO DESIGNED THE SEMI-AUTOMATIC RIFLE. IN HIS HEAD.
TO KEEP SANE DURING A LONG STRETCH IN SOLITARY WITHOUT EVEN PENCIL AND PAPER TO OCCUPY HIM.
RAINES GRADUATED TOP OF HIS CLASS WITH DEGREES IN MECHANICAL ENGINEERING AND APPLIED PHYSICS. HOPEFULLY, THEY DIDN'T GO TO WASTE.

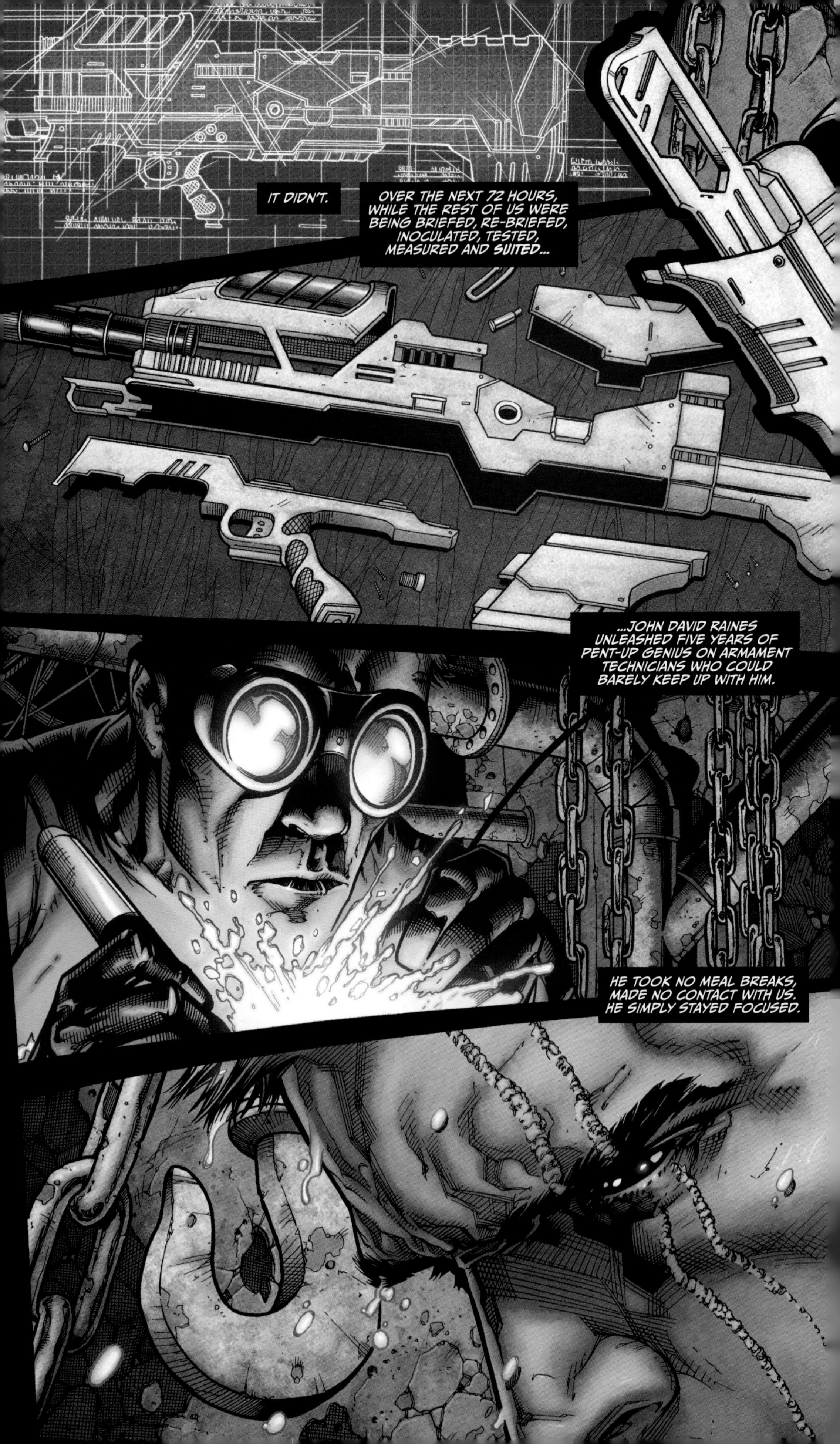
IT DIDN'T.
OVER THE NEXT 72 HOURS, WHILE THE REST OF US WERE BEING BRIEFED, RE-BRIEFED, INOCULATED, TESTED, MEASURED AND SUITED...
...JOHN DAVID RAINES UNLEASHED FIVE YEARS OF PENT-UP GENIUS ON ARMAMENT TECHNICIANS WHO COULD BARELY KEEP UP WITH HIM.
HE TOOK NO MEAL BREAKS, MADE NO CONTACT WITH US. HE SIMPLY STAYED FOCUSED.

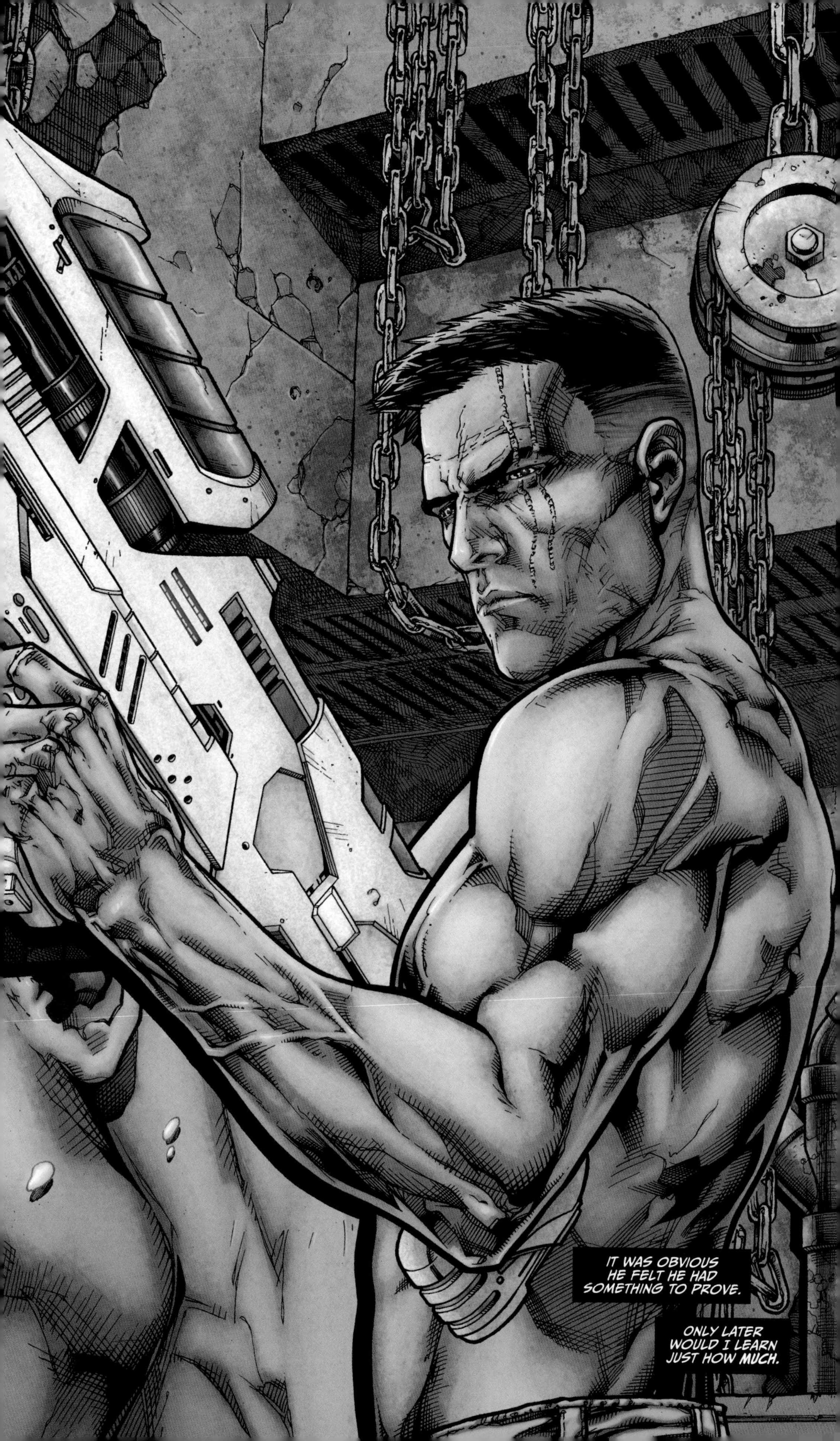
IT WAS OBVIOUS HE FELT HE HAD SOMETHING TO PROVE.
ONLY LATER WOULD I LEARN JUST HOW MUCH.

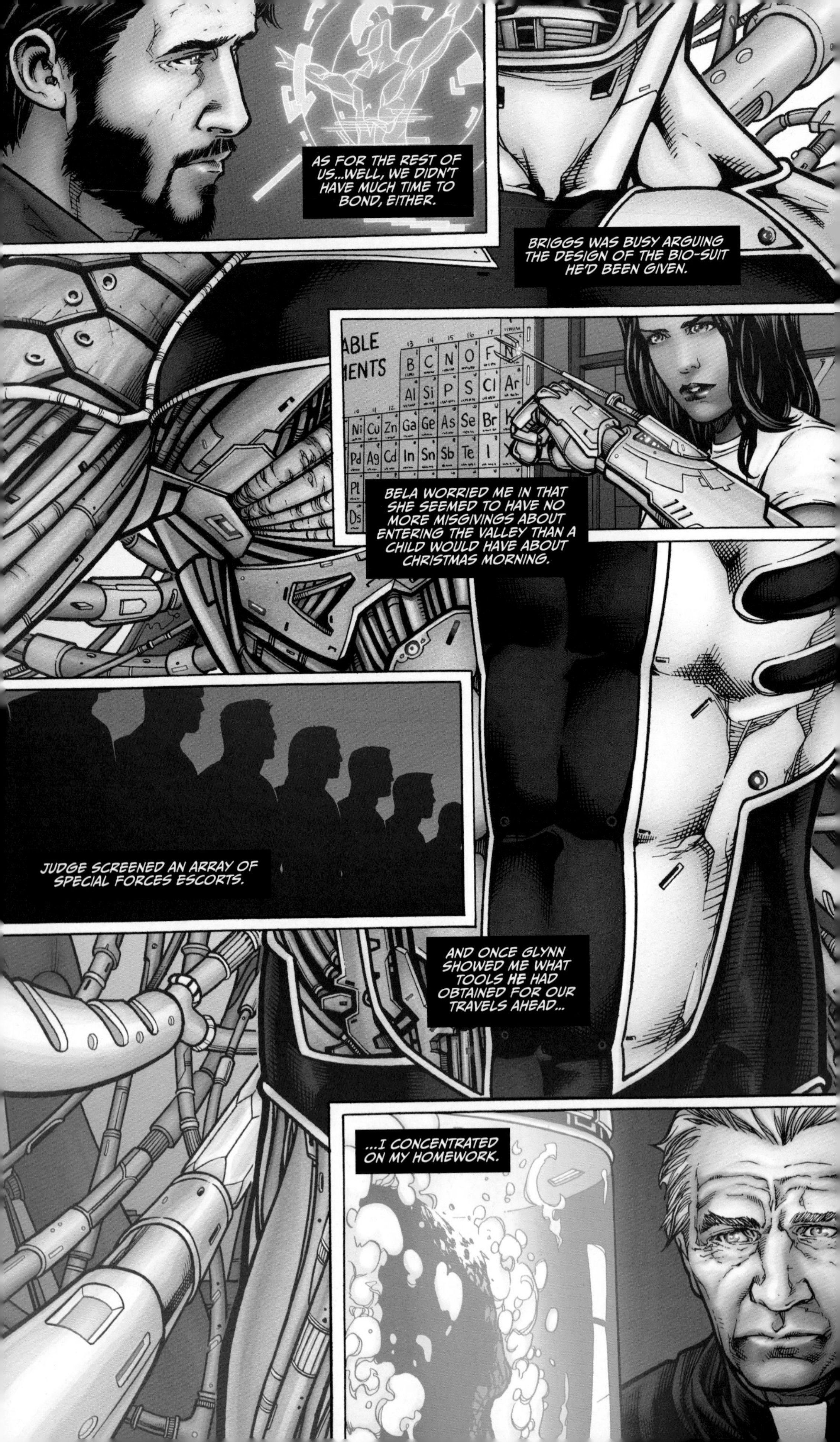
AS FOR THE REST OF US...WELL, WE DIDN'T HAVE MUCH TIME TO BOND, EITHER.
BRIGGS WAS BUSY ARGUING THE DESIGN OF THE BIO-SUIT HE'D BEEN GIVEN.
ABLE
MENTS
B C N O F
Al Si P S Cl Ar
Ni Cu Zn Ga Ge As Se Br
Pd Ag Cd In Sn Sb Te I
BELA WORRIED ME IN THAT SHE SEEMED TO HAVE NO MORE MISGIVINGS ABOUT ENTERING THE VALLEY THAN A CHILD WOULD HAVE ABOUT CHRISTMAS MORNING.
JUDGE SCREENED AN ARRAY OF SPECIAL FORCES ESCORTS.
AND ONCE GLYNN SHOWED ME WHAT TOOLS HE HAD OBTAINED FOR OUR TRAVELS AHEAD...
...I CONCENTRATED ON MY HOMEWORK.

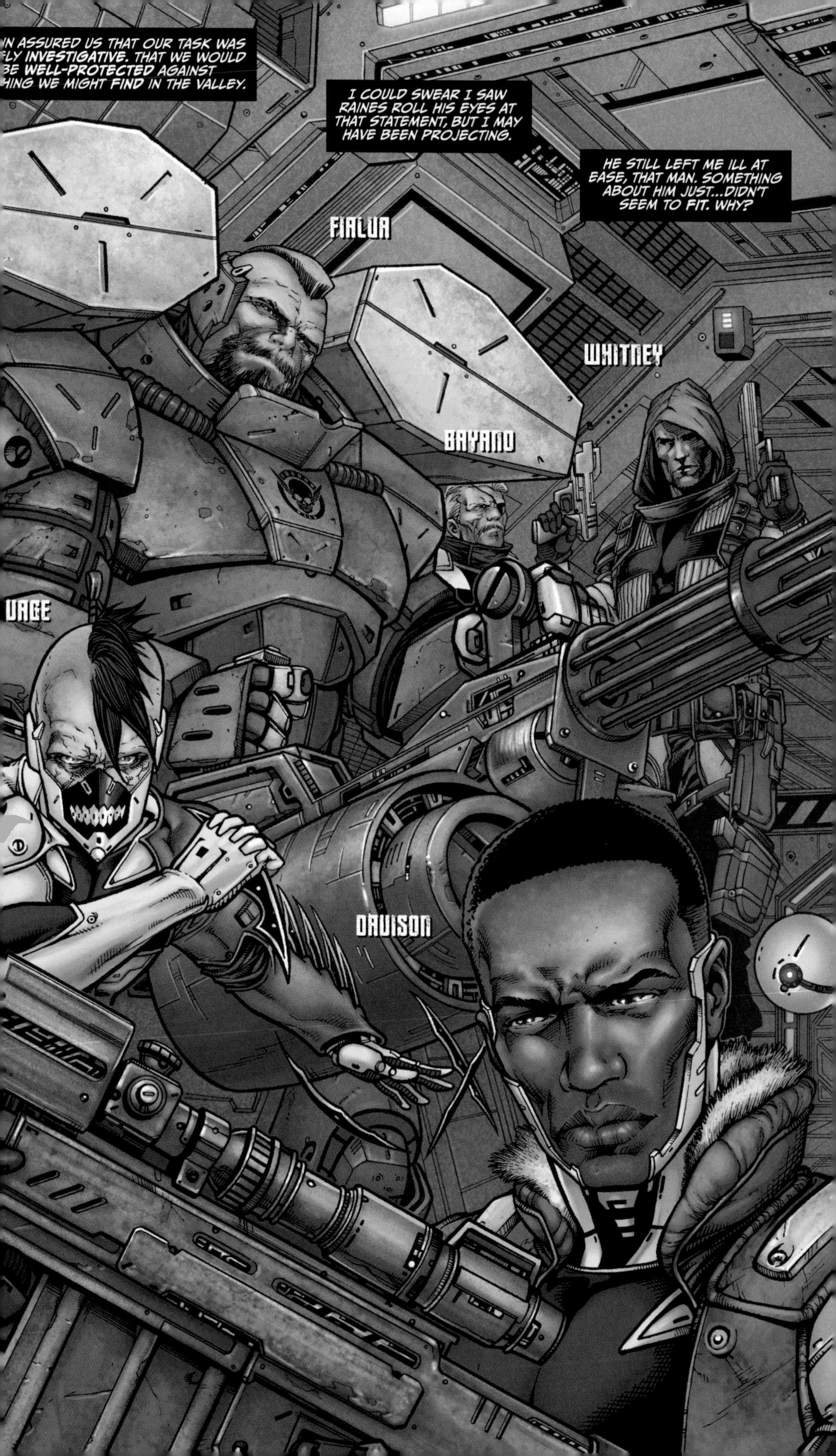

N ASSURED US THAT OUR TASK WAS
LY INVESTIGATIVE. THAT WE WOULD
BE WELL-PROTECTED AGAINST
HING WE MIGHT FIND IN THE VALLEY.
I COULD SWEAR I SAW RAINES ROLL HIS EYES AT THAT STATEMENT, BUT I MAY HAVE BEEN PROJECTING.
HE STILL LEFT ME ILL AT EASE, THAT MAN. SOMETHING ABOUT HIM JUST...DIDN'T SEEM TO FIT. WHY?
FIALUA
WHITNEY
BAYANO
VAGE
DAVISON

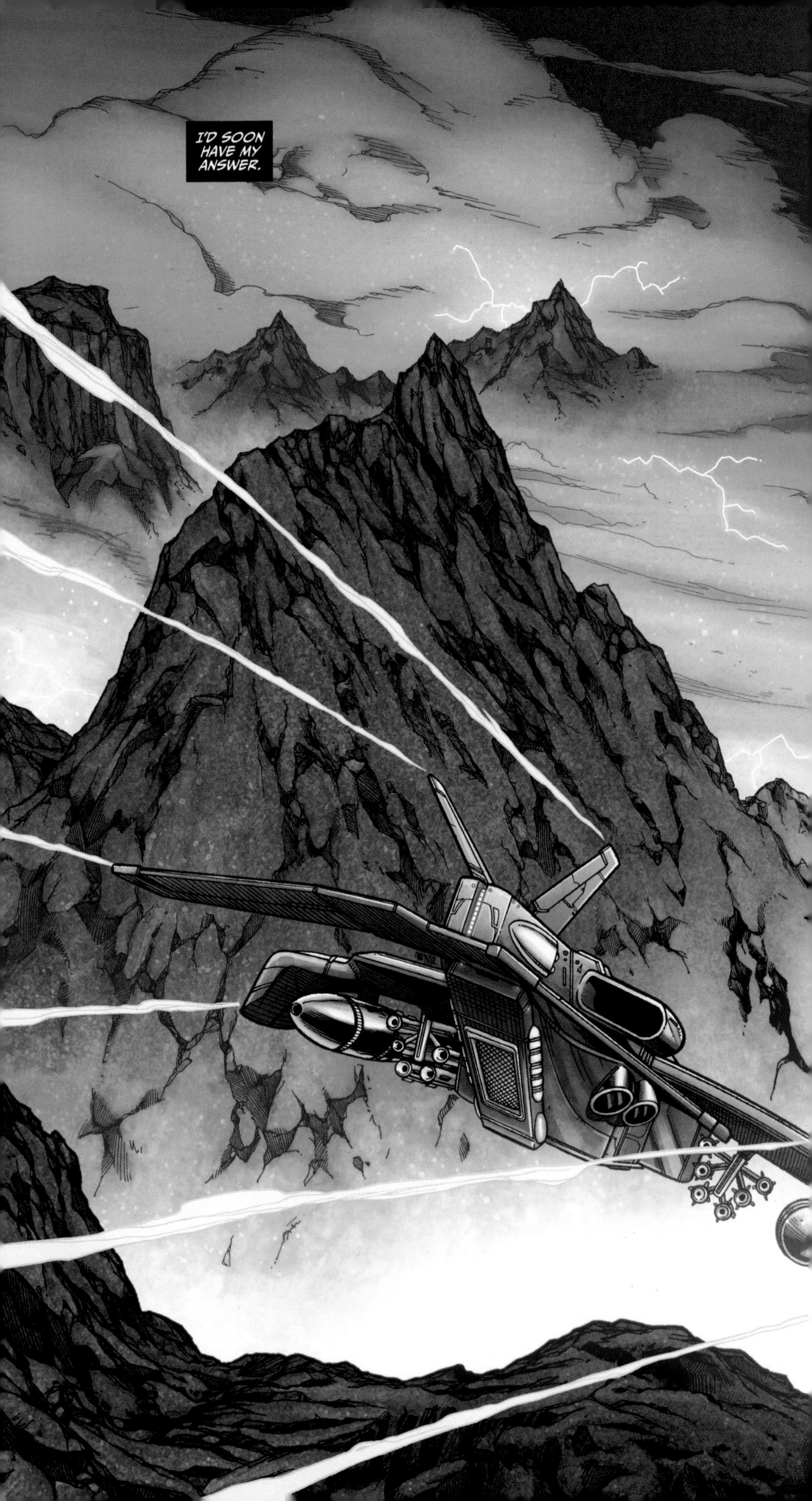
I'D SOON HAVE MY ANSWER.

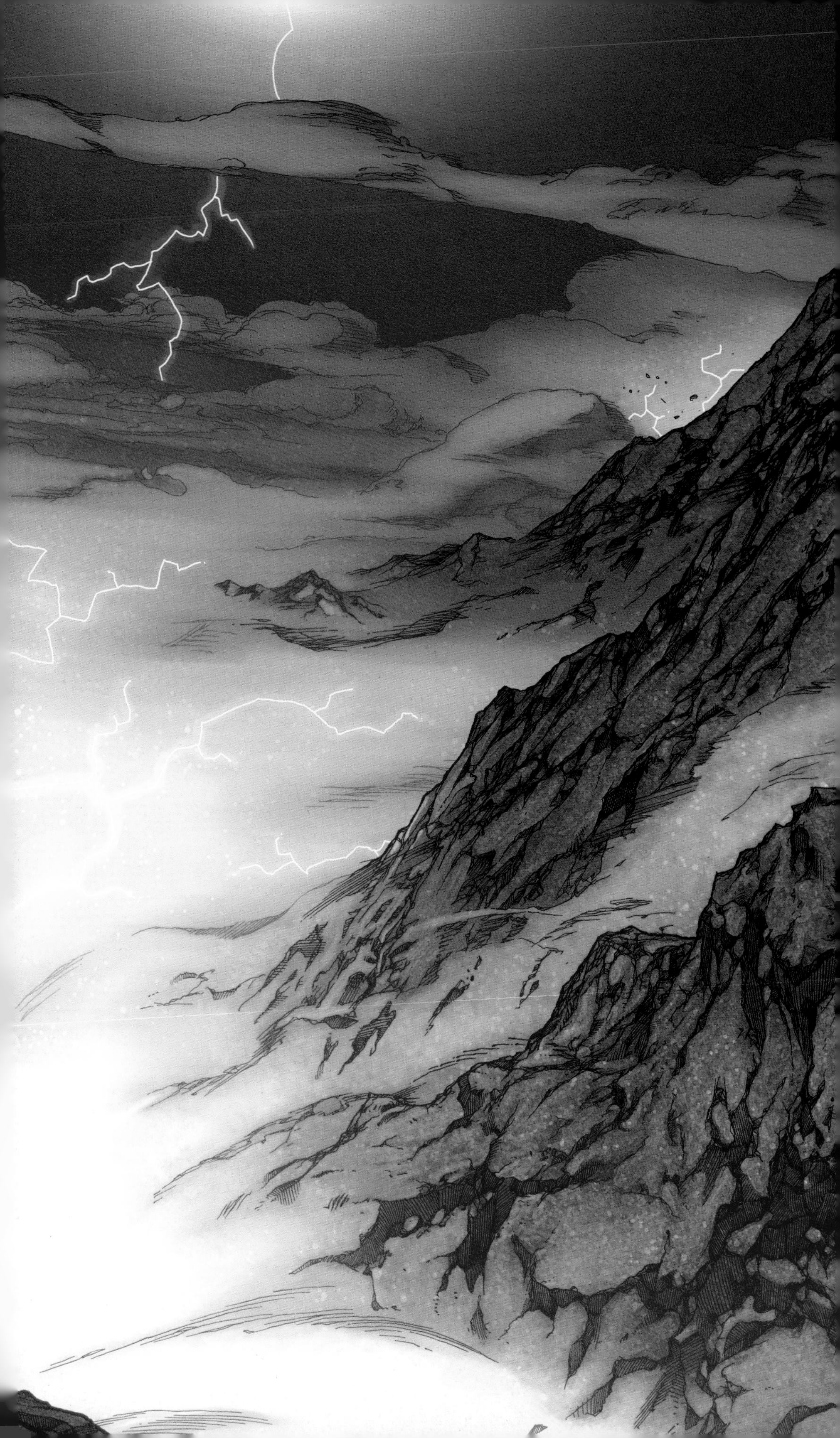

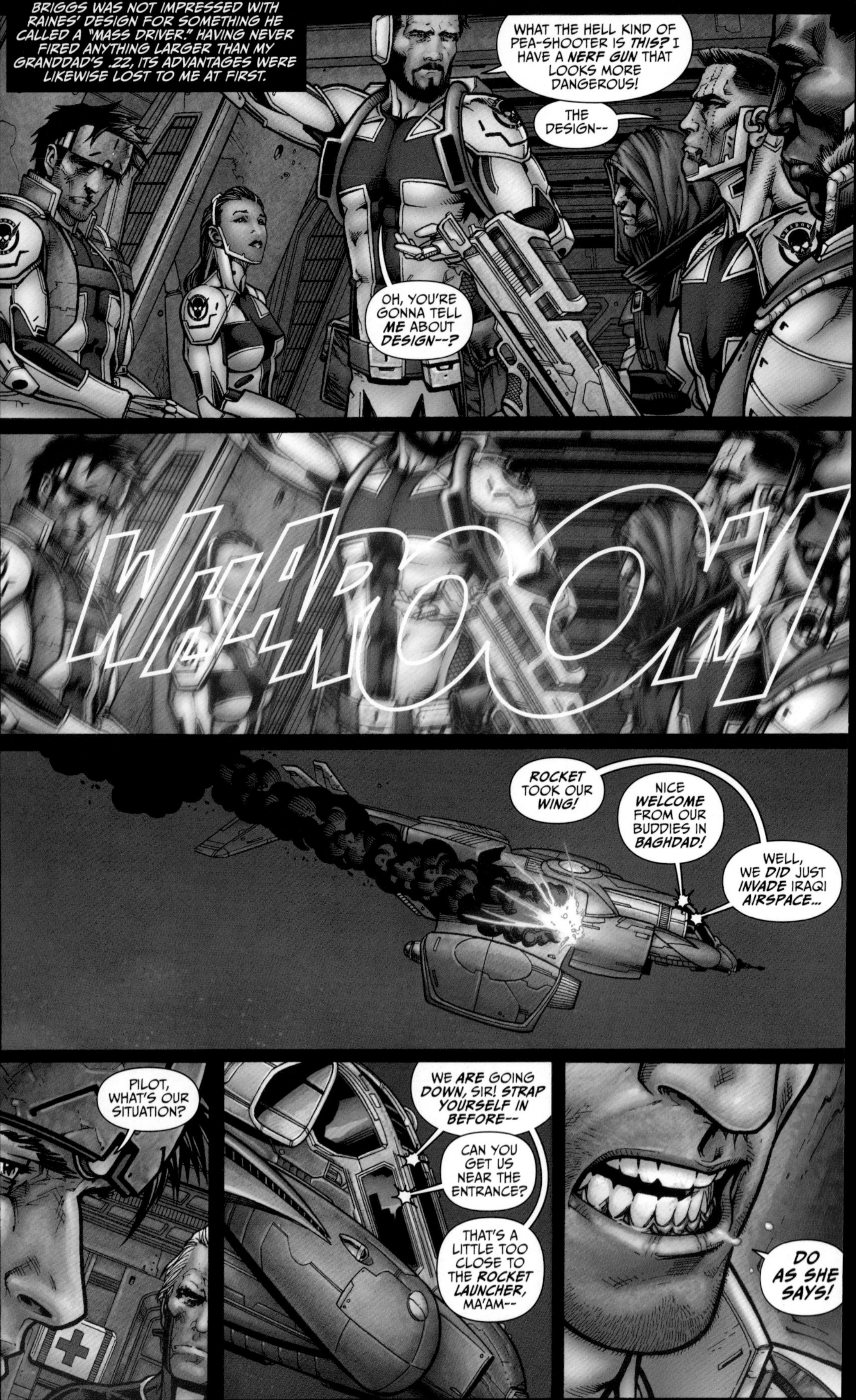
BRIGGS WAS NOT IMPRESSED WITH RAINES' DESIGN FOR SOMETHING HE CALLED A "MASS DRIVER." HAVING NEVER FIRED ANYTHING LARGER THAN MY GRANDDAD'S .22, ITS ADVANTAGES WERE LIKEWISE LOST TO ME AT FIRST.
WHAT THE HELL KIND OF PEA-SHOOTER IS THIS? I HAVE A NERF GUN THAT LOOKS MORE DANGEROUS!
THE DESIGN--
OH, YOU'RE GONNA TELL ME ABOUT DESIGN--?
WHROOM
ROCKET TOOK OUR WING!
NICE WELCOME FROM OUR BUDDIES IN BAGHDAD!
WELL, WE DID JUST INVADE IRAQI AIRSPACE...
PILOT, WHAT'S OUR SITUATION?
WE ARE GOING DOWN, SIR! STRAP YOURSELF IN BEFORE--
CAN YOU GET US NEAR THE ENTRANCE?
THAT'S A LITTLE TOO CLOSE TO THE ROCKET LAUNCHER, MA'AM--
DO AS SHE SAYS!

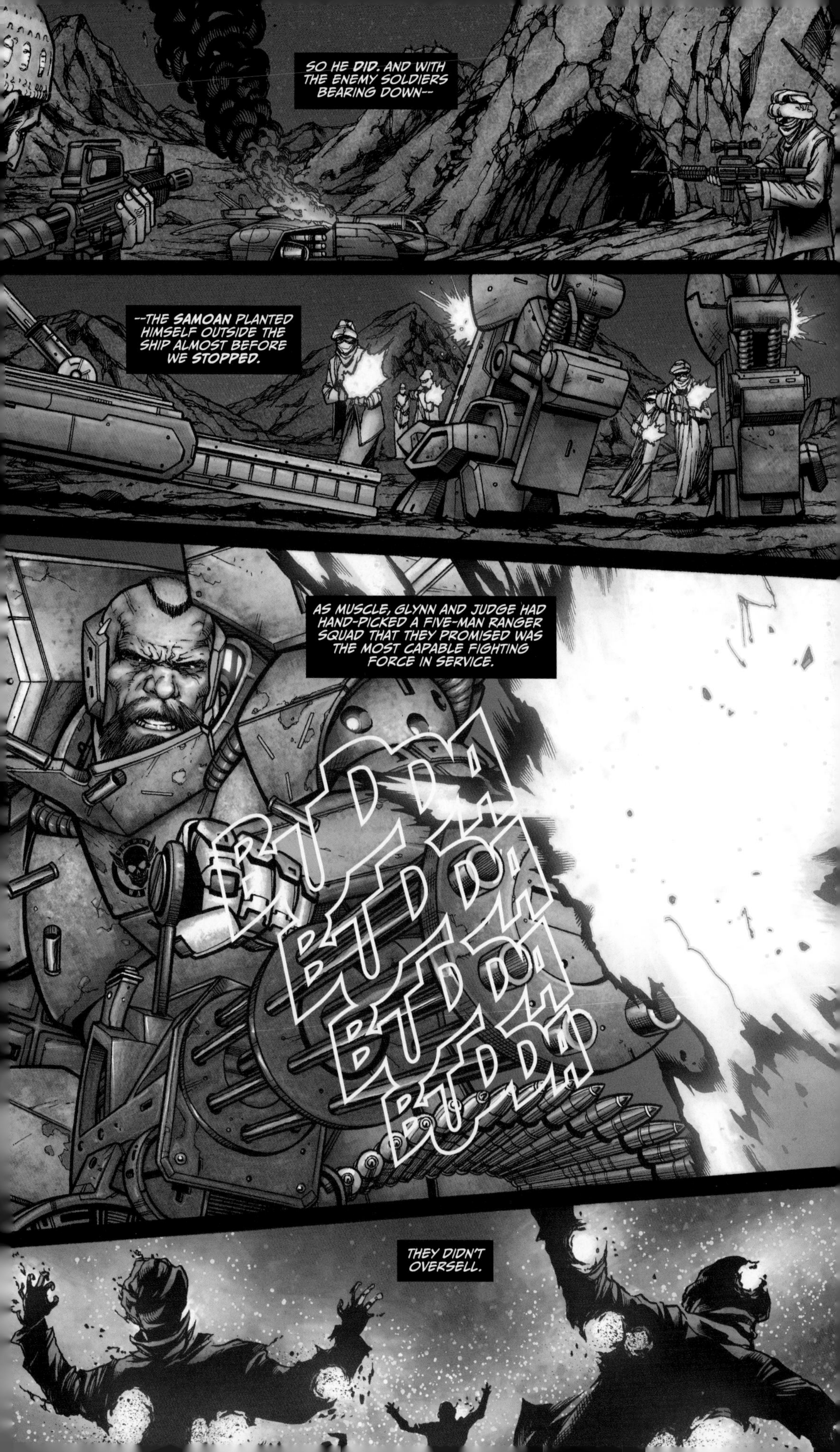
SO HE DID. AND WITH THE ENEMY SOLDIERS BEARING DOWN--
--THE SAMOAN PLANTED HIMSELF OUTSIDE THE SHIP ALMOST BEFORE WE STOPPED.
AS MUSCLE, GLYNN AND JUDGE HAD HAND-PICKED A FIVE-MAN RANGER SQUAD THAT THEY PROMISED WAS THE MOST CAPABLE FIGHTING FORCE IN SERVICE.
BUDDA BUDDA BUDDA BUDDA BUDDA
THEY DIDN'T OVERSELL.

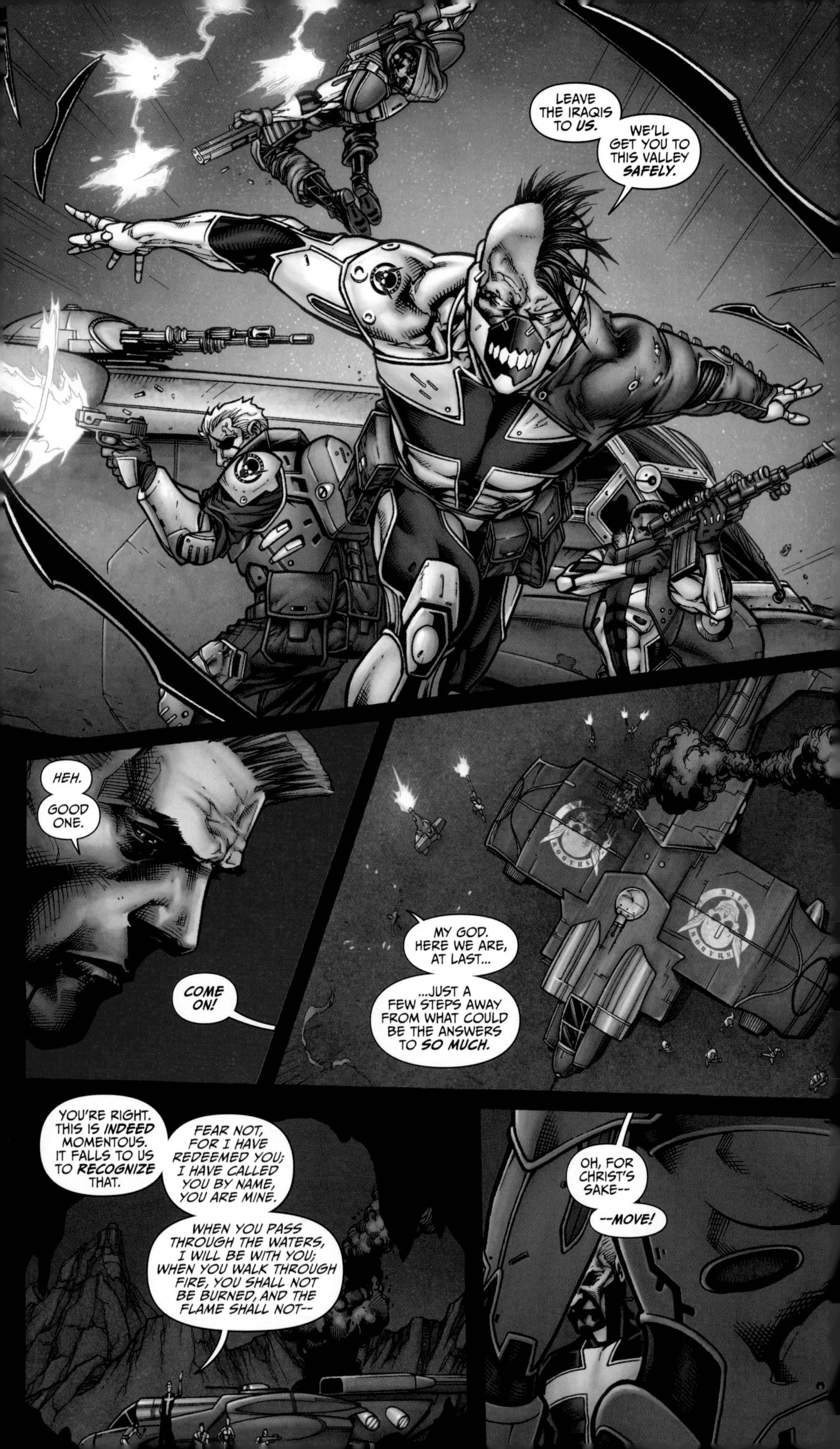
LEAVE THE IRAQIS TO US.
WE'LL GET YOU TO THIS VALLEY SAFELY.
HEH.
GOOD ONE.
COME ON!
MY GOD. HERE WE ARE, AT LAST...
...JUST A FEW STEPS AWAY FROM WHAT COULD BE THE ANSWERS TO SO MUCH.
YOU'RE RIGHT. THIS IS INDEED MOMENTOUS. IT FALLS TO US TO RECOGNIZE THAT.
FEAR NOT, FOR I HAVE REDEEMED YOU; I HAVE CALLED YOU BY NAME, YOU ARE MINE.
WHEN YOU PASS THROUGH THE WATERS, I WILL BE WITH YOU; WHEN YOU WALK THROUGH FIRE, YOU SHALL NOT BE BURNED, AND THE FLAME SHALL NOT--
OH, FOR CHRIST'S SAKE--
--MOVE!

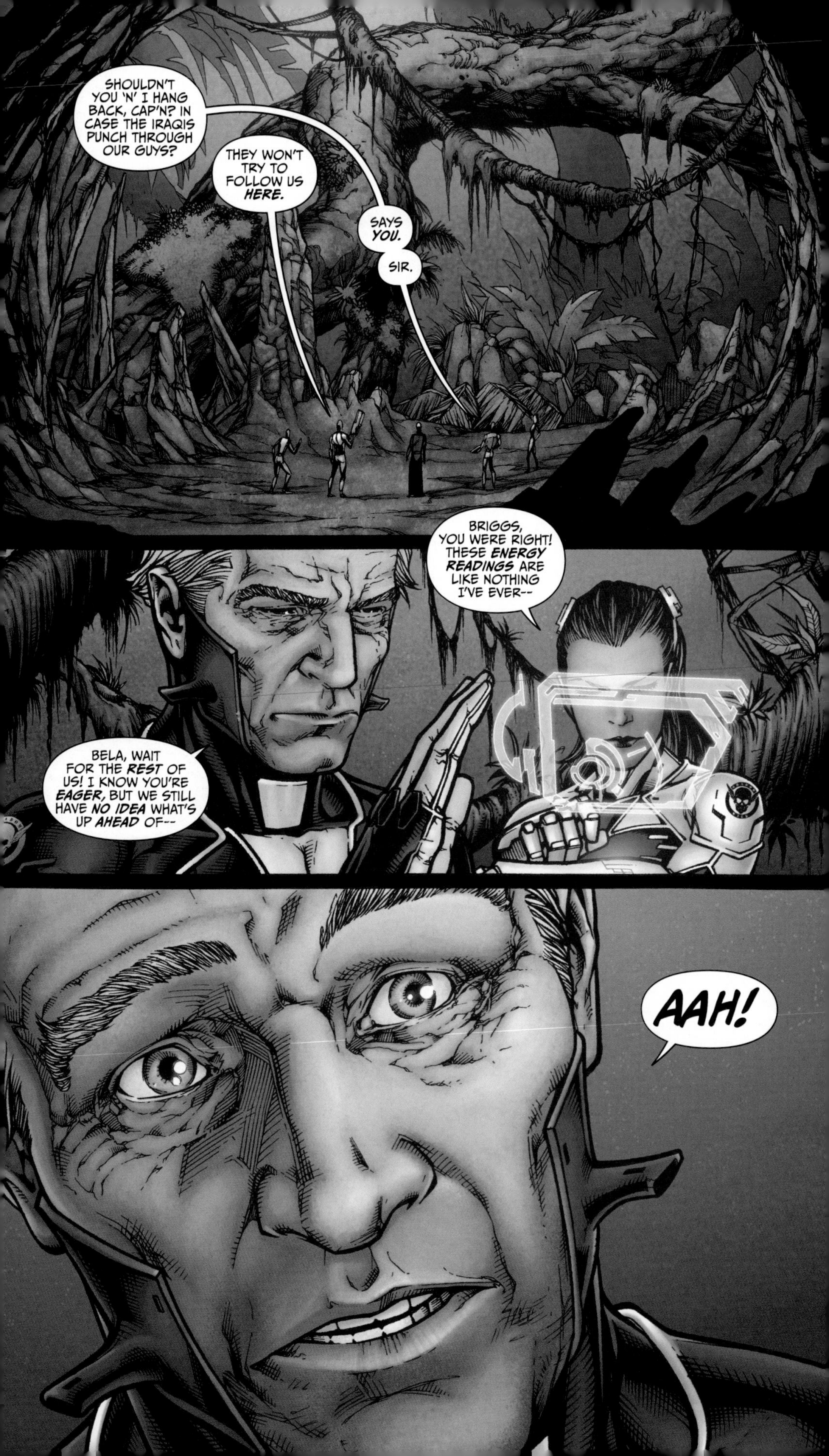
SHOULDN'T YOU 'N' I HANG BACK, CAP'N? IN CASE THE IRAQIS PUNCH THROUGH OUR GUYS?
THEY WON'T TRY TO FOLLOW US HERE.
SAYS YOU.
SIR.
BRIGGS, YOU WERE RIGHT! THESE ENERGY READINGS ARE LIKE NOTHING I'VE EVER--
BELA, WAIT FOR THE REST OF US! I KNOW YOU'RE EAGER, BUT WE STILL HAVE NO IDEA WHAT'S UP AHEAD OF--
AAH!

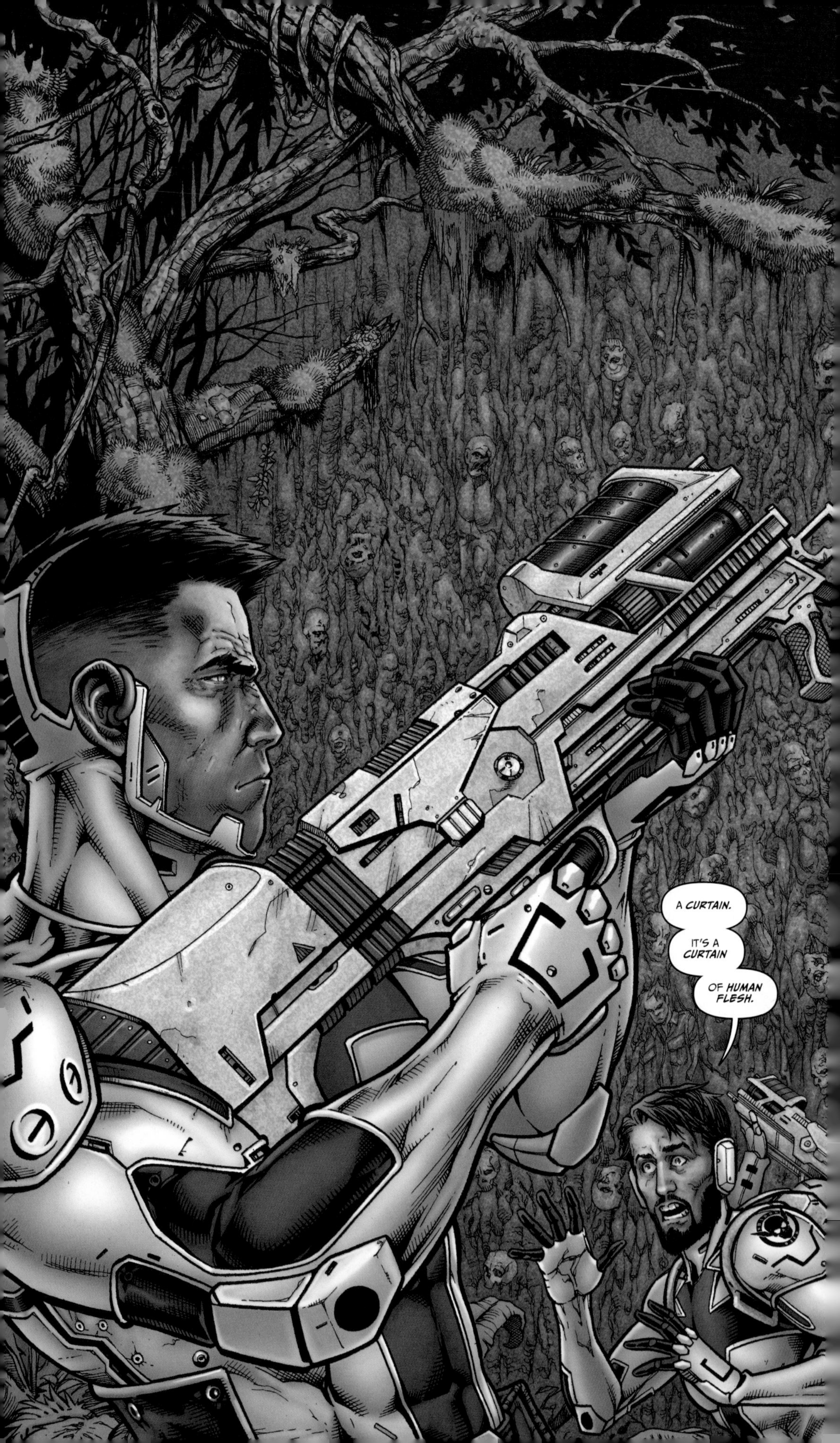
A CURTAIN.
IT'S A CURTAIN
OF HUMAN FLESH.

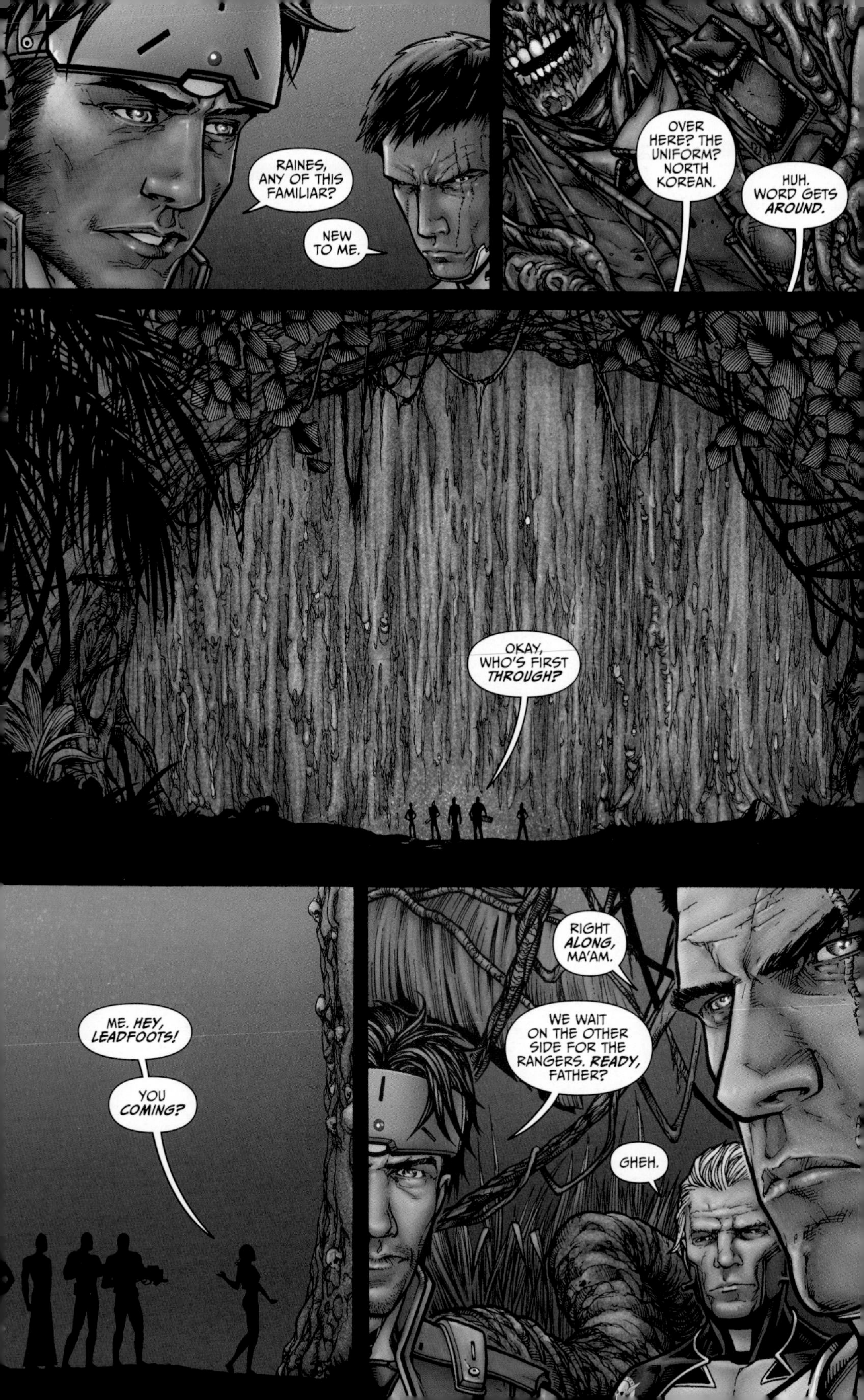
RAINES, ANY OF THIS FAMILIAR?
NEW TO ME.
OVER HERE? THE UNIFORM? NORTH KOREAN.
HUH. WORD GETS AROUND.
OKAY, WHO'S FIRST THROUGH?
ME. HEY, LEADFOOTS!
YOU COMING?
RIGHT ALONG, MA'AM.
WE WAIT ON THE OTHER SIDE FOR THE RANGERS. READY, FATHER?
GHEH.

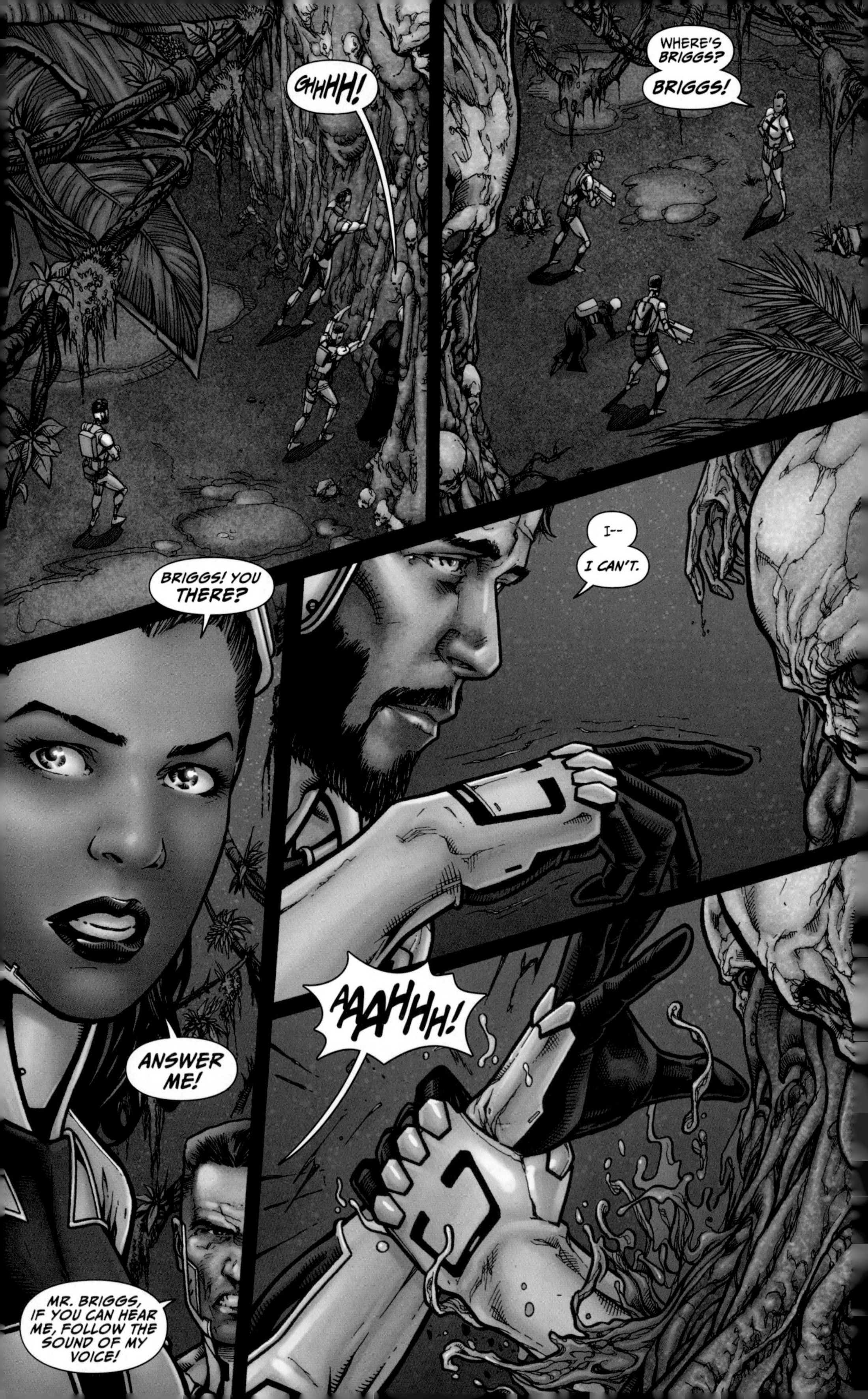
GHHHH!
WHERE'S BRIGGS?
BRIGGS!
BRIGGS! YOU THERE?
I--
I CAN'T.
ANSWER ME!
AAAHHH!
MR. BRIGGS, IF YOU CAN HEAR ME, FOLLOW THE SOUND OF MY VOICE!

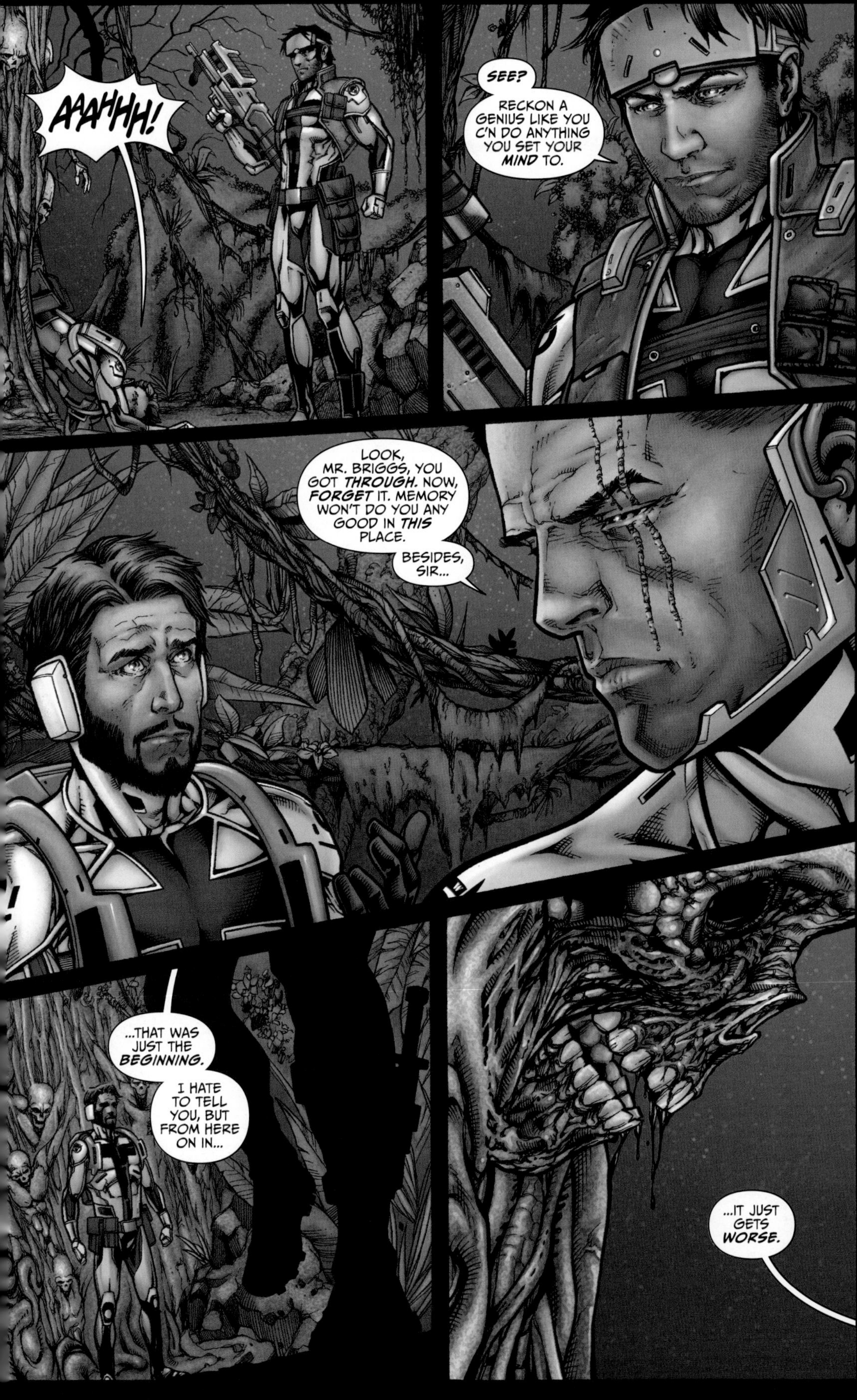
AAAHHH!
SEE?
RECKON A GENIUS LIKE YOU C'N DO ANYTHING YOU SET YOUR MIND TO.
LOOK, MR. BRIGGS, YOU GOT THROUGH. NOW, FORGET IT. MEMORY WON'T DO YOU ANY GOOD IN THIS PLACE.
BESIDES, SIR...
...THAT WAS JUST THE BEGINNING.
I HATE TO TELL YOU, BUT FROM HERE ON IN...
...IT JUST GETS WORSE.

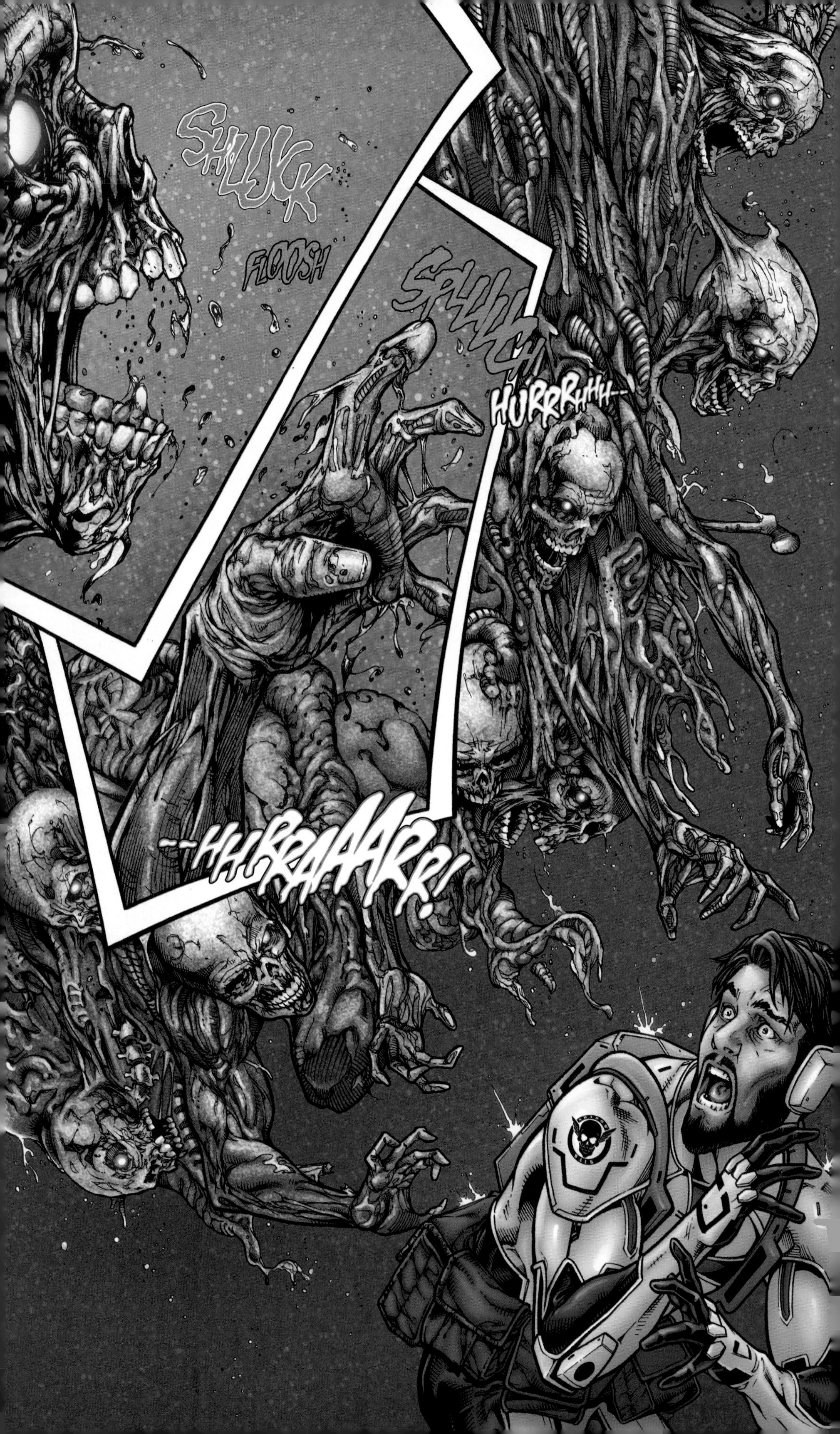
SHLUKCK
FLOOSH
SPLUTCH
HURRRHHH--
--HHRRAAAARR!

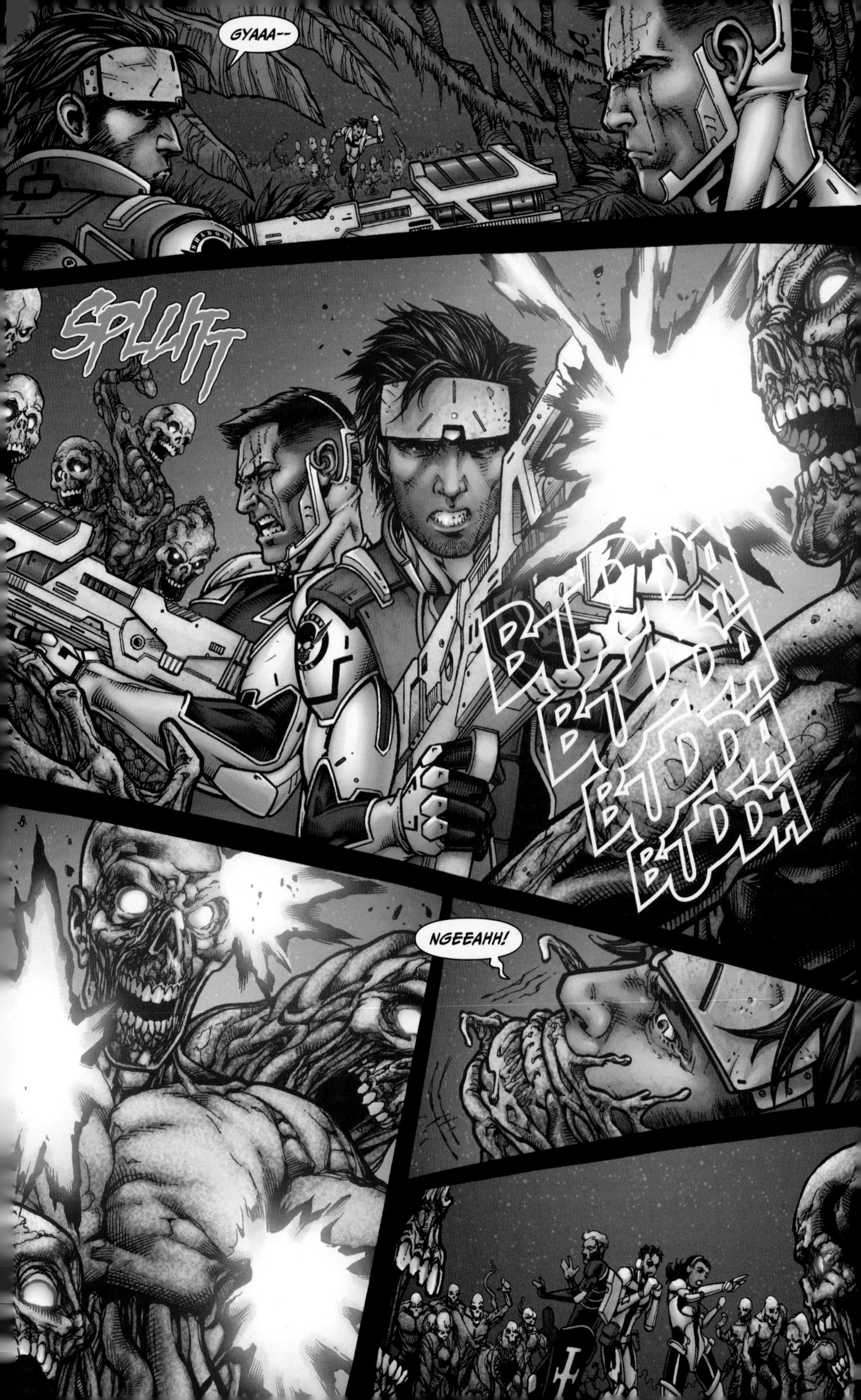
GYAAA--
SPLUTT
BUDDA
BUDDA
BUDDA
BUDDA
NGEEAHH!

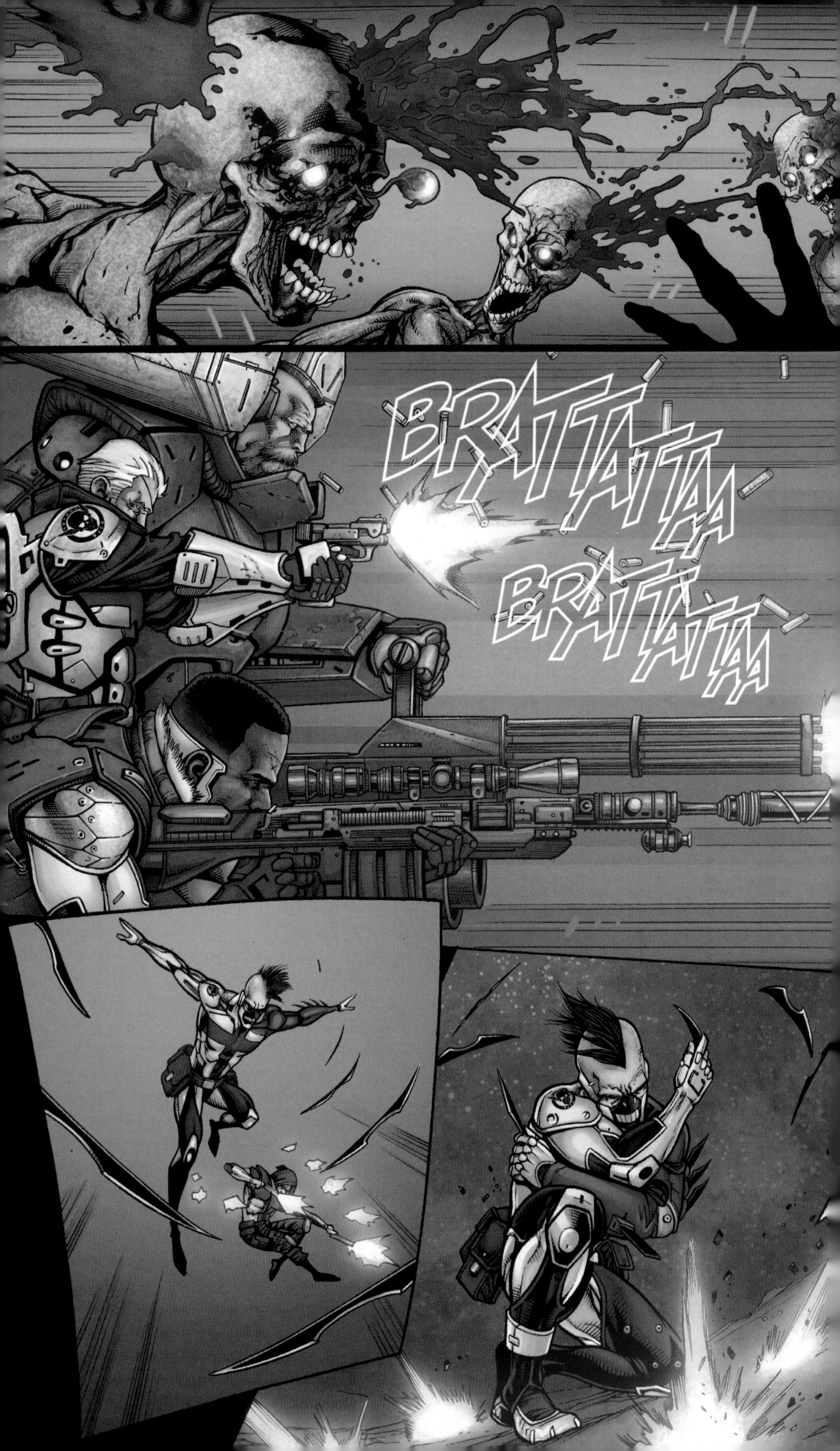
BRATTATTAA
BRATTATTA

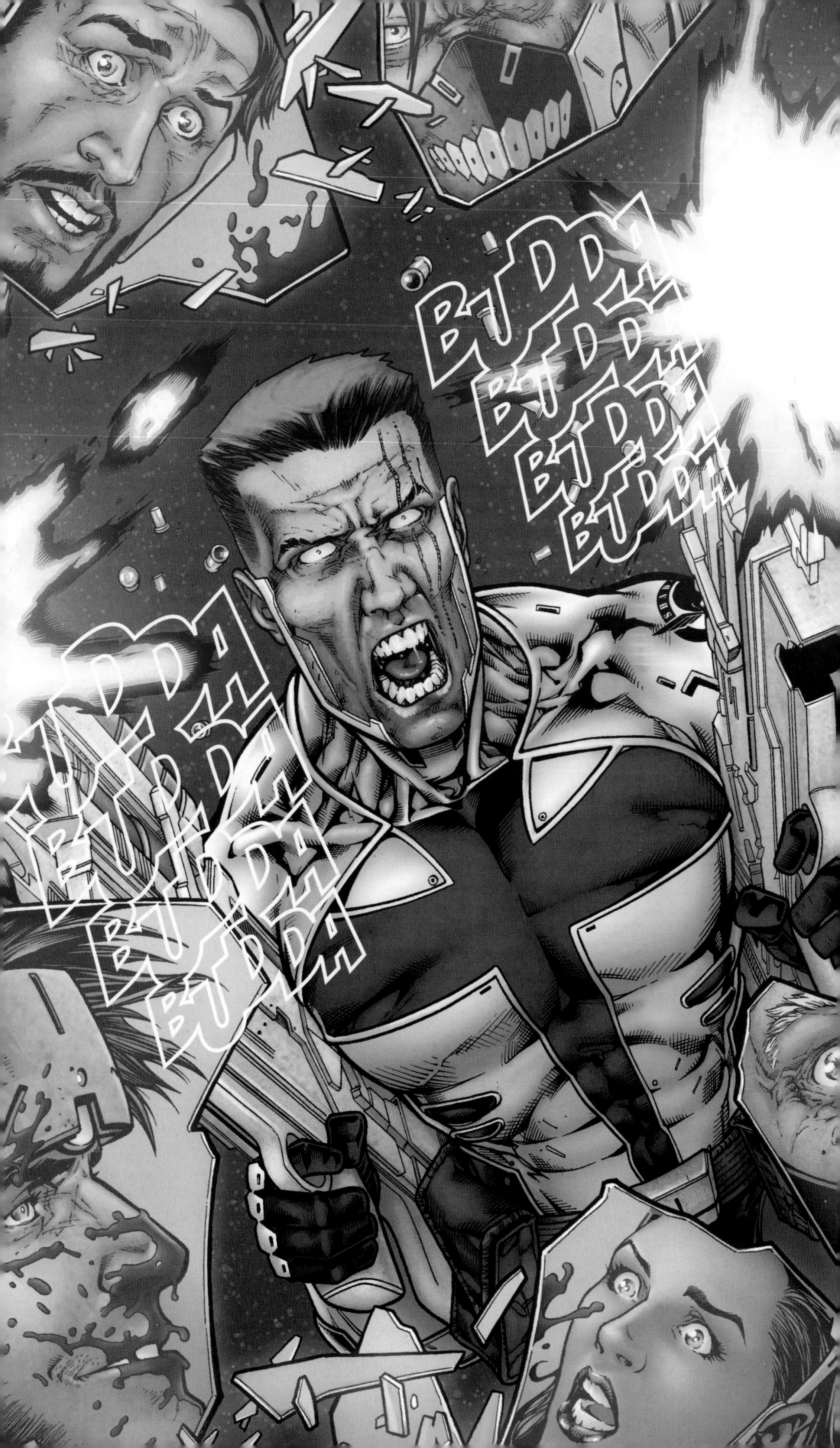
BUDDA
BUDDA
BUDDA
BUDDA
BUDDA
BUDDA
BUDDA
BUDDA
BUDDA

NICE *SHOOTIN'* THERE, DEADEYE.

Y'ALRIGHT?

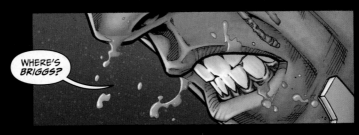

WHERE'S *BRIGGS?*

WHAT'S HE WANT WITH ME?

GO *ASK* HIM.

NO. HE'S *CRAZY,* I CAN'T--

THAT MAN JUST SAVED YOUR *LIFE.*

AAH!

BRIGGS.

MAGNETIC RAIL GUN. ZERO RECOIL DESPITE THE SIZE OF THE AMMO.

KILLING POWER OF A 20MM CHAIN GUN, WEIGHT OF A .45.

WH-WHAT?

YOU WANTED TO KNOW.

YES.

YES, I DID.

THAT'S GOOD.

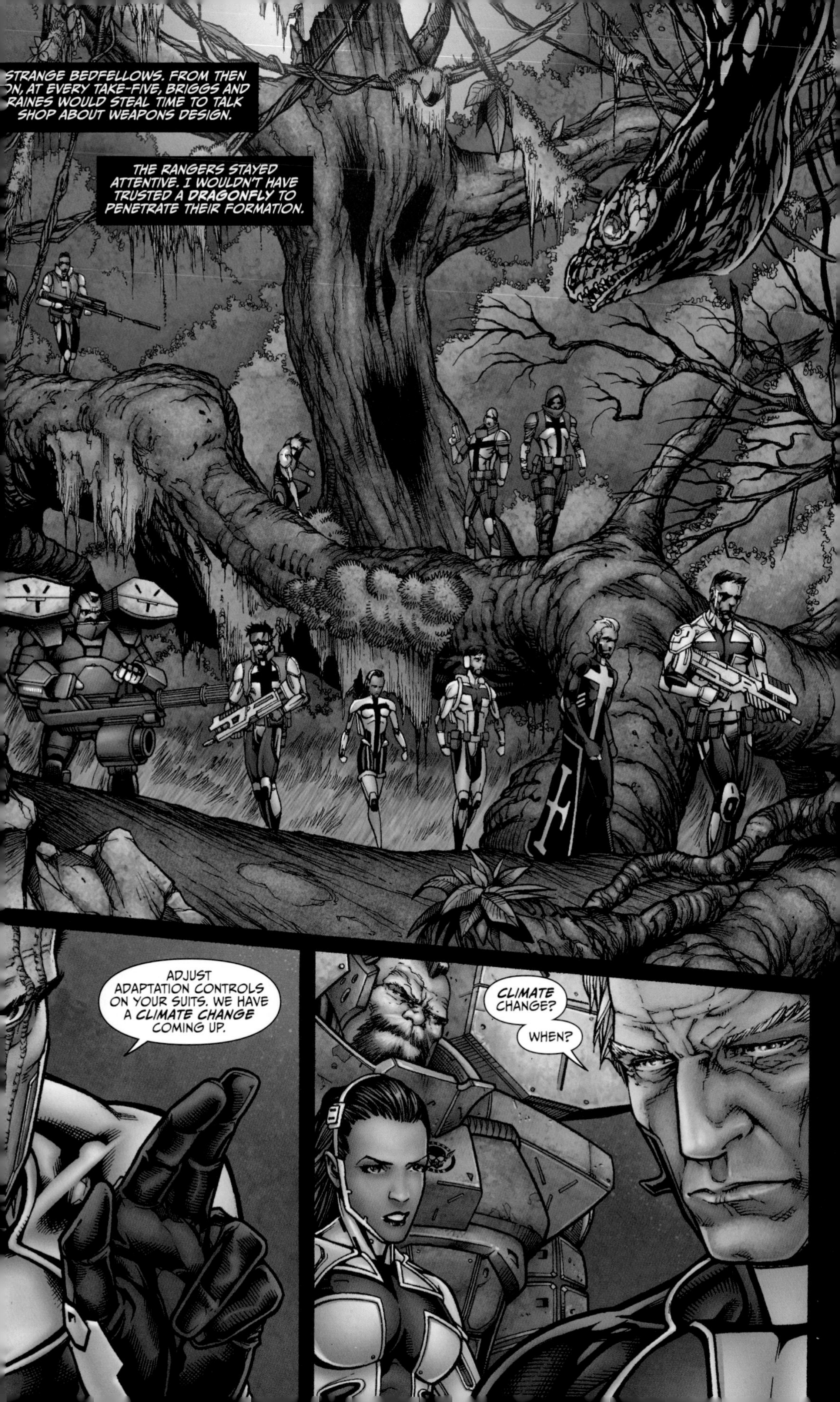
STRANGE BEDFELLOWS. FROM THEN ON, AT EVERY TAKE-FIVE, BRIGGS AND RAINES WOULD STEAL TIME TO TALK SHOP ABOUT WEAPONS DESIGN.
THE RANGERS STAYED ATTENTIVE. I WOULDN'T HAVE TRUSTED A DRAGONFLY TO PENETRATE THEIR FORMATION.
ADJUST ADAPTATION CONTROLS ON YOUR SUITS. WE HAVE A CLIMATE CHANGE COMING UP.
CLIMATE CHANGE?
WHEN?

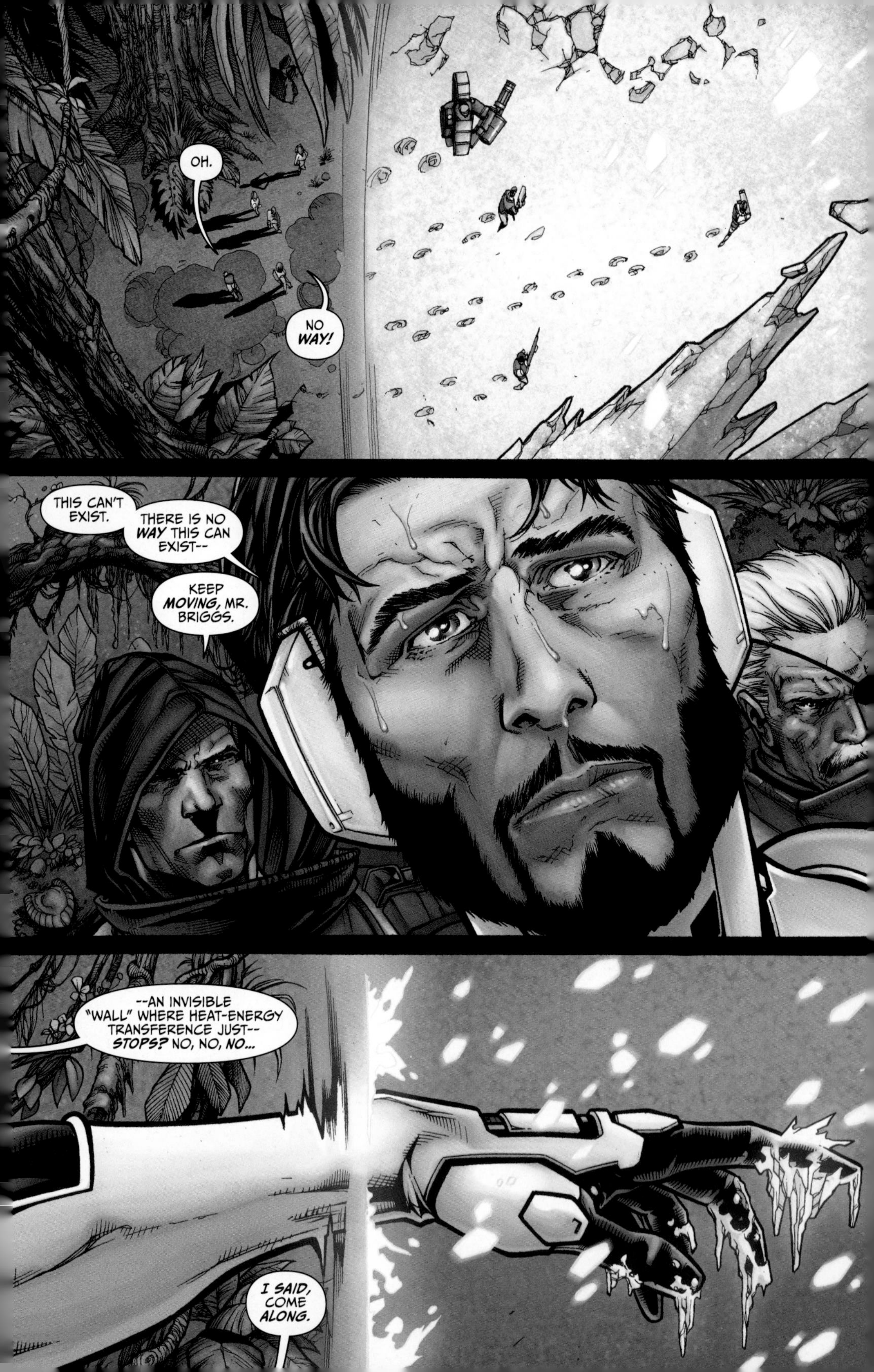
OH.
NO WAY!
THIS CAN'T EXIST.
THERE IS NO WAY THIS CAN EXIST--
KEEP MOVING, MR. BRIGGS.
--AN INVISIBLE "WALL" WHERE HEAT-ENERGY TRANSFERENCE JUST--STOPS? NO, NO, NO...
I SAID, COME ALONG.

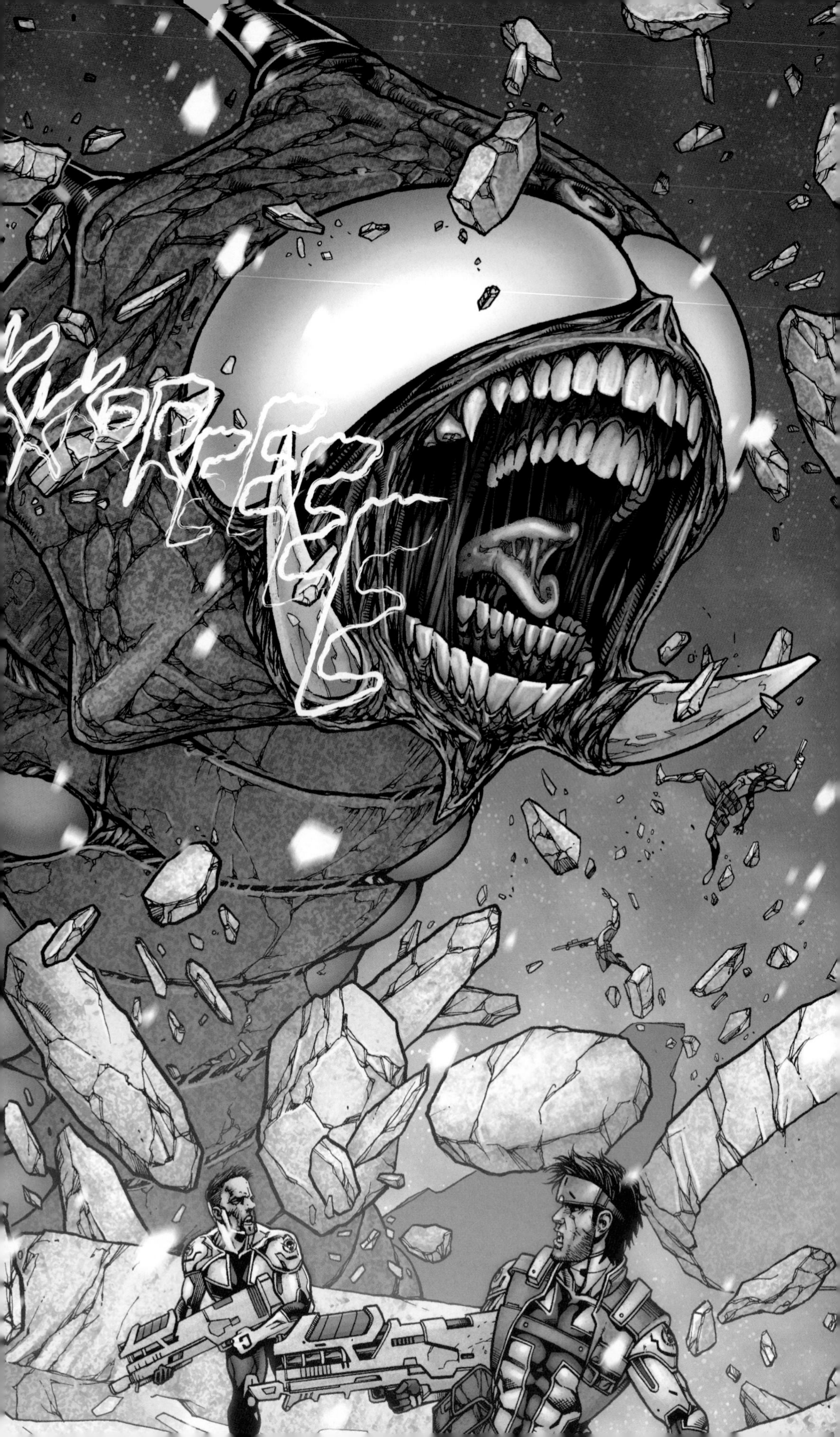
WORREEEE

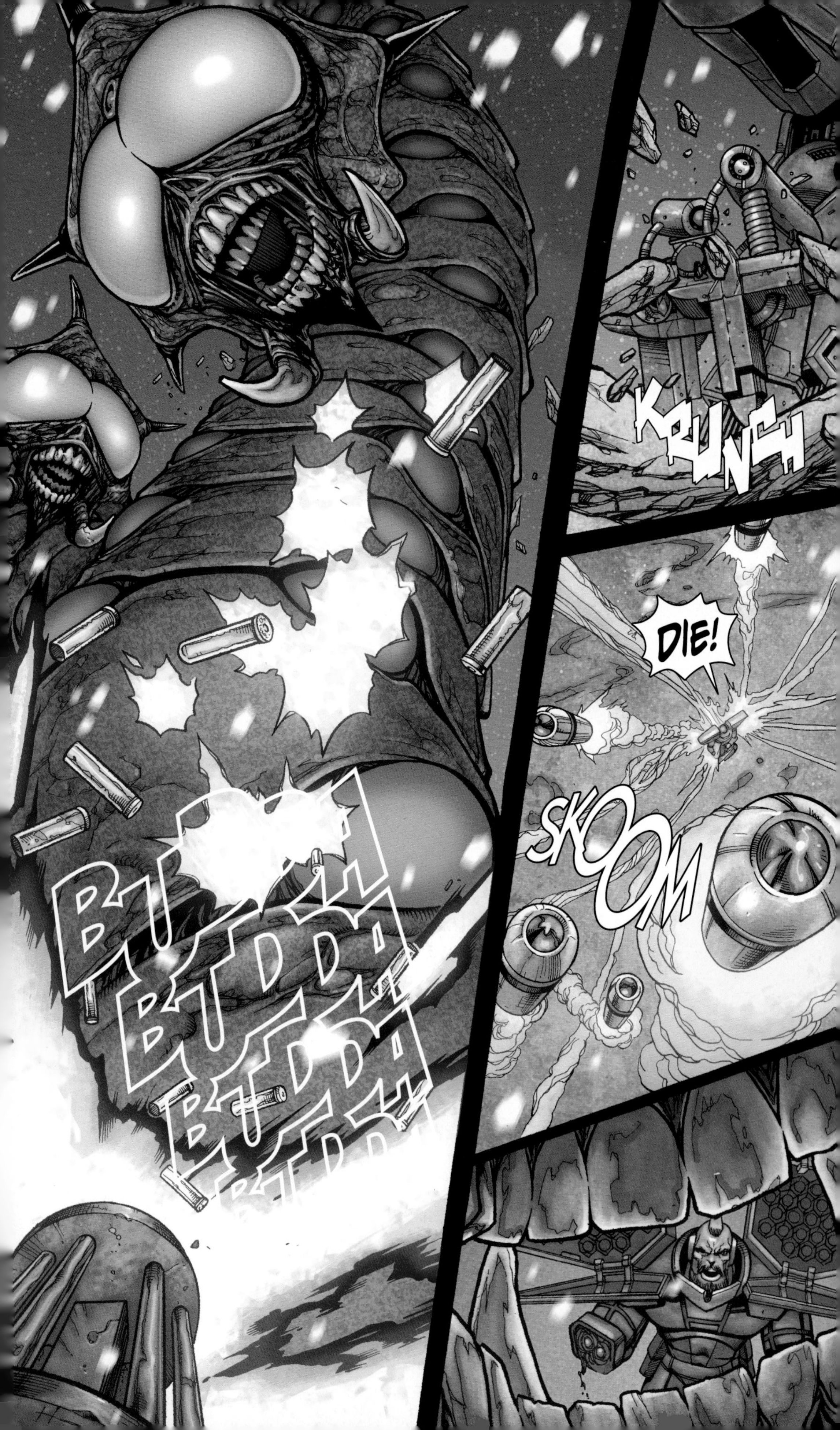
KRUNCH
DIE!
SKOOOM
BUDDA
BUDDA
BUDDA

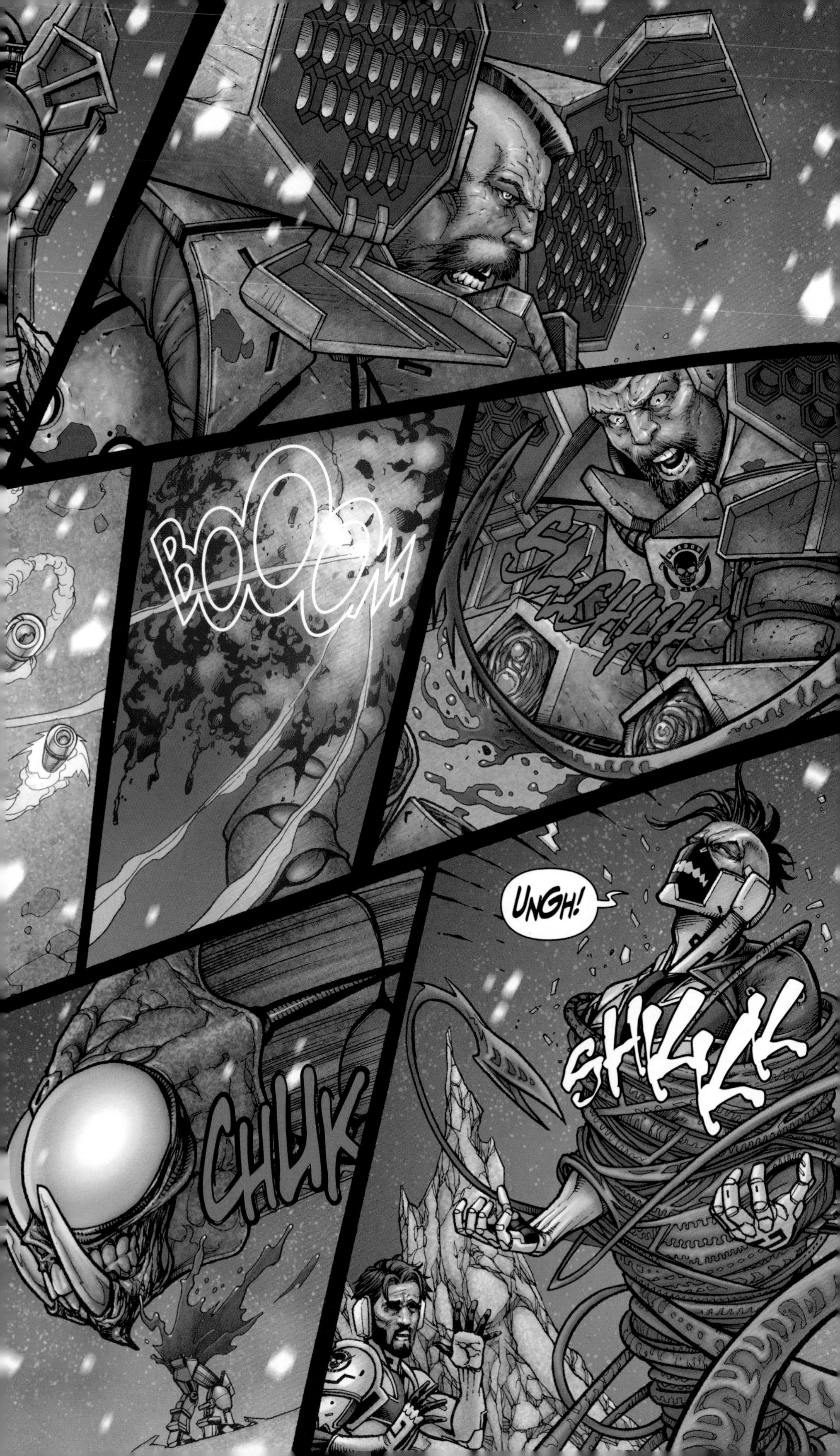
BOOOM
SSCHHH
UNGH!
SHKK
CHUK

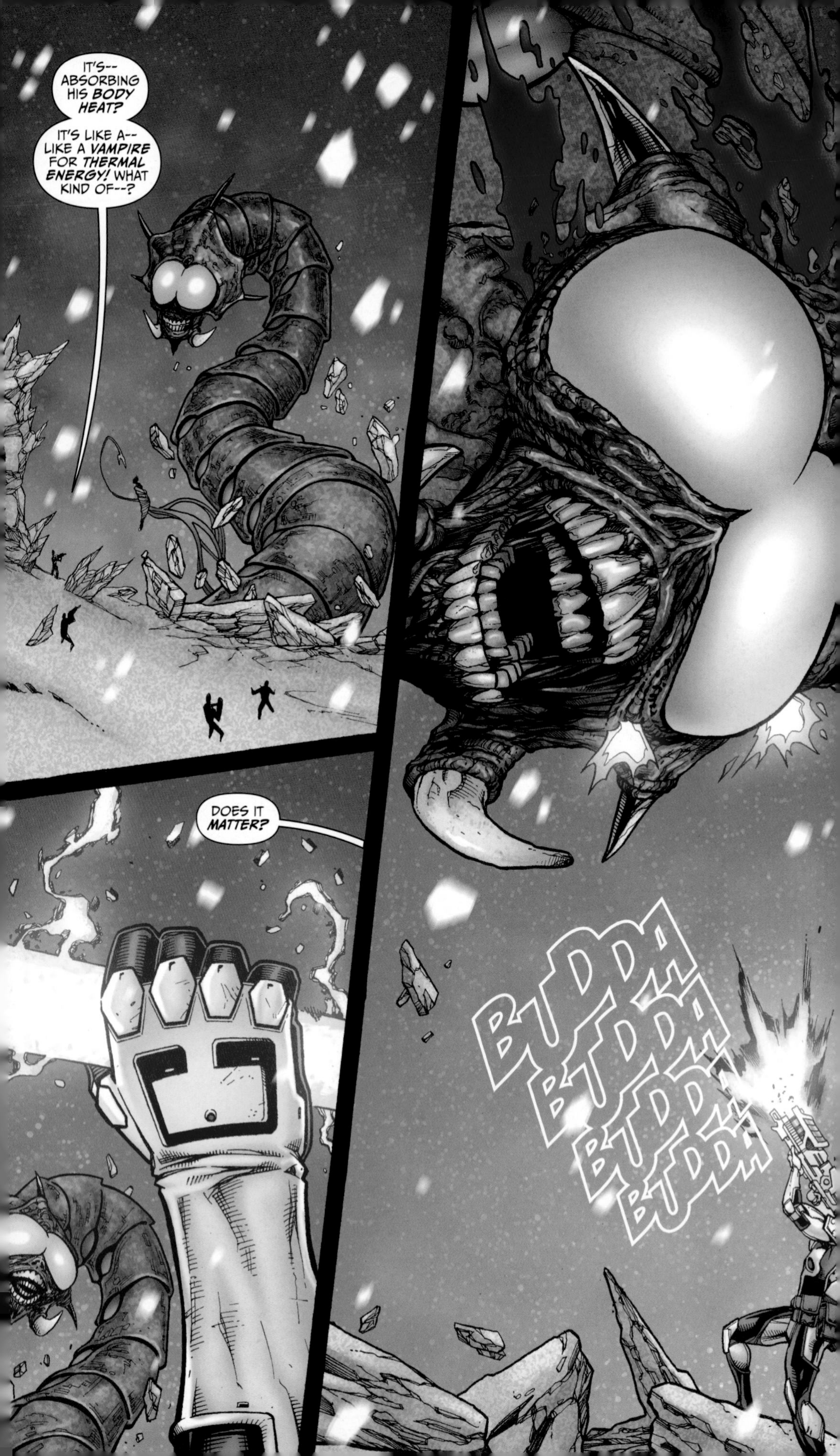
IT'S--
ABSORBING HIS BODY HEAT?
IT'S LIKE A-- LIKE A VAMPIRE FOR THERMAL ENERGY! WHAT KIND OF--?
DOES IT MATTER?
BUDDA BUDDA BUDDA BUDDA BUDDA

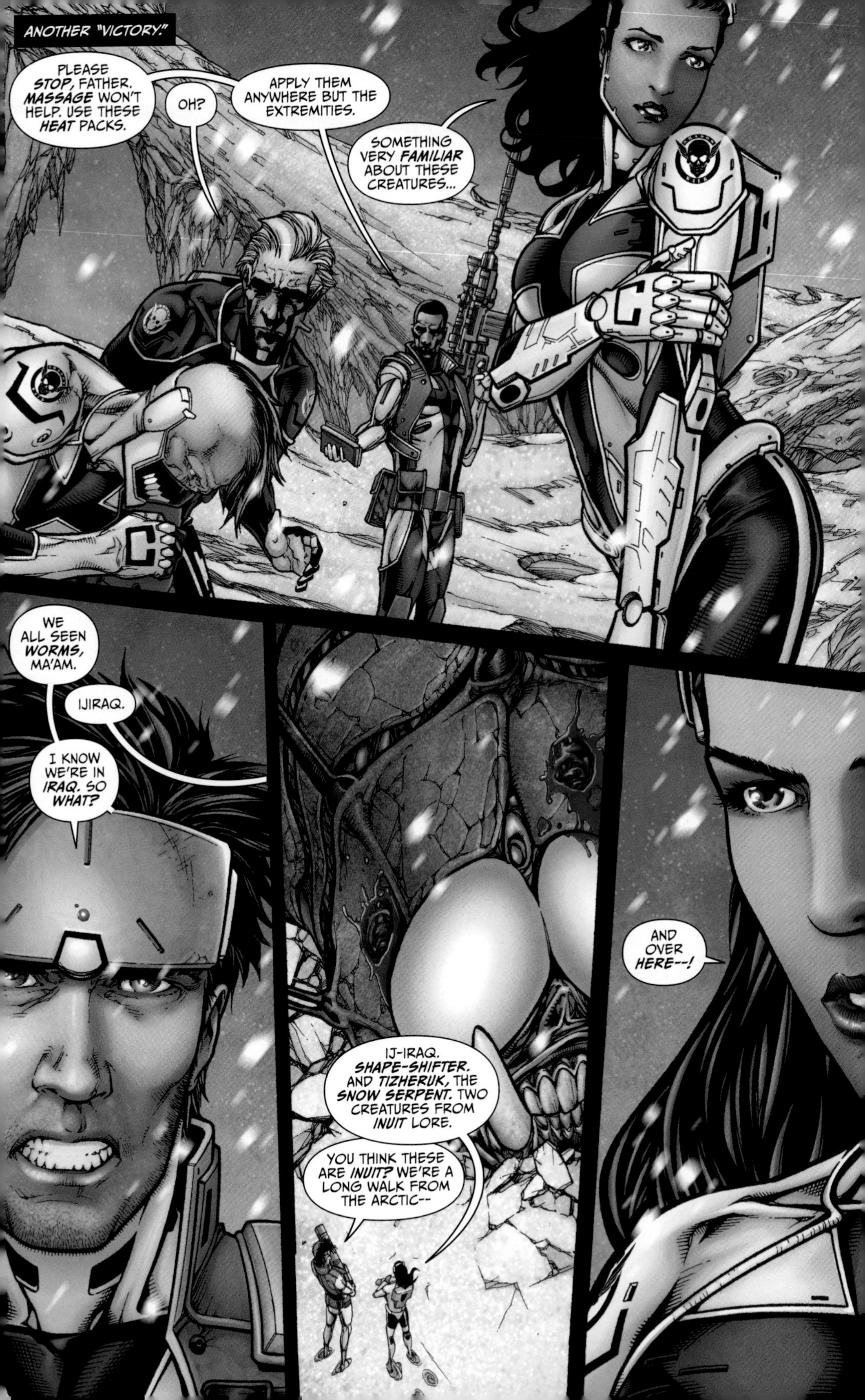
ANOTHER "VICTORY."
PLEASE STOP, FATHER. MASSAGE WON'T HELP. USE THESE HEAT PACKS.
OH?
APPLY THEM ANYWHERE BUT THE EXTREMITIES.
SOMETHING VERY FAMILIAR ABOUT THESE CREATURES...
WE ALL SEEN WORMS, MA'AM.
IJIRAQ.
I KNOW WE'RE IN IRAQ. SO WHAT?
AND OVER HERE--!
IJ-IRAQ. SHAPE-SHIFTER. AND TIZHERUK, THE SNOW SERPENT. TWO CREATURES FROM INUIT LORE.
YOU THINK THESE ARE INUIT? WE'RE A LONG WALK FROM THE ARCTIC--

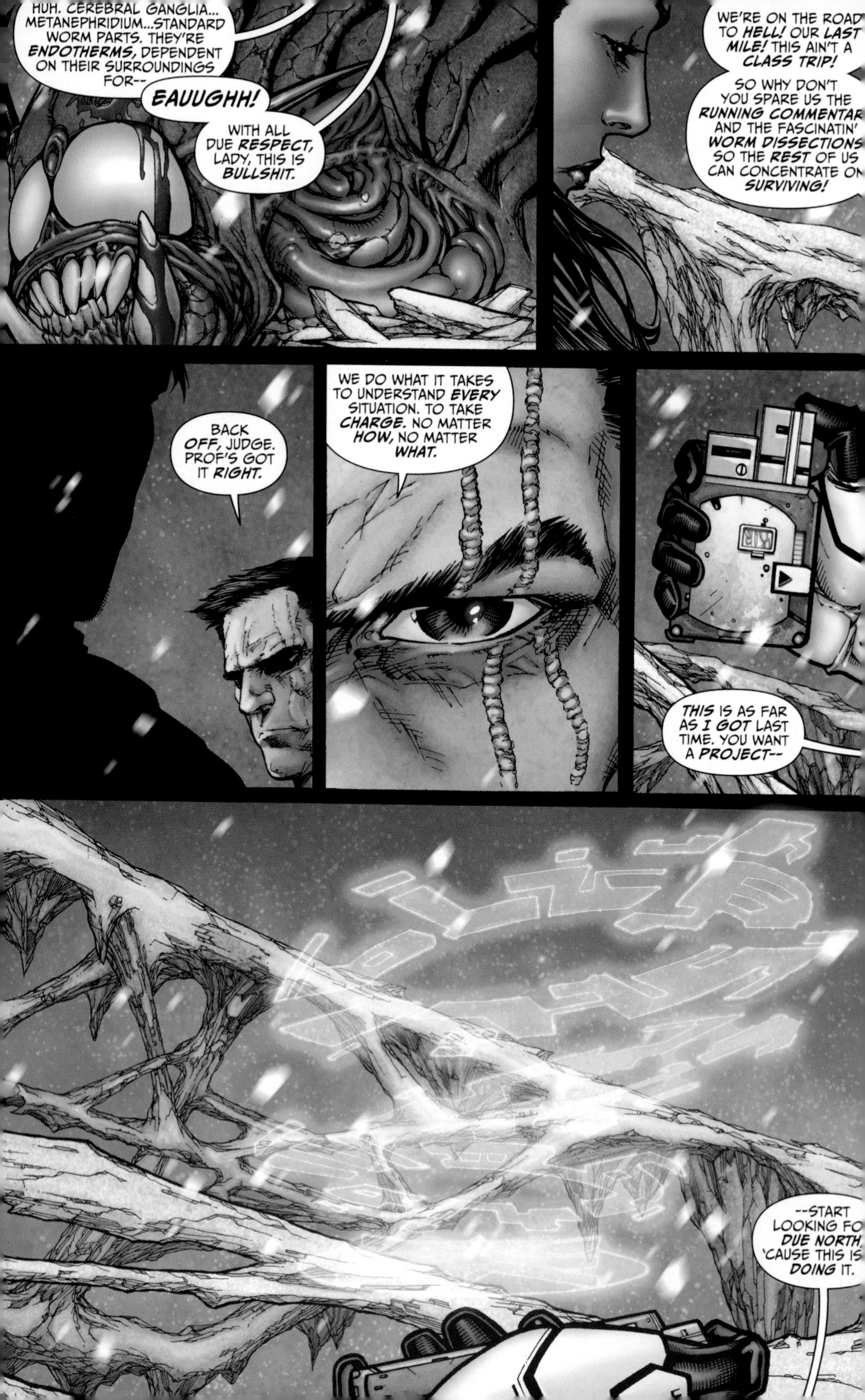
HUH. CEREBRAL GANGLIA... METANEPHRIDIUM...STANDARD WORM PARTS. THEY'RE ENDOTHERMS, DEPENDENT ON THEIR SURROUNDINGS FOR--
EAUUGHH!
WITH ALL DUE RESPECT, LADY, THIS IS BULLSHIT.
WE'RE ON THE ROAD TO HELL! OUR LAST MILE! THIS AIN'T A CLASS TRIP!
SO WHY DON'T YOU SPARE US THE RUNNING COMMENTAR AND THE FASCINATIN' WORM DISSECTIONS SO THE REST OF US CAN CONCENTRATE O SURVIVING!
BACK OFF, JUDGE. PROF'S GOT IT RIGHT.
WE DO WHAT IT TAKES TO UNDERSTAND EVERY SITUATION. TO TAKE CHARGE. NO MATTER HOW, NO MATTER WHAT.
THIS IS AS FAR AS I GOT LAST TIME. YOU WANT A PROJECT--
--START LOOKING FO DUE NORTH, 'CAUSE THIS IS DOING IT.

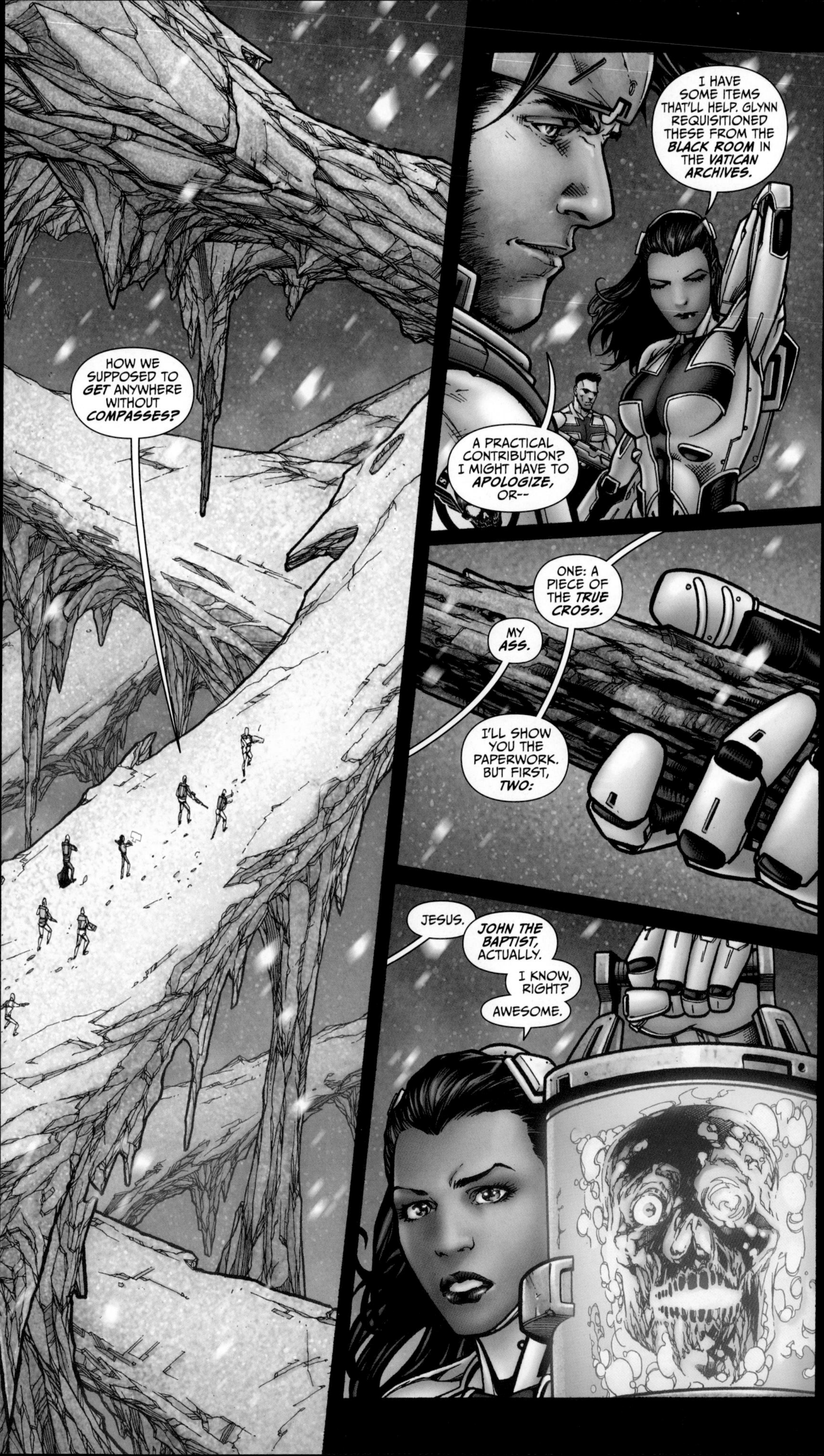

HOW WE SUPPOSED TO GET ANYWHERE WITHOUT COMPASSES?
I HAVE SOME ITEMS THAT'LL HELP. GLYNN REQUISITIONED THESE FROM THE BLACK ROOM IN THE VATICAN ARCHIVES.
A PRACTICAL CONTRIBUTION? I MIGHT HAVE TO APOLOGIZE, OR--
ONE: A PIECE OF THE TRUE CROSS.
MY ASS.
I'LL SHOW YOU THE PAPERWORK. BUT FIRST, TWO:
JESUS.
JOHN THE BAPTIST, ACTUALLY.
I KNOW, RIGHT?
AWESOME.

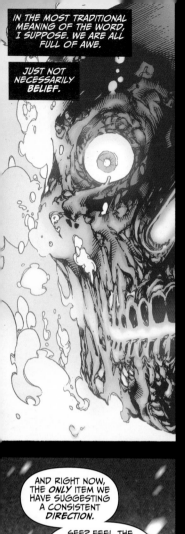

IN THE MOST TRADITIONAL MEANING OF THE WORD, I SUPPOSE. WE ARE ALL FULL OF AWE.

JUST NOT NECESSARILY BELIEF.

BACK TO *SCRIPTURE.* THE PHRASE *"THY ROD AND THY STAFF, THEY COMFORT ME"* GOT MANGLED IN TRANSLATION. RIGHT, FATHER?

IT'S SAID.

JEWISH TARGUM INTERPRETS "ROD AND STAFF" AS, MORE LITERALLY, "WORD AND LAW"... OR BETTER YET, "GUIDANCE AND DEFENSE."

SO I GIVE YOU *DEFENSE:* SHARDS OF THE CRUCIFIX UPON WHICH *JESUS* DIED, FEARED BY *COUNTLESS* CREATURES OF MYTH...

....AND *GUIDANCE:* THE PRESERVED HEAD OF JOHN THE BAPTIST, PURPORTEDLY A TRUE-SIGHT PROPHET.

AND RIGHT NOW, THE *ONLY* ITEM WE HAVE SUGGESTING A CONSISTENT *DIRECTION.*

SEE? FEEL THE *TUG?* WHEREVER WE GO--OR MORE CORRECTLY, WHEREVER HE *WANTS* US TO GO-- HE'LL *LEAD* US.

PADRE! SHE *SHITTIN'* US?

LORD, LET THIS SOUL AND LET THIS FLESH PRESS ON AMID THE PROFANE AND THE VULGAR--

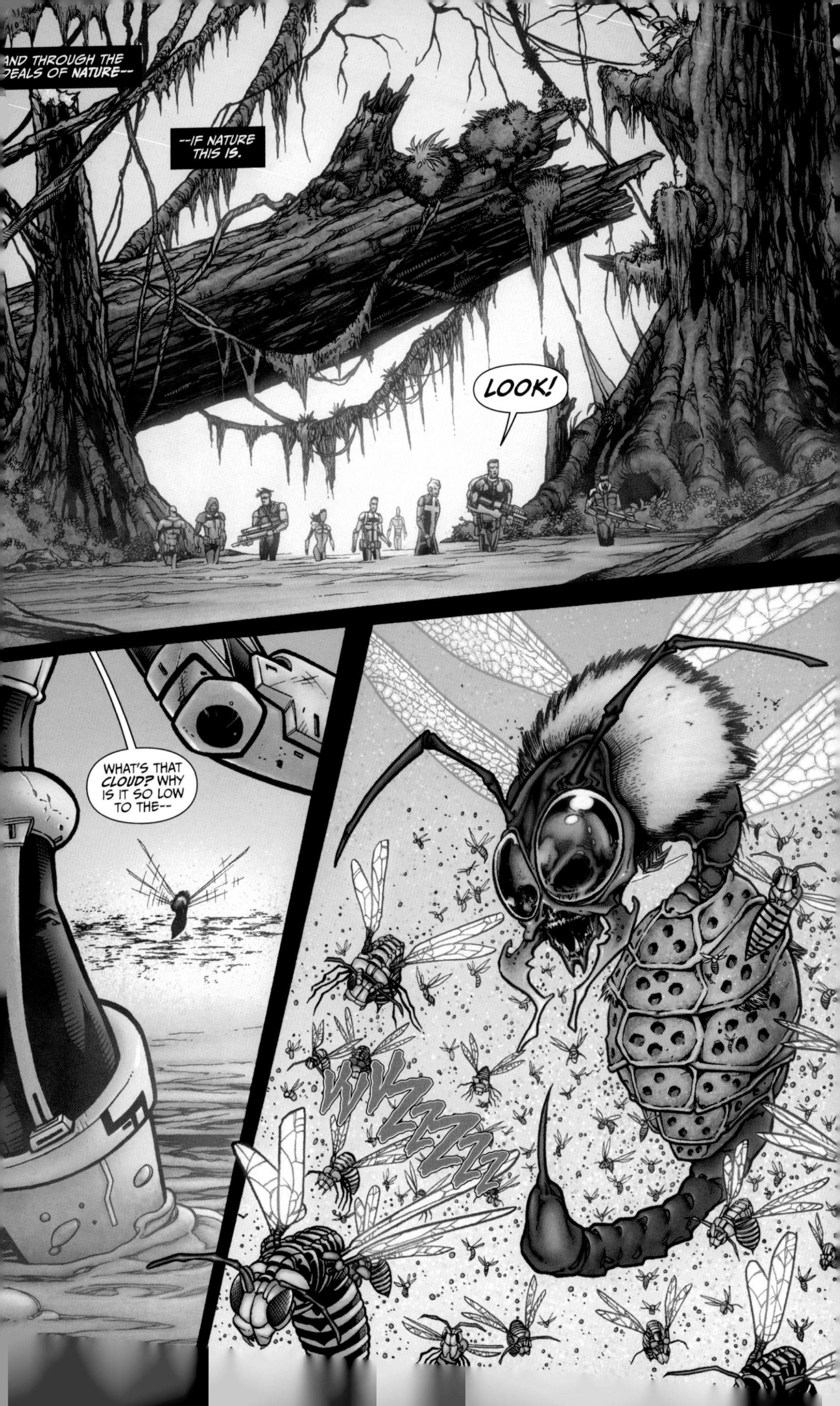
AND THROUGH THE
DEALS OF NATURE--
--IF NATURE
THIS IS.
LOOK!
WHAT'S THAT
CLOUD? WHY
IS IT SO LOW
TO THE--
WKZZZZZ

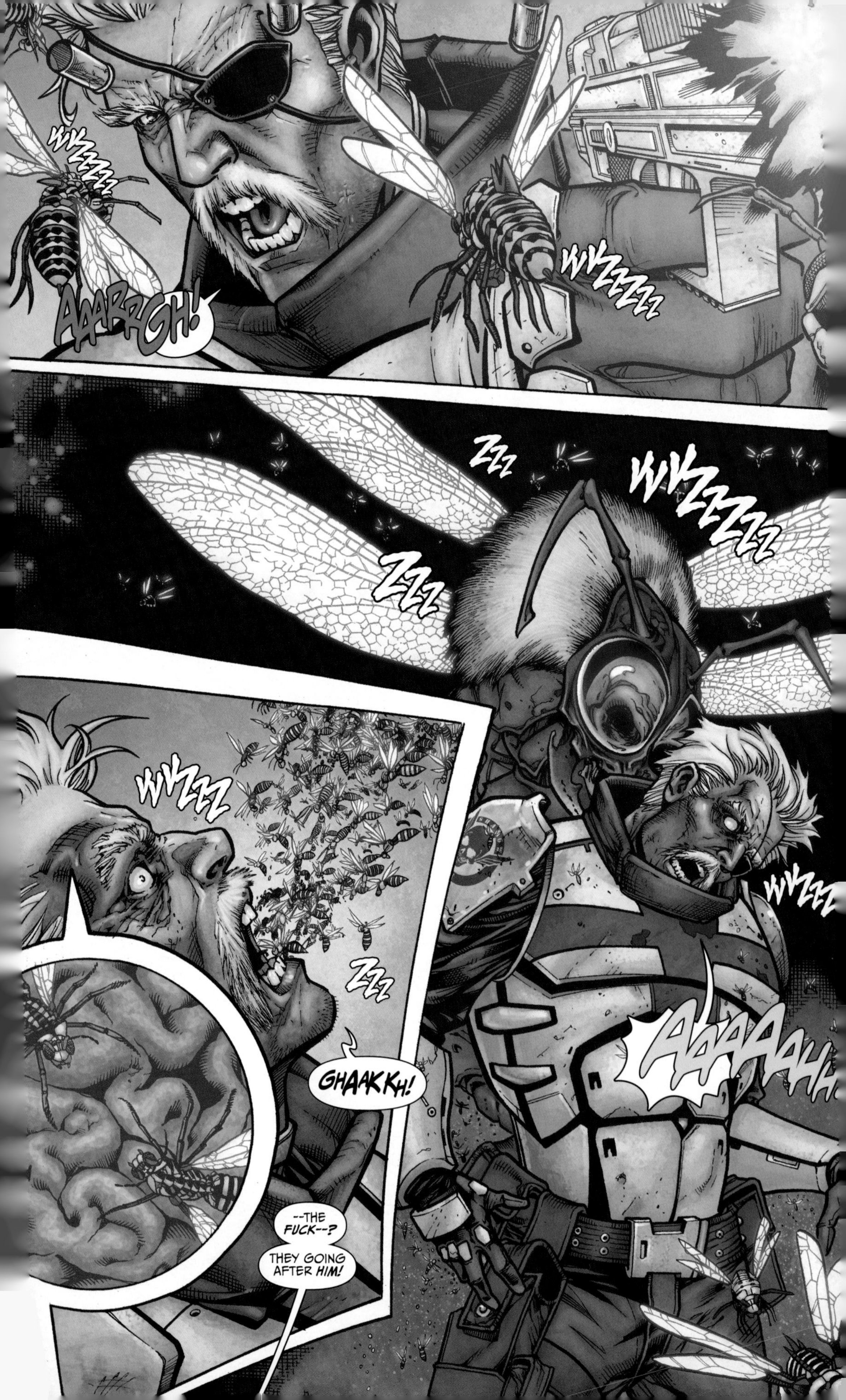
WVZZZZZ
AAARRGH!
WVZZZZZZ
ZZZ
WVZZZZZZ
ZZZ
WVZZZ
ZZZ
GHAAKKH!
--THE FUCK--?
THEY GOING AFTER HIM!
WVZZZ
AAAAAAHH

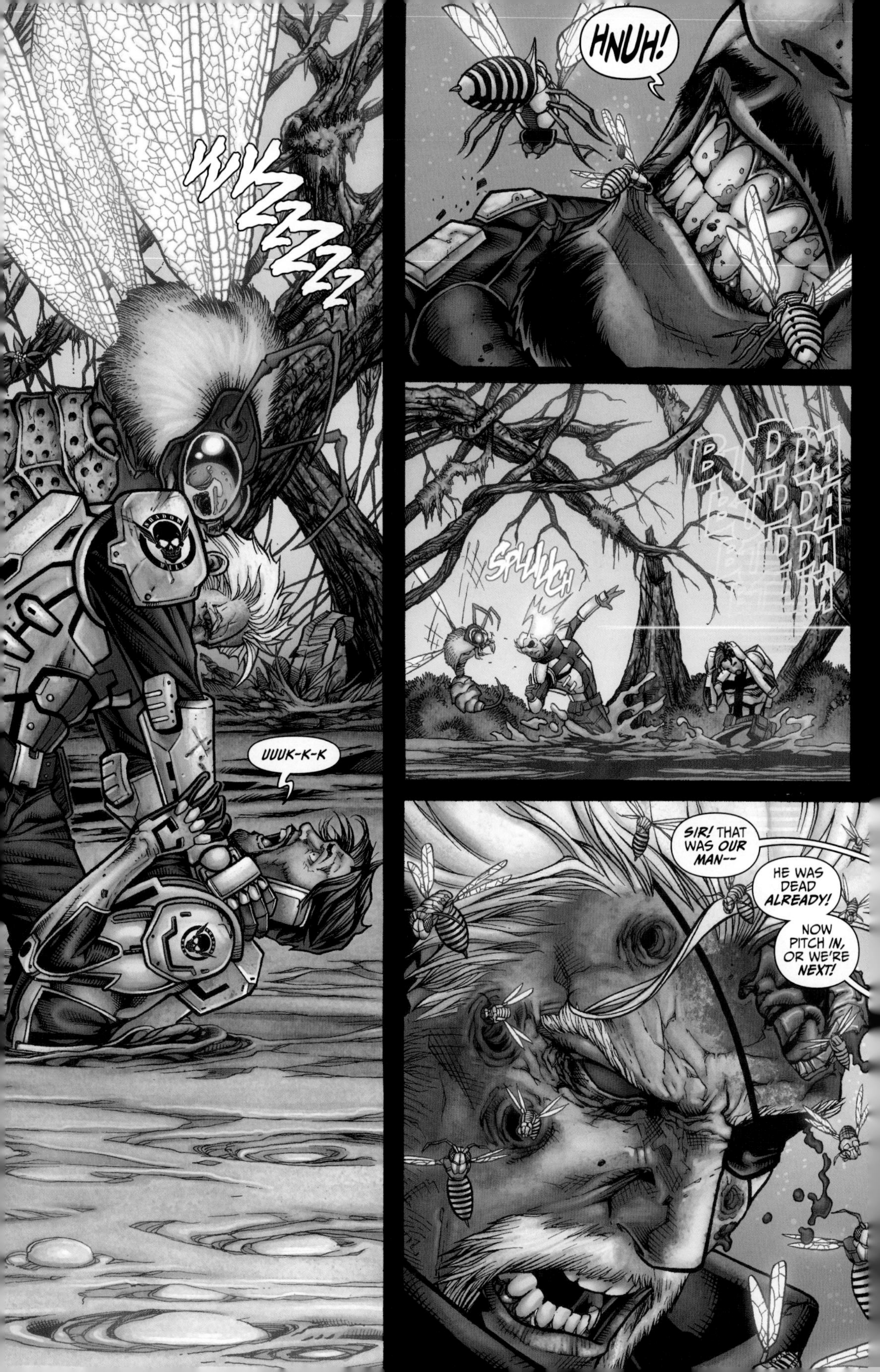

WHZZZZZZ
UUUK-K-K
HNUH!
SPLUUCH
BUDDA BUDDA BUDDA
SIR! THAT WAS OUR MAN--
HE WAS DEAD ALREADY!
NOW PITCH IN, OR WE'RE NEXT!

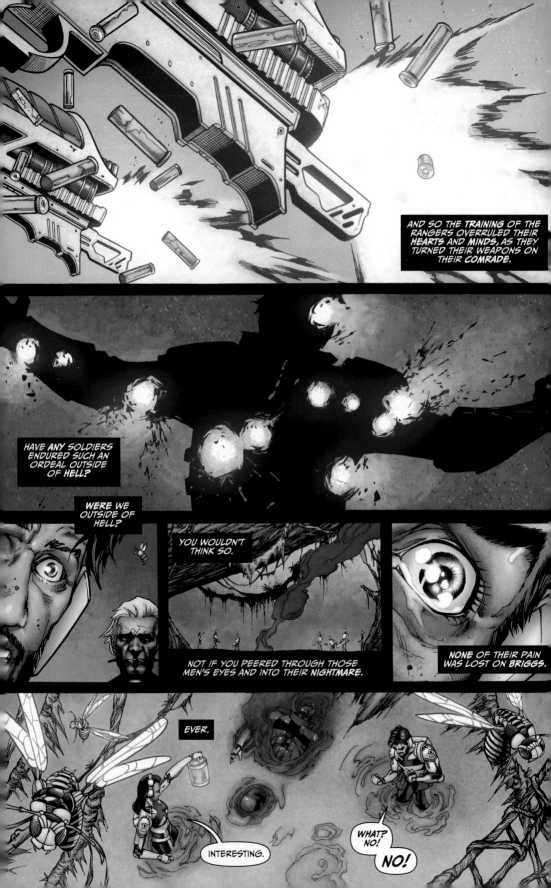

AND SO THE *TRAINING* OF THE RANGERS OVERRULED THEIR *HEARTS* AND *MINDS*, AS THEY TURNED THEIR WEAPONS ON THEIR *COMRADE*.

HAVE *ANY* SOLDIERS ENDURED SUCH AN ORDEAL OUTSIDE OF HELL?

WERE WE OUTSIDE OF HELL?

YOU WOULDN'T THINK SO.

NOT IF YOU PEERED THROUGH THOSE MEN'S EYES AND INTO THEIR *NIGHTMARE*.

NONE OF THEIR PAIN WAS LOST ON BRIGGS.

EVER.

INTERESTING.

WHAT? NO!

NO!

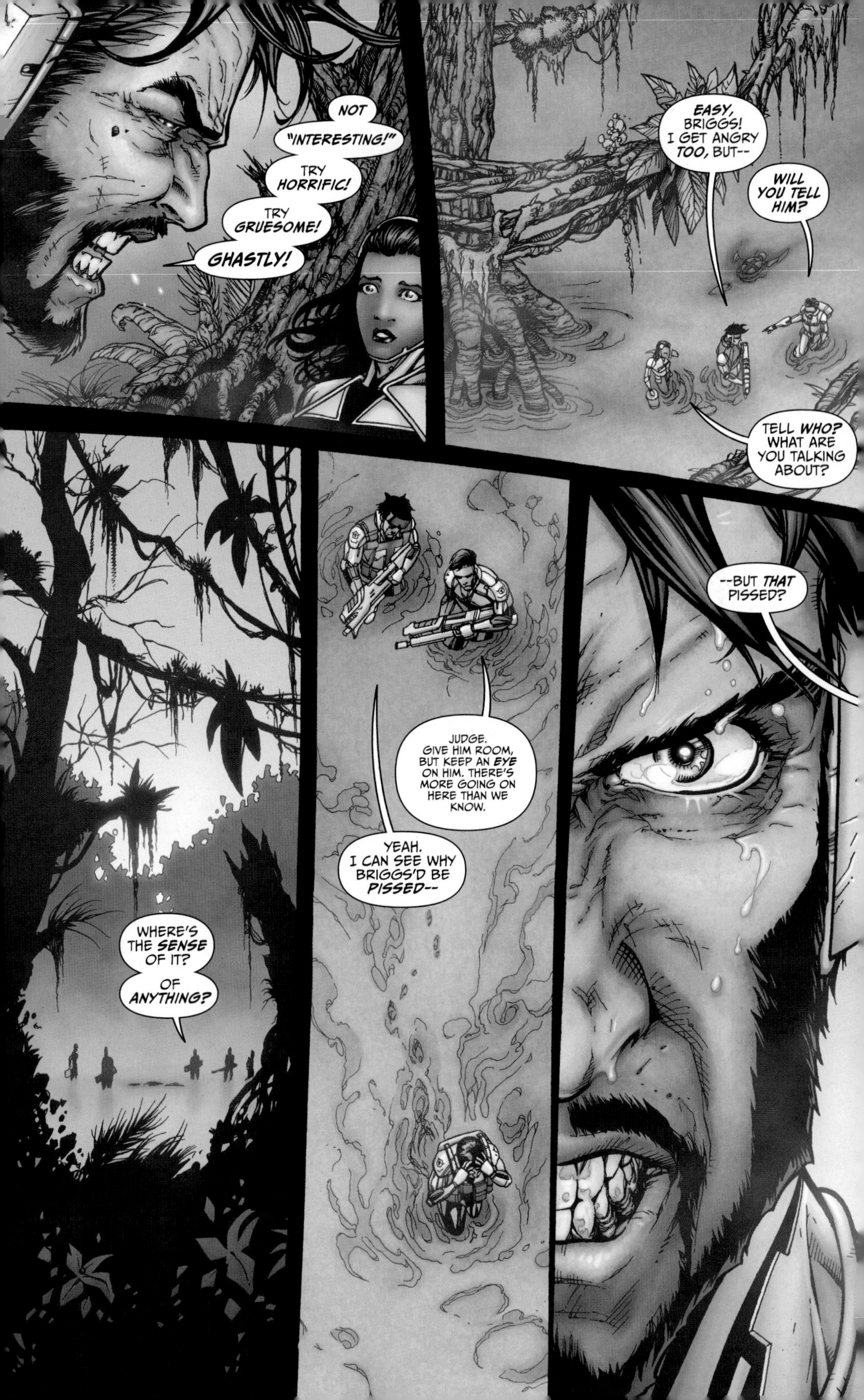
NOT "INTERESTING!"
TRY HORRIFIC!
TRY GRUESOME!
GHASTLY!
EASY, BRIGGS! I GET ANGRY TOO, BUT--
WILL YOU TELL HIM?
TELL WHO? WHAT ARE YOU TALKING ABOUT?
WHERE'S THE SENSE OF IT?
OF ANYTHING?
JUDGE. GIVE HIM ROOM, BUT KEEP AN EYE ON HIM. THERE'S MORE GOING ON HERE THAN WE KNOW.
YEAH. I CAN SEE WHY BRIGGS'D BE PISSED--
--BUT THAT PISSED?

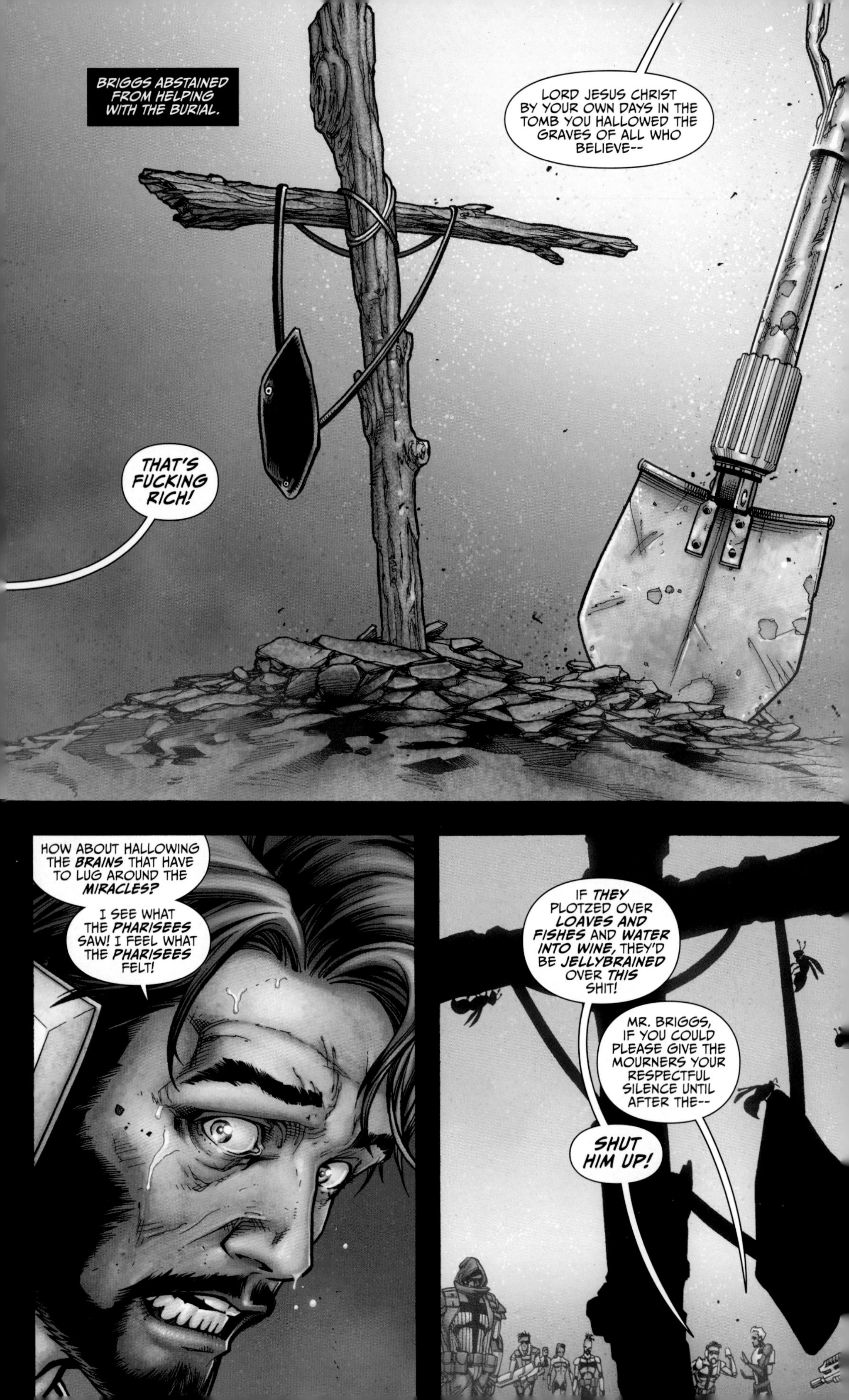

BRIGGS ABSTAINED FROM HELPING WITH THE BURIAL.
LORD JESUS CHRIST BY YOUR OWN DAYS IN THE TOMB YOU HALLOWED THE GRAVES OF ALL WHO BELIEVE--
THAT'S FUCKING RICH!
HOW ABOUT HALLOWING THE BRAINS THAT HAVE TO LUG AROUND THE MIRACLES?
I SEE WHAT THE PHARISEES SAW! I FEEL WHAT THE PHARISEES FELT!
IF THEY PLOTZED OVER LOAVES AND FISHES AND WATER INTO WINE, THEY'D BE JELLYBRAINED OVER THIS SHIT!
MR. BRIGGS, IF YOU COULD PLEASE GIVE THE MOURNERS YOUR RESPECTFUL SILENCE UNTIL AFTER THE--
SHUT HIM UP!

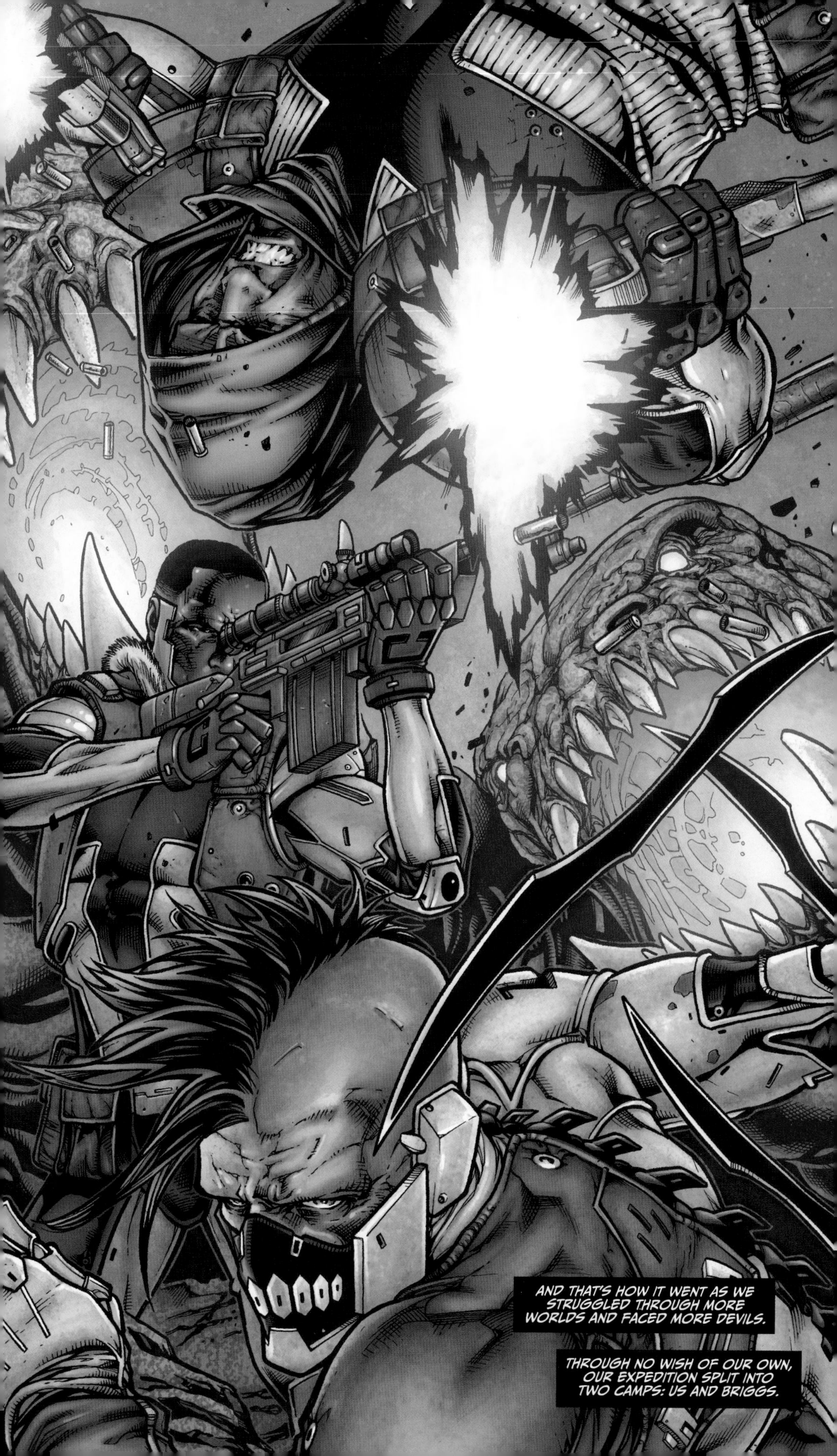

AND THAT'S HOW IT WENT AS WE STRUGGLED THROUGH MORE WORLDS AND FACED MORE DEVILS.
THROUGH NO WISH OF OUR OWN, OUR EXPEDITION SPLIT INTO TWO CAMPS: US AND BRIGGS.

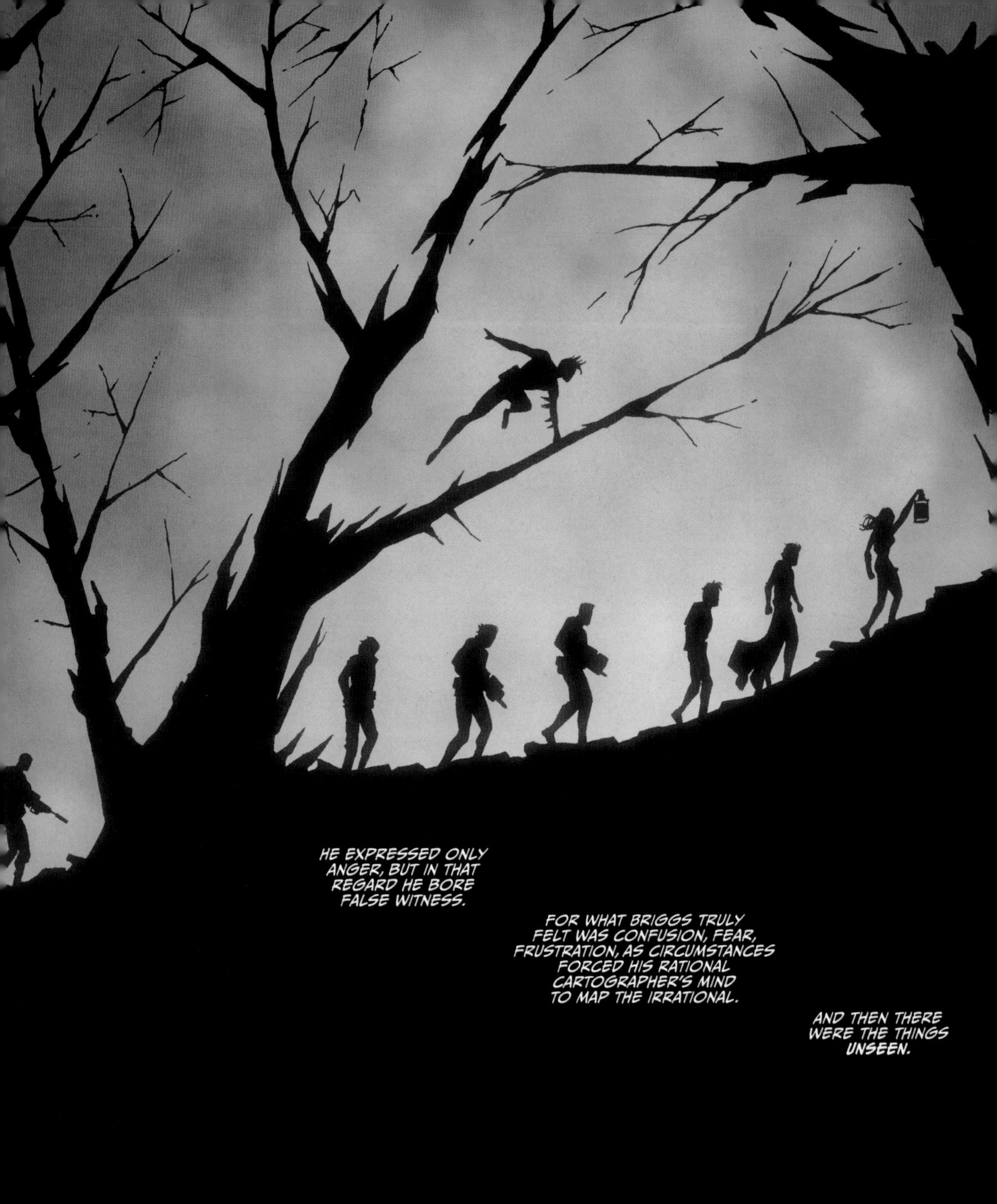
HE EXPRESSED ONLY ANGER, BUT IN THAT REGARD HE BORE FALSE WITNESS.
FOR WHAT BRIGGS TRULY FELT WAS CONFUSION, FEAR, FRUSTRATION, AS CIRCUMSTANCES FORCED HIS RATIONAL CARTOGRAPHER'S MIND TO MAP THE IRRATIONAL.
AND THEN THERE WERE THE THINGS UNSEEN.

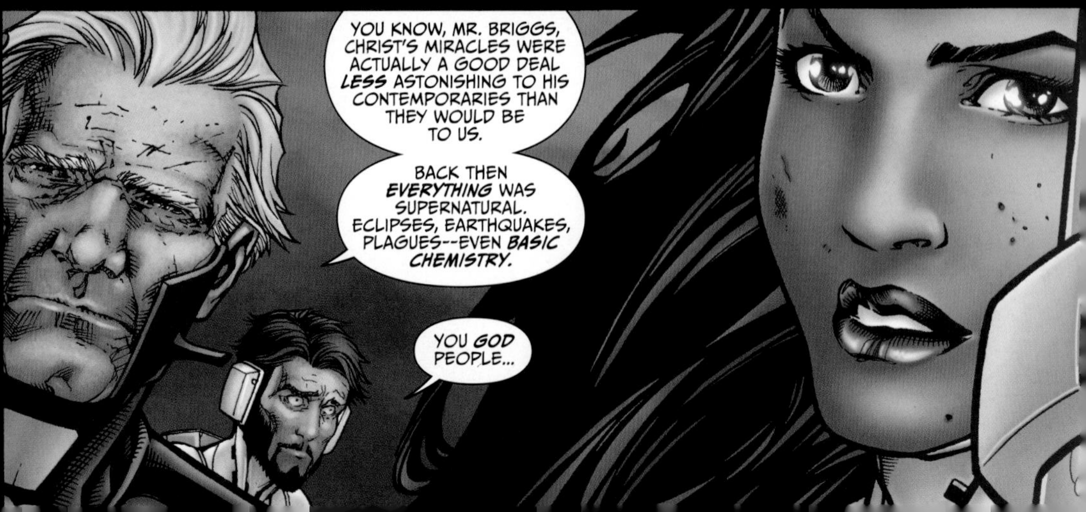
YOU KNOW, MR. BRIGGS, CHRIST'S MIRACLES WERE ACTUALLY A GOOD DEAL LESS ASTONISHING TO HIS CONTEMPORARIES THAN THEY WOULD BE TO US.
BACK THEN EVERYTHING WAS SUPERNATURAL. ECLIPSES, EARTHQUAKES, PLAGUES--EVEN BASIC CHEMISTRY.
YOU GOD PEOPLE...

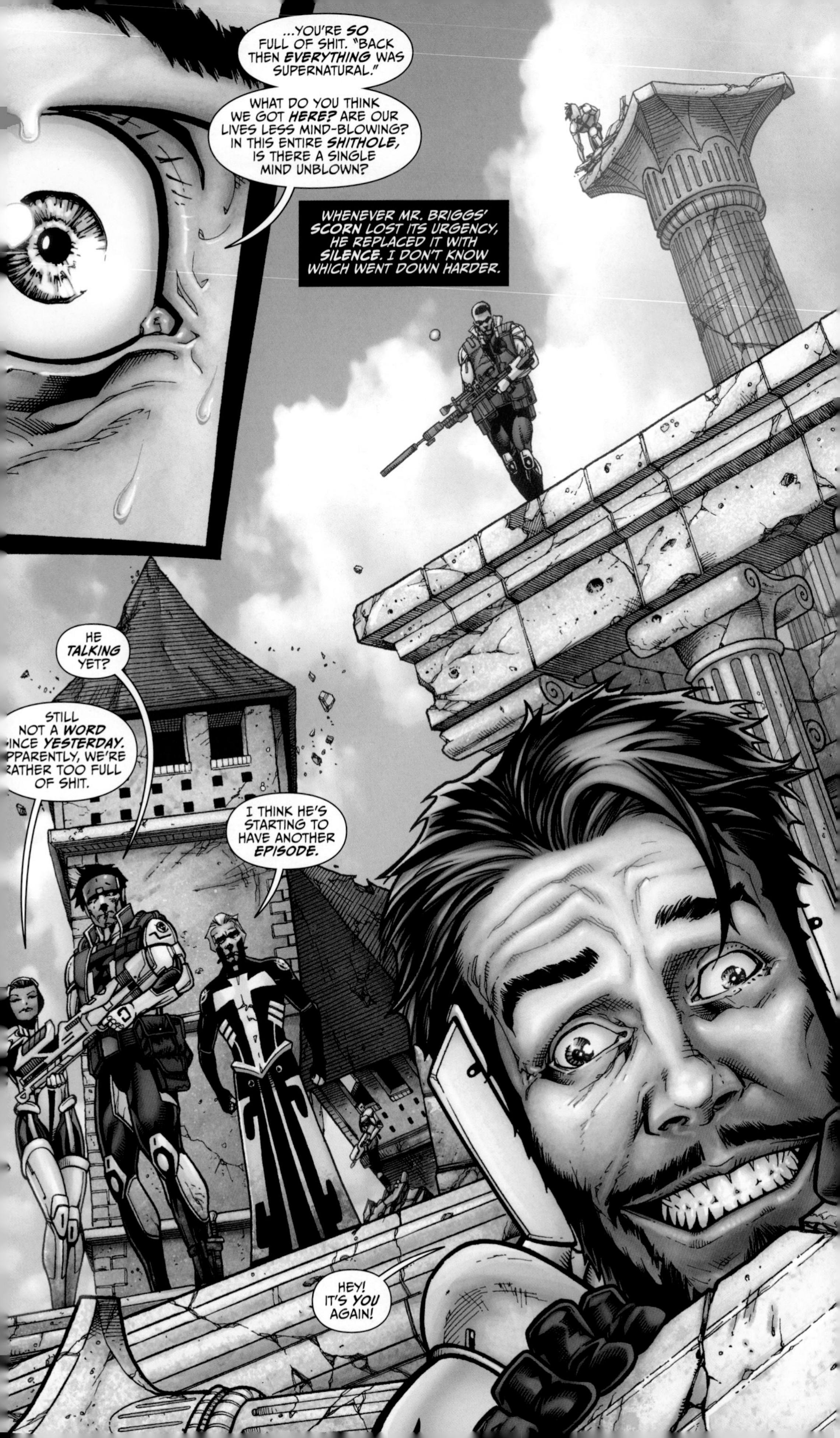
...YOU'RE SO FULL OF SHIT. "BACK THEN EVERYTHING WAS SUPERNATURAL."
WHAT DO YOU THINK WE GOT HERE? ARE OUR LIVES LESS MIND-BLOWING? IN THIS ENTIRE SHITHOLE, IS THERE A SINGLE MIND UNBLOWN?
WHENEVER MR. BRIGGS' SCORN LOST ITS URGENCY, HE REPLACED IT WITH SILENCE. I DON'T KNOW WHICH WENT DOWN HARDER.
HE TALKING YET?
STILL NOT A WORD SINCE YESTERDAY. APPARENTLY, WE'RE RATHER TOO FULL OF SHIT.
I THINK HE'S STARTING TO HAVE ANOTHER EPISODE.
HEY! IT'S YOU AGAIN!

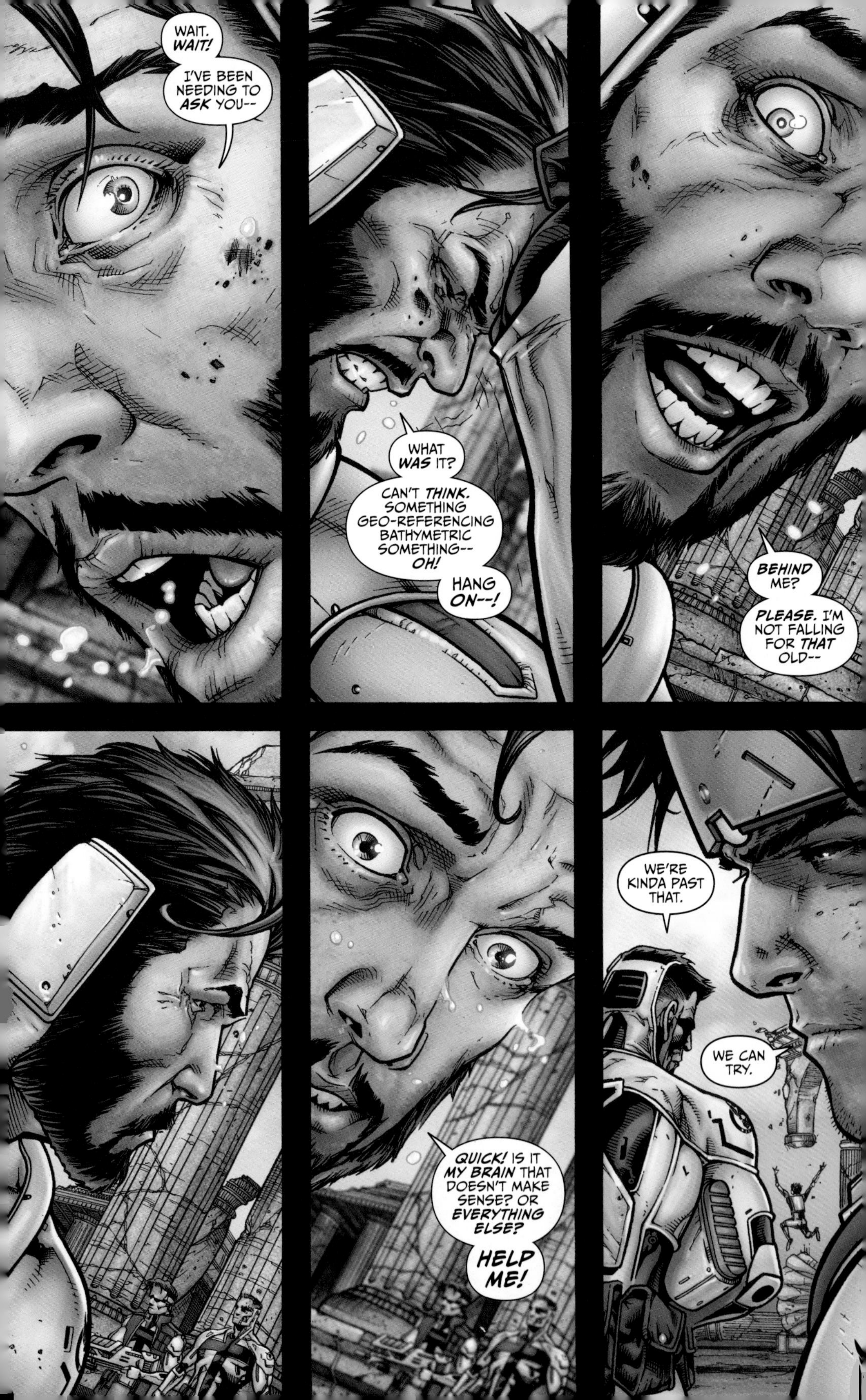
WAIT. WAIT!
I'VE BEEN NEEDING TO ASK YOU--
WHAT WAS IT?
CAN'T THINK. SOMETHING GEO-REFERENCING BATHYMETRIC SOMETHING-- OH!
HANG ON--!
BEHIND ME?
PLEASE. I'M NOT FALLING FOR THAT OLD--
QUICK! IS IT MY BRAIN THAT DOESN'T MAKE SENSE? OR EVERYTHING ELSE?
HELP ME!
WE'RE KINDA PAST THAT.
WE CAN TRY.

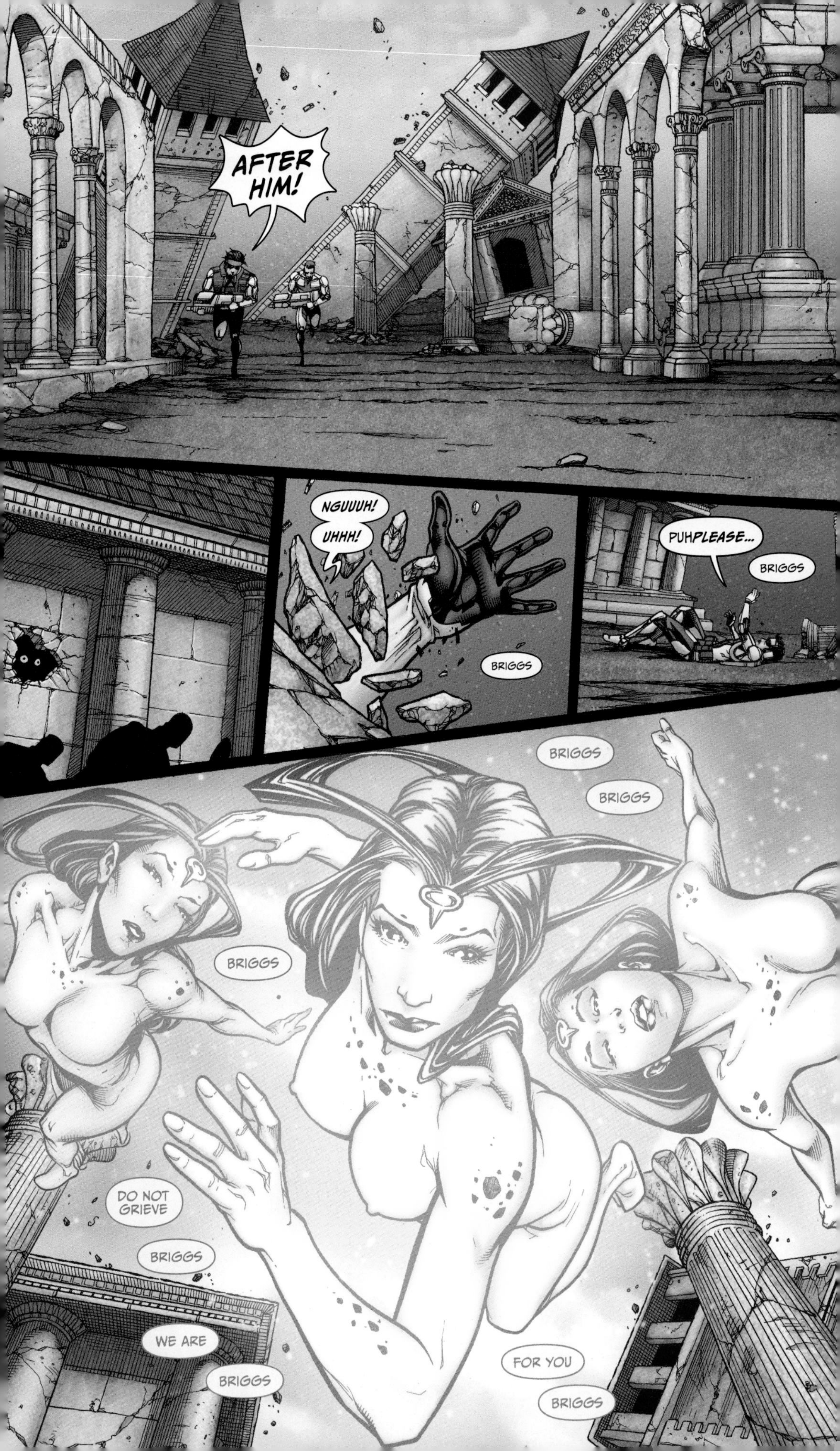

AFTER HIM!
NGUUUH!
UHHH!
BRIGGS
PUHPLEASE...
BRIGGS
BRIGGS
BRIGGS
BRIGGS
DO NOT GRIEVE
BRIGGS
WE ARE
BRIGGS
FOR YOU
BRIGGS

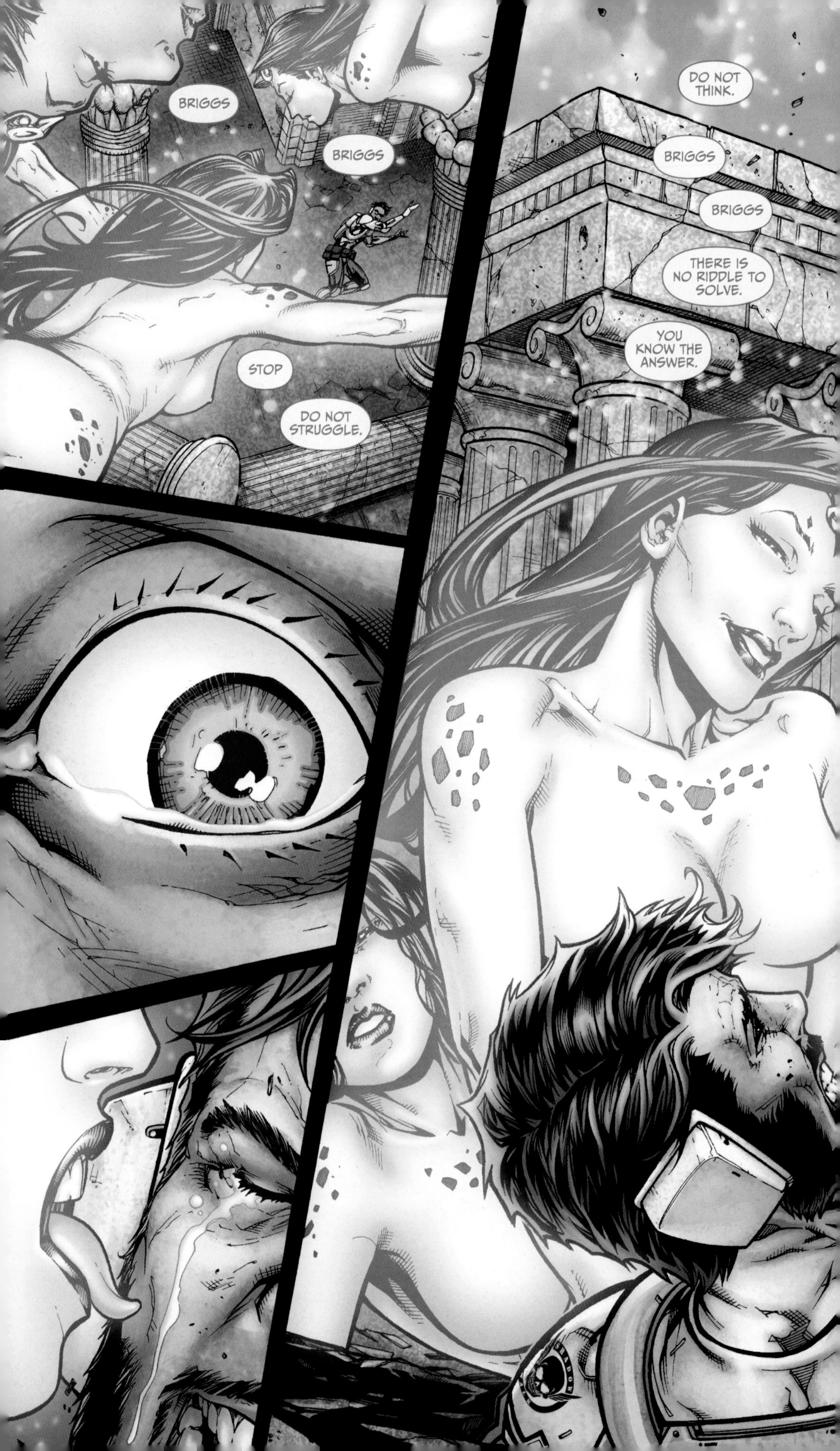
BRIGGS
BRIGGS
STOP
DO NOT STRUGGLE.
DO NOT THINK.
BRIGGS
BRIGGS
THERE IS NO RIDDLE TO SOLVE.
YOU KNOW THE ANSWER.

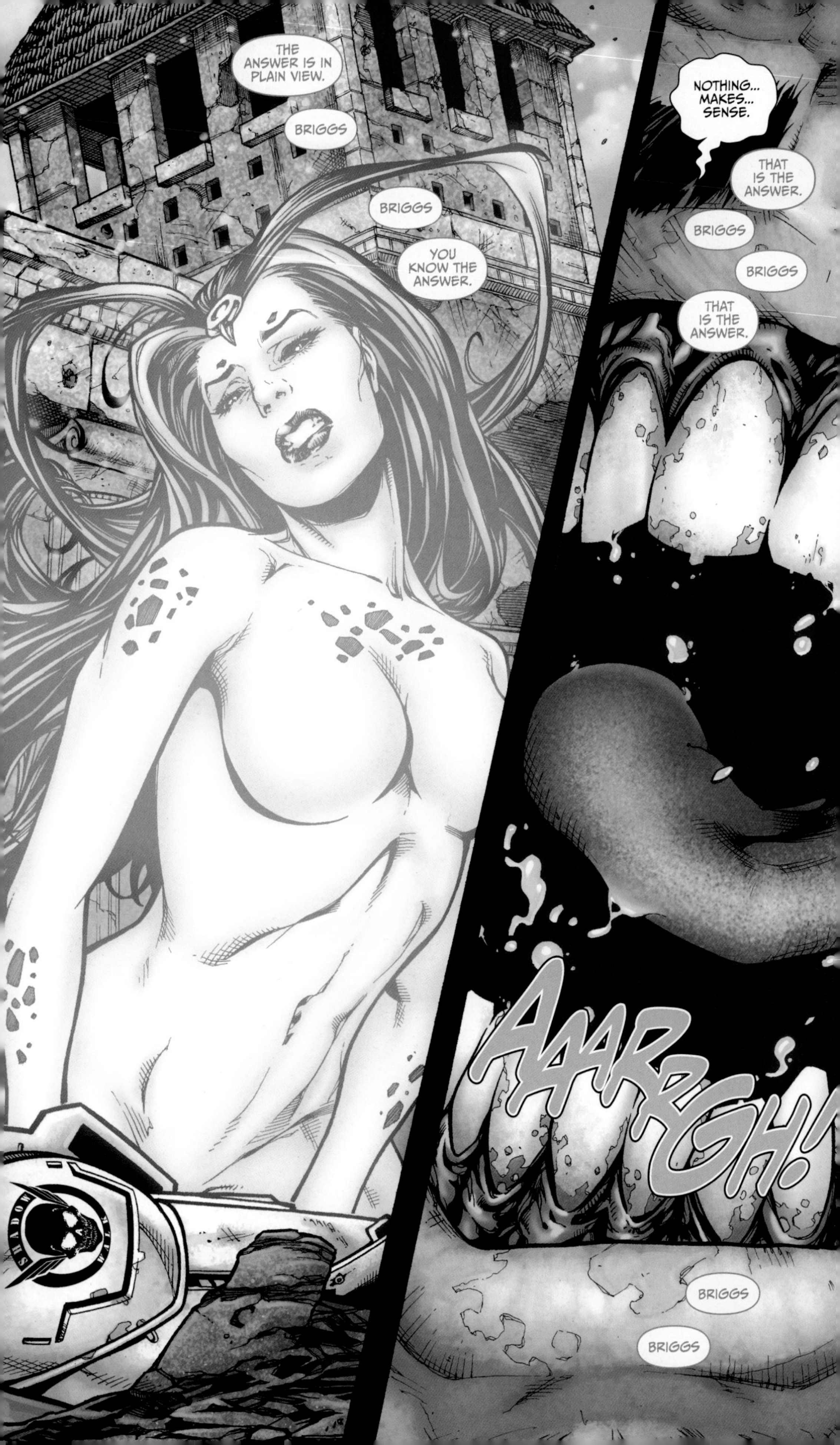
THE ANSWER IS IN PLAIN VIEW.
BRIGGS
BRIGGS
YOU KNOW THE ANSWER.
NOTHING... MAKES... SENSE.
THAT IS THE ANSWER.
BRIGGS
BRIGGS
THAT IS THE ANSWER.
AAARRGH!
BRIGGS
BRIGGS

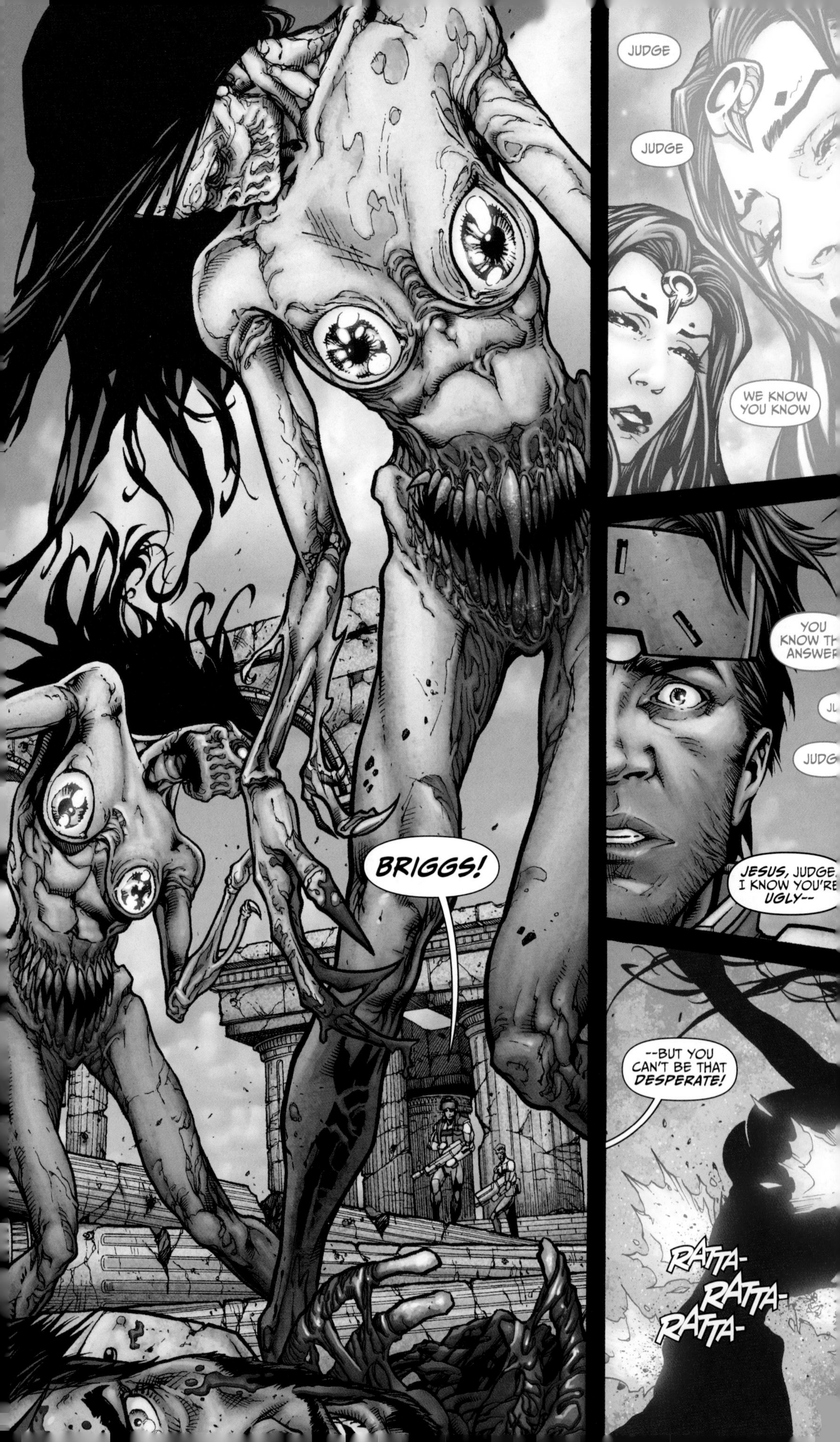
JUDGE
JUDGE
WE KNOW YOU KNOW
BRIGGS!
YOU KNOW TH ANSWER
JUDG
JESUS, JUDGE. I KNOW YOU'RE UGLY--
--BUT YOU CAN'T BE THAT DESPERATE!
RATTA-RATTA-RATTA-

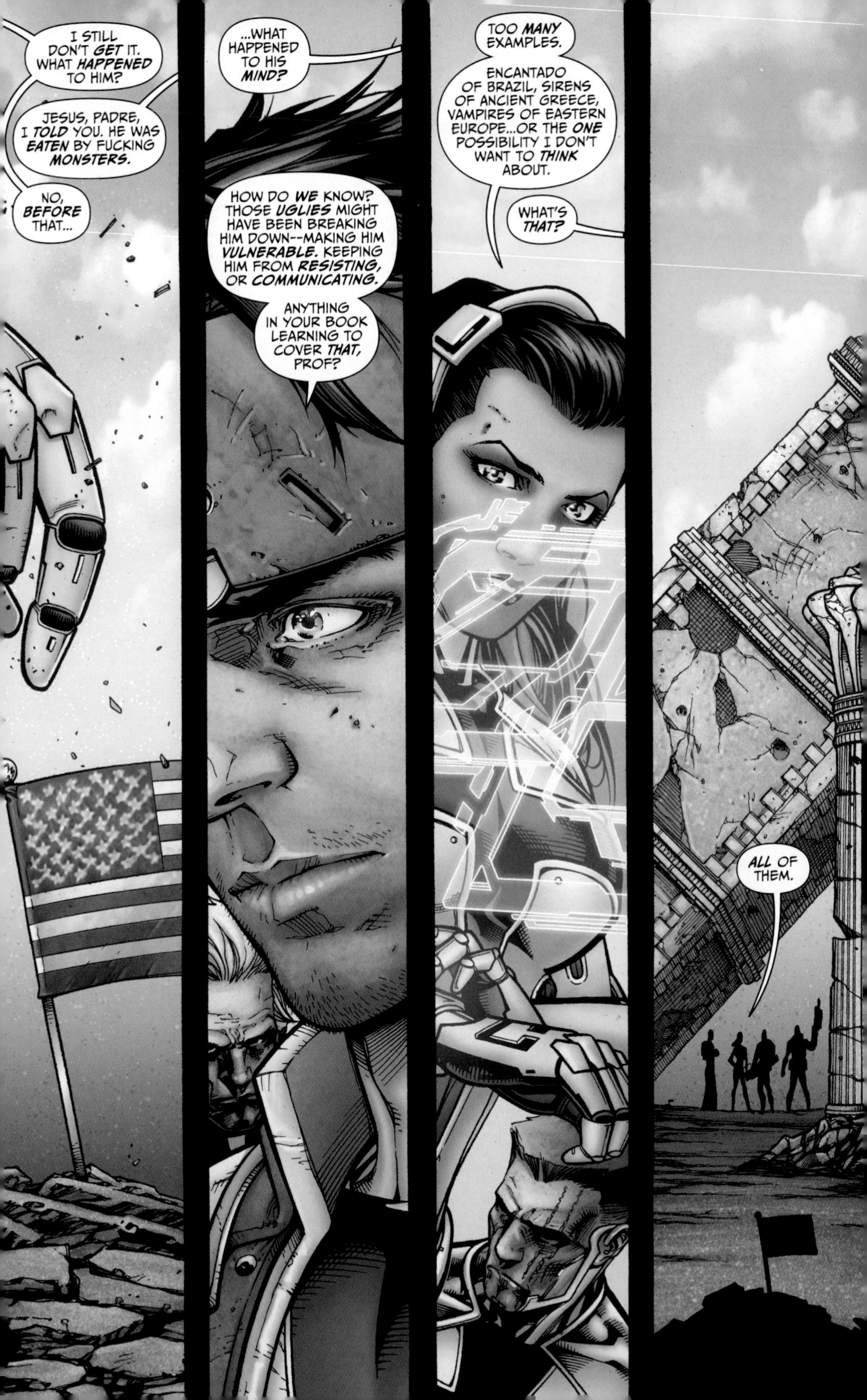
I STILL DON'T GET IT. WHAT HAPPENED TO HIM?
JESUS, PADRE, I TOLD YOU. HE WAS EATEN BY FUCKING MONSTERS.
NO, BEFORE THAT...
...WHAT HAPPENED TO HIS MIND?
HOW DO WE KNOW? THOSE UGLIES MIGHT HAVE BEEN BREAKING HIM DOWN--MAKING HIM VULNERABLE. KEEPING HIM FROM RESISTING, OR COMMUNICATING.
ANYTHING IN YOUR BOOK LEARNING TO COVER THAT, PROF?
TOO MANY EXAMPLES.
ENCANTADO OF BRAZIL, SIRENS OF ANCIENT GREECE, VAMPIRES OF EASTERN EUROPE...OR THE ONE POSSIBILITY I DON'T WANT TO THINK ABOUT.
WHAT'S THAT?
ALL OF THEM.

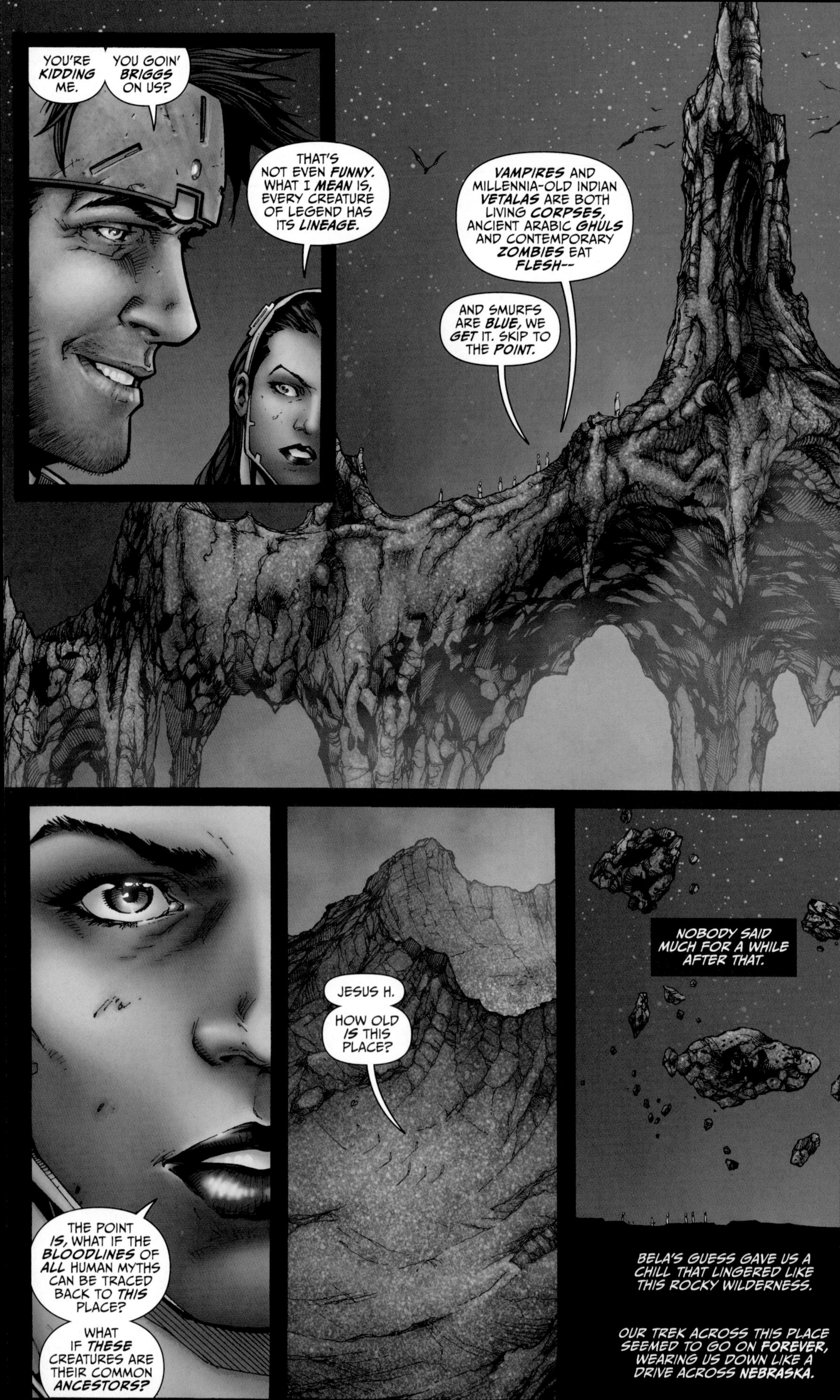

YOU'RE KIDDING ME.
YOU GOIN' BRIGGS ON US?
THAT'S NOT EVEN FUNNY. WHAT I MEAN IS, EVERY CREATURE OF LEGEND HAS ITS LINEAGE.
VAMPIRES AND MILLENNIA-OLD INDIAN VETALAS ARE BOTH LIVING CORPSES, ANCIENT ARABIC GHULS AND CONTEMPORARY ZOMBIES EAT FLESH--
AND SMURFS ARE BLUE, WE GET IT. SKIP TO THE POINT.
THE POINT IS, WHAT IF THE BLOODLINES OF ALL HUMAN MYTHS CAN BE TRACED BACK TO THIS PLACE?
WHAT IF THESE CREATURES ARE THEIR COMMON ANCESTORS?
JESUS H.
HOW OLD IS THIS PLACE?
NOBODY SAID MUCH FOR A WHILE AFTER THAT.
BELA'S GUESS GAVE US A CHILL THAT LINGERED LIKE THIS ROCKY WILDERNESS.
OUR TREK ACROSS THIS PLACE SEEMED TO GO ON FOREVER, WEARING US DOWN LIKE A DRIVE ACROSS NEBRASKA.

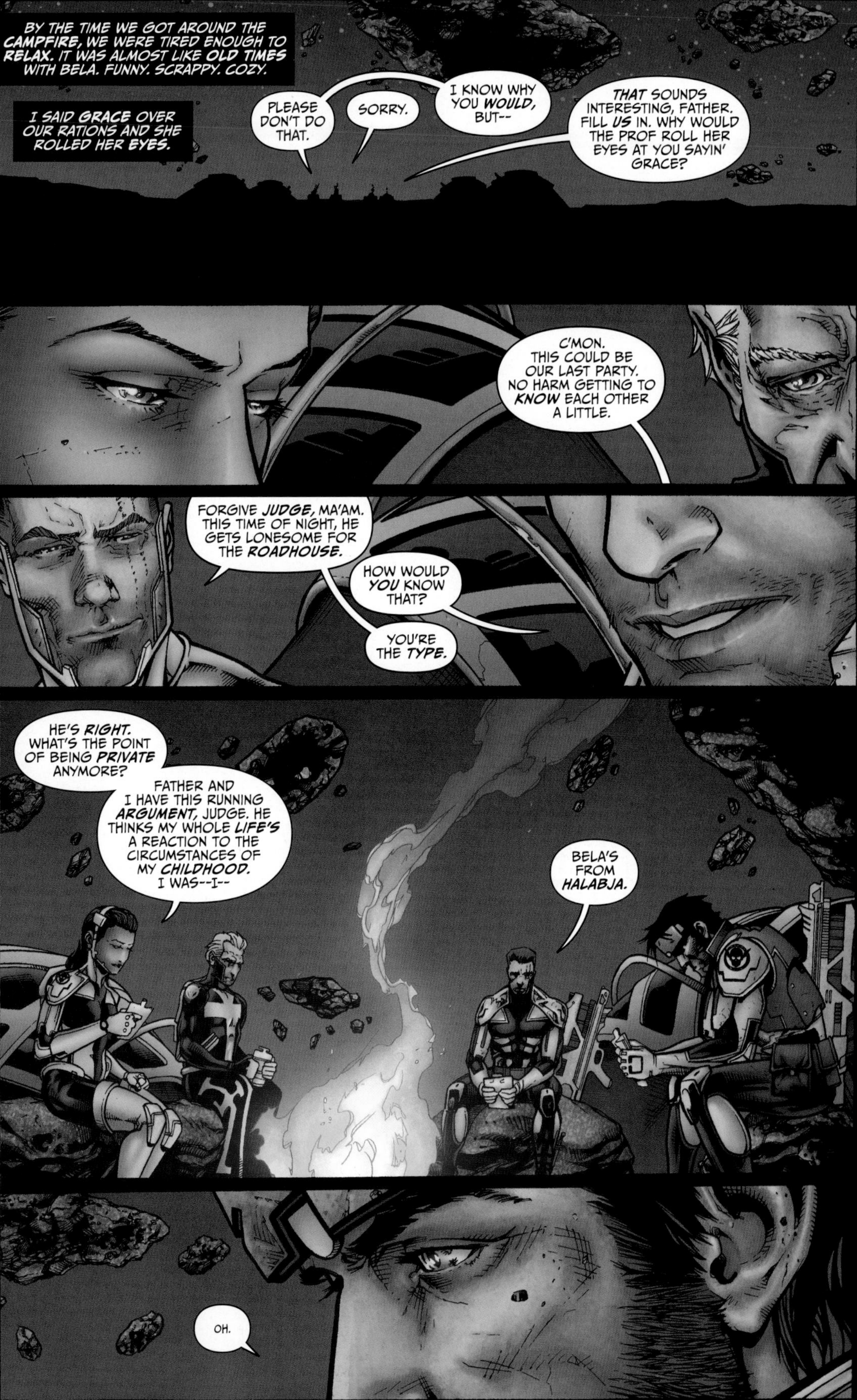
BY THE TIME WE GOT AROUND THE CAMPFIRE, WE WERE TIRED ENOUGH TO RELAX. IT WAS ALMOST LIKE OLD TIMES WITH BELA. FUNNY. SCRAPPY. COZY.
I SAID GRACE OVER OUR RATIONS AND SHE ROLLED HER EYES.
PLEASE DON'T DO THAT.
SORRY.
I KNOW WHY YOU WOULD, BUT--
THAT SOUNDS INTERESTING, FATHER. FILL US IN. WHY WOULD THE PROF ROLL HER EYES AT YOU SAYIN' GRACE?
C'MON. THIS COULD BE OUR LAST PARTY. NO HARM GETTING TO KNOW EACH OTHER A LITTLE.
FORGIVE JUDGE, MA'AM. THIS TIME OF NIGHT, HE GETS LONESOME FOR THE ROADHOUSE.
HOW WOULD YOU KNOW THAT?
YOU'RE THE TYPE.
HE'S RIGHT. WHAT'S THE POINT OF BEING PRIVATE ANYMORE?
FATHER AND I HAVE THIS RUNNING ARGUMENT, JUDGE. HE THINKS MY WHOLE LIFE'S A REACTION TO THE CIRCUMSTANCES OF MY CHILDHOOD. I WAS--I--
BELA'S FROM HALABJA.
OH.

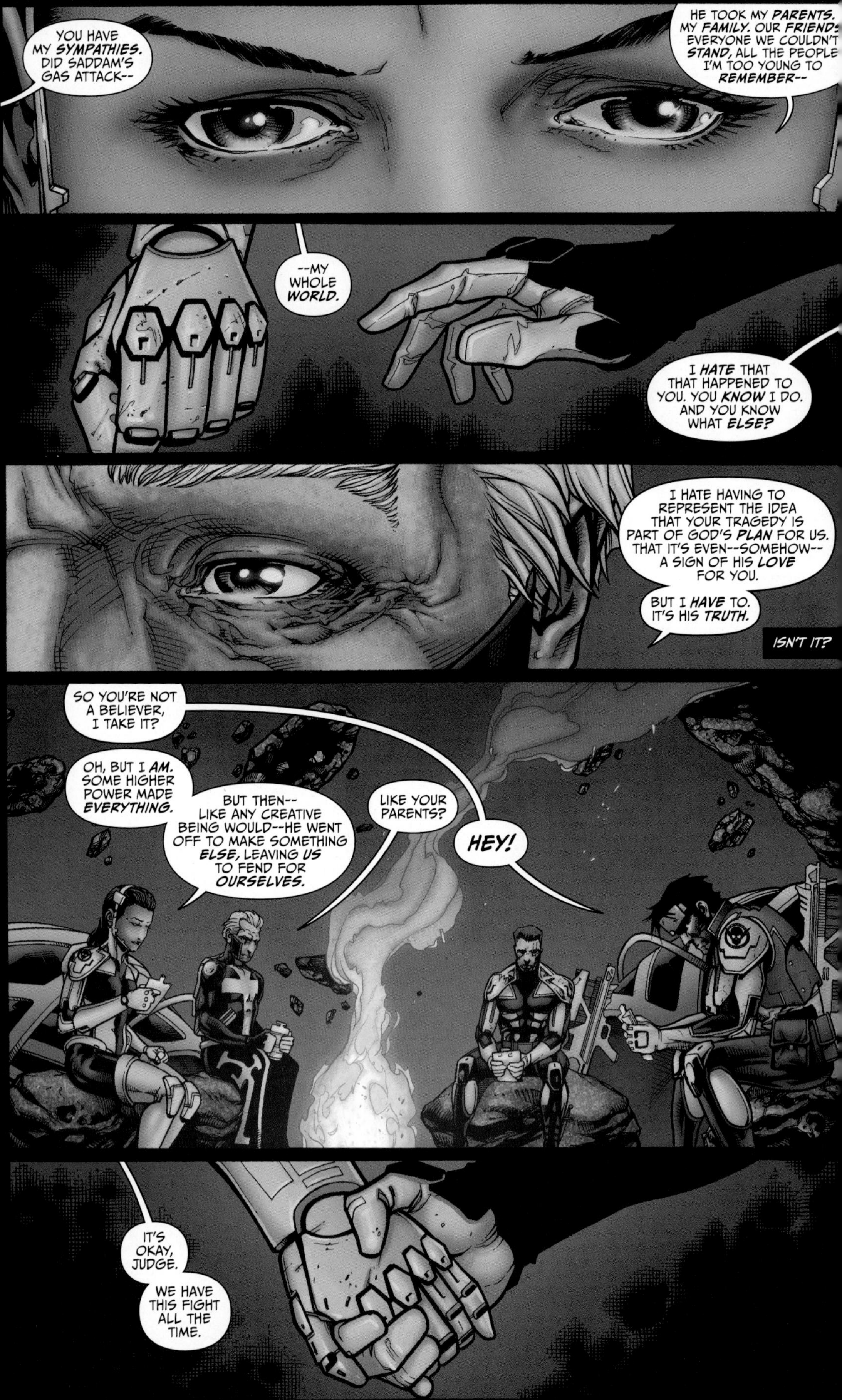
YOU HAVE MY SYMPATHIES. DID SADDAM'S GAS ATTACK--
HE TOOK MY PARENTS. MY FAMILY. OUR FRIENDS. EVERYONE WE COULDN'T STAND, ALL THE PEOPLE I'M TOO YOUNG TO REMEMBER--
--MY WHOLE WORLD.
I HATE THAT THAT HAPPENED TO YOU. YOU KNOW I DO. AND YOU KNOW WHAT ELSE?
I HATE HAVING TO REPRESENT THE IDEA THAT YOUR TRAGEDY IS PART OF GOD'S PLAN FOR US. THAT IT'S EVEN--SOMEHOW--A SIGN OF HIS LOVE FOR YOU.
BUT I HAVE TO. IT'S HIS TRUTH.
ISN'T IT?
SO YOU'RE NOT A BELIEVER, I TAKE IT?
OH, BUT I AM. SOME HIGHER POWER MADE EVERYTHING.
BUT THEN--LIKE ANY CREATIVE BEING WOULD--HE WENT OFF TO MAKE SOMETHING ELSE, LEAVING US TO FEND FOR OURSELVES.
LIKE YOUR PARENTS?
HEY!
IT'S OKAY, JUDGE.
WE HAVE THIS FIGHT ALL THE TIME.

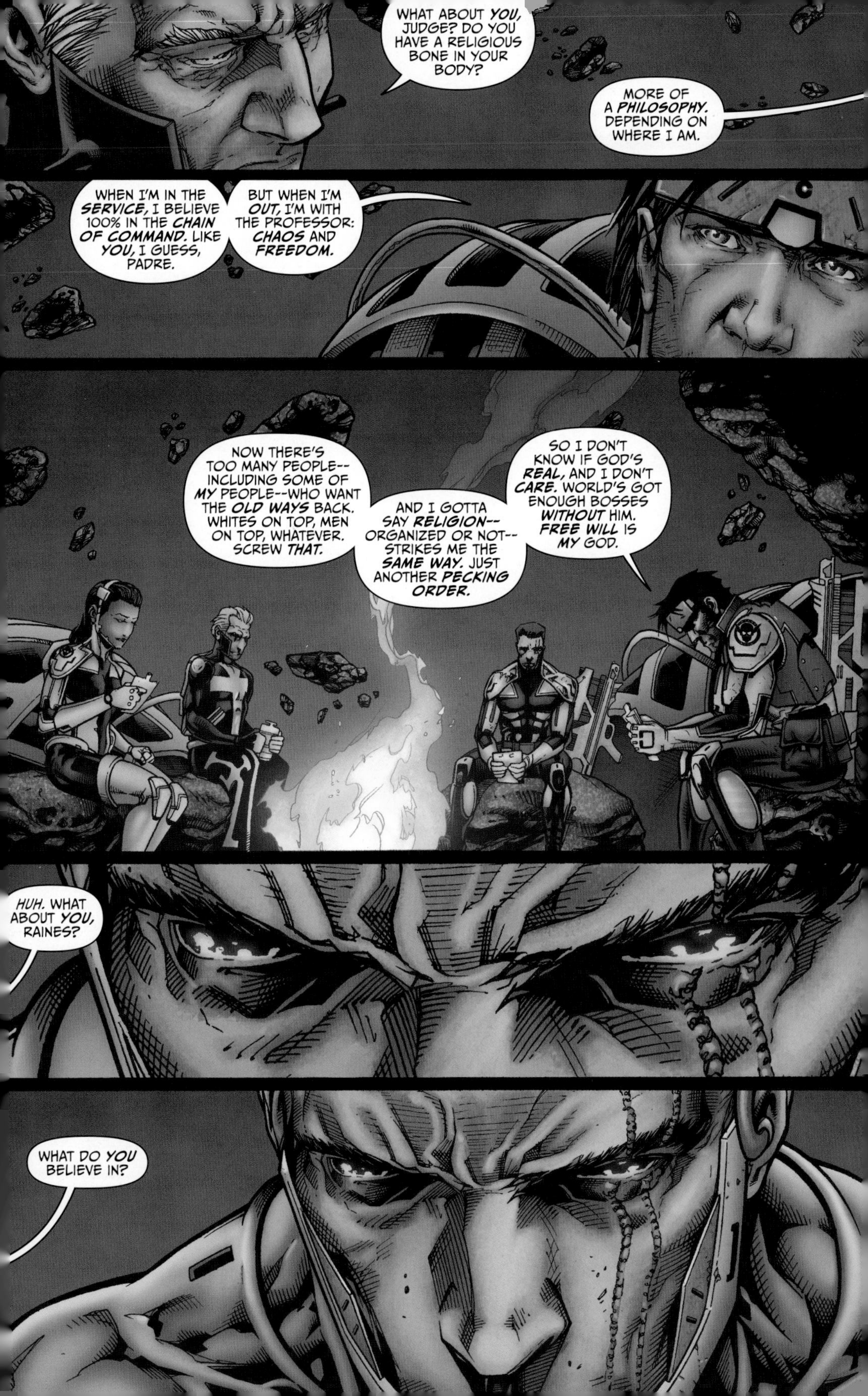
WHAT ABOUT YOU, JUDGE? DO YOU HAVE A RELIGIOUS BONE IN YOUR BODY?
MORE OF A PHILOSOPHY. DEPENDING ON WHERE I AM.
WHEN I'M IN THE SERVICE, I BELIEVE 100% IN THE CHAIN OF COMMAND. LIKE YOU, I GUESS, PADRE.
BUT WHEN I'M OUT, I'M WITH THE PROFESSOR: CHAOS AND FREEDOM.
NOW THERE'S TOO MANY PEOPLE--INCLUDING SOME OF MY PEOPLE--WHO WANT THE OLD WAYS BACK. WHITES ON TOP, MEN ON TOP, WHATEVER. SCREW THAT.
AND I GOTTA SAY RELIGION--ORGANIZED OR NOT--STRIKES ME THE SAME WAY. JUST ANOTHER PECKING ORDER.
SO I DON'T KNOW IF GOD'S REAL, AND I DON'T CARE. WORLD'S GOT ENOUGH BOSSES WITHOUT HIM. FREE WILL IS MY GOD.
HUH. WHAT ABOUT YOU, RAINES?
WHAT DO YOU BELIEVE IN?

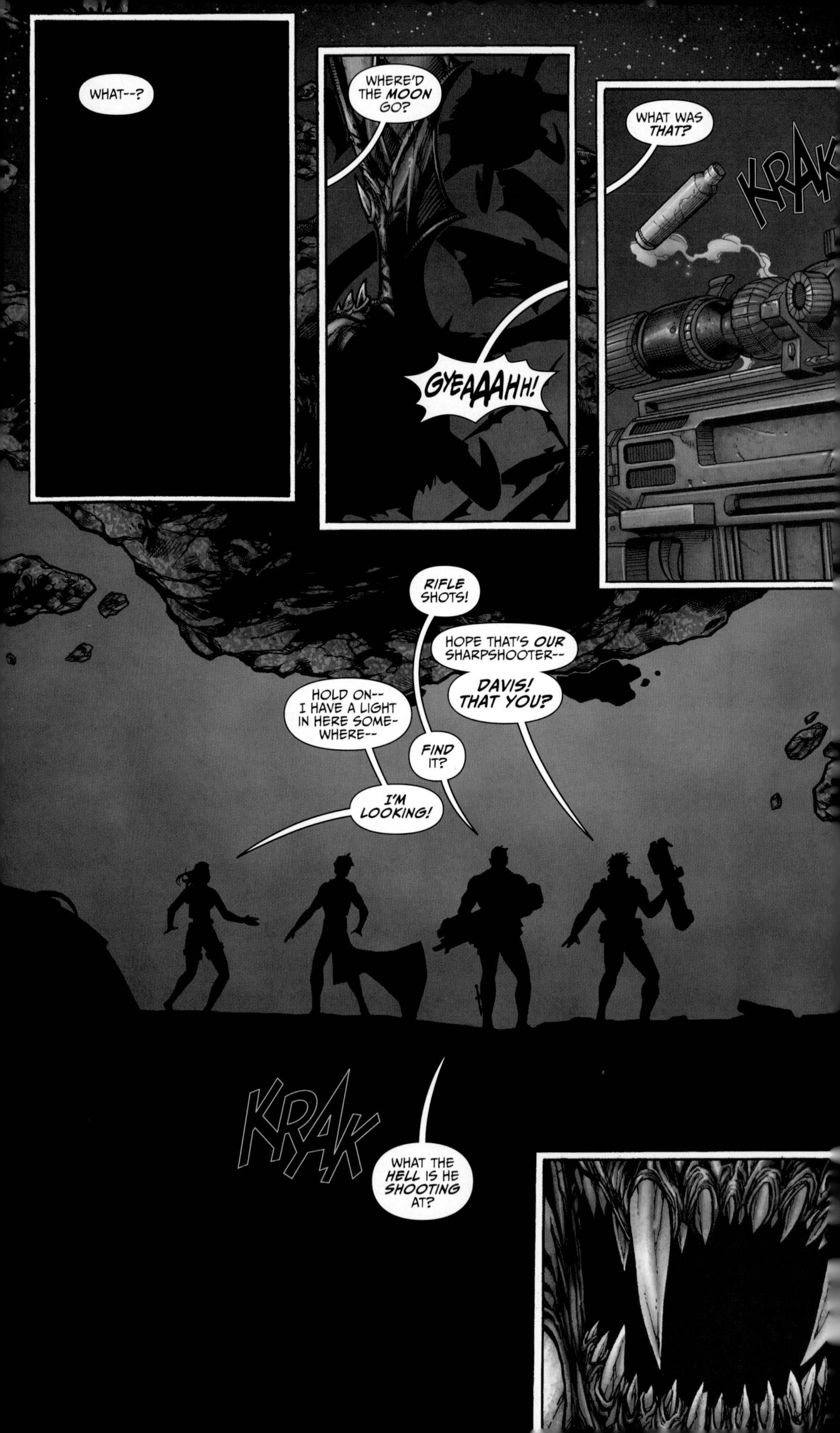
WHAT--?
WHERE'D THE MOON GO?
GYEAAAHH!
WHAT WAS THAT?
KRAK
RIFLE SHOTS!
HOPE THAT'S OUR SHARPSHOOTER--
DAVIS! THAT YOU?
HOLD ON-- I HAVE A LIGHT IN HERE SOME-WHERE--
FIND IT?
I'M LOOKING!
KRAK
WHAT THE HELL IS HE SHOOTING AT?

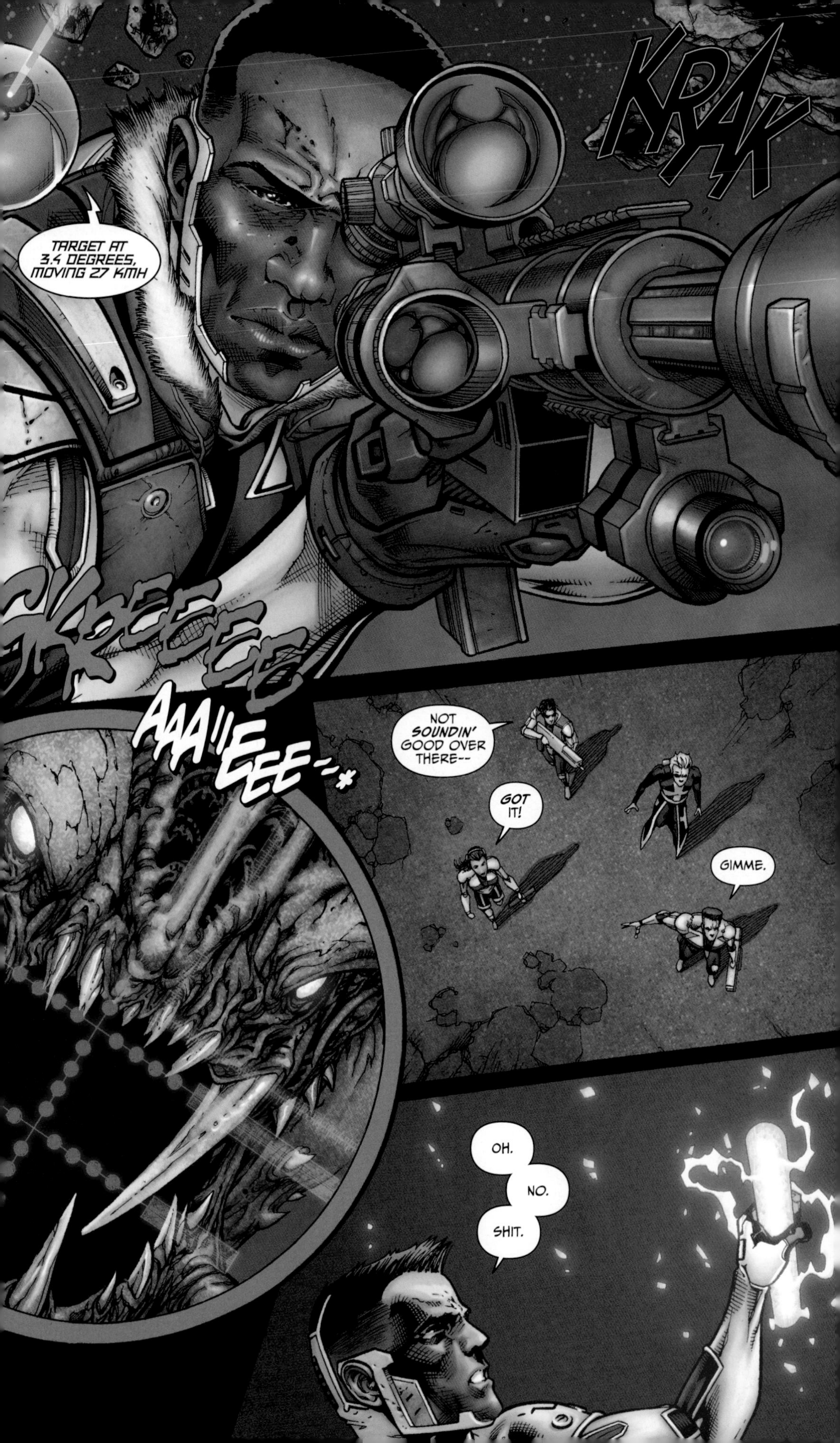
KRAK
TARGET AT 3.4 DEGREES, MOVING 27 KMH
SKREEEEEE
AAA'''EEE--*
NOT SOUNDIN' GOOD OVER THERE--
GOT IT!
GIMME.
OH.
NO.
SHIT.

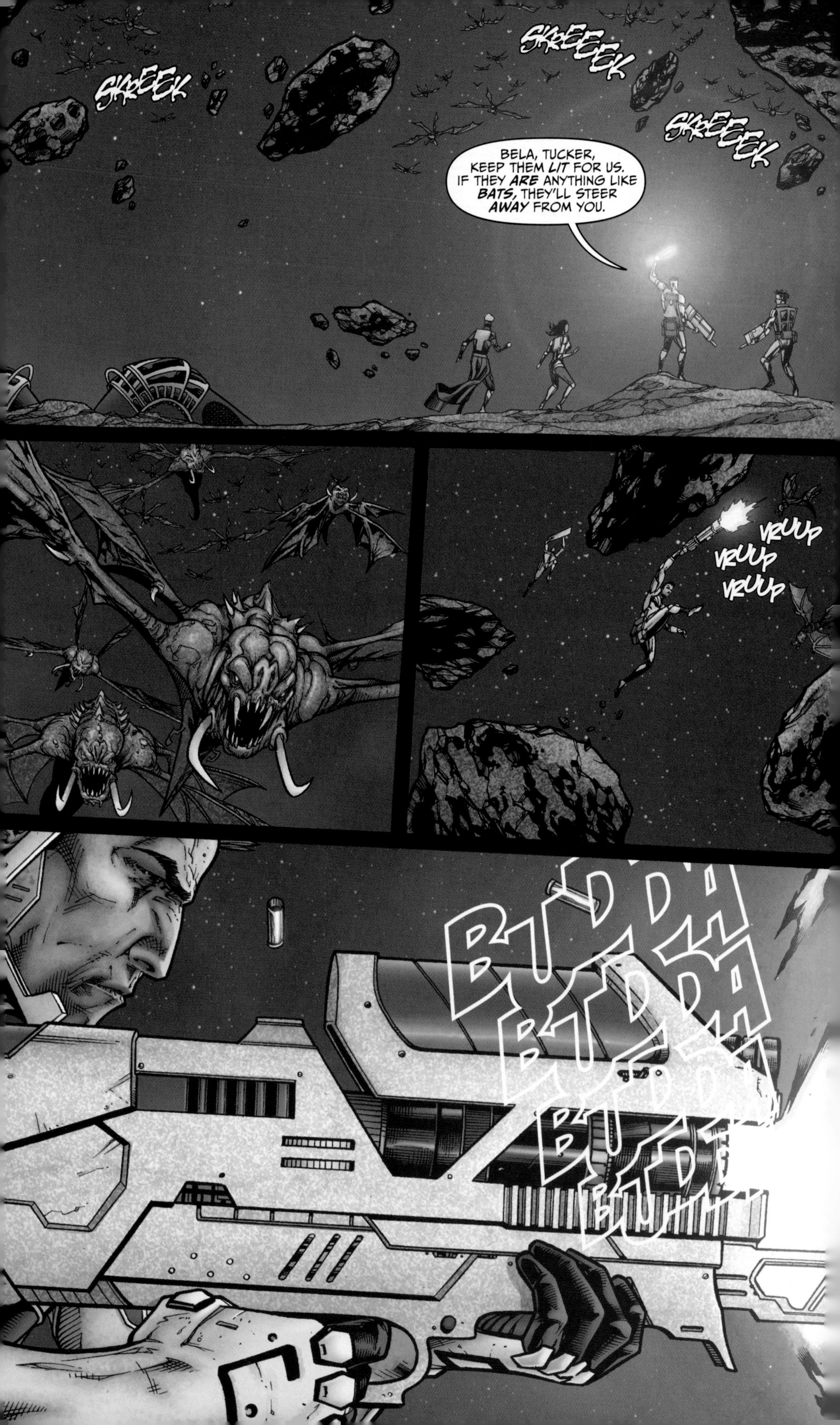
SKREEK
SKREEEEK
SKREEEEK
BELA, TUCKER, KEEP THEM LIT FOR US. IF THEY ARE ANYTHING LIKE BATS, THEY'LL STEER AWAY FROM YOU.
VRUUP
VRUUP
VRUUP
BUDDA
BUDDA
BUDDA

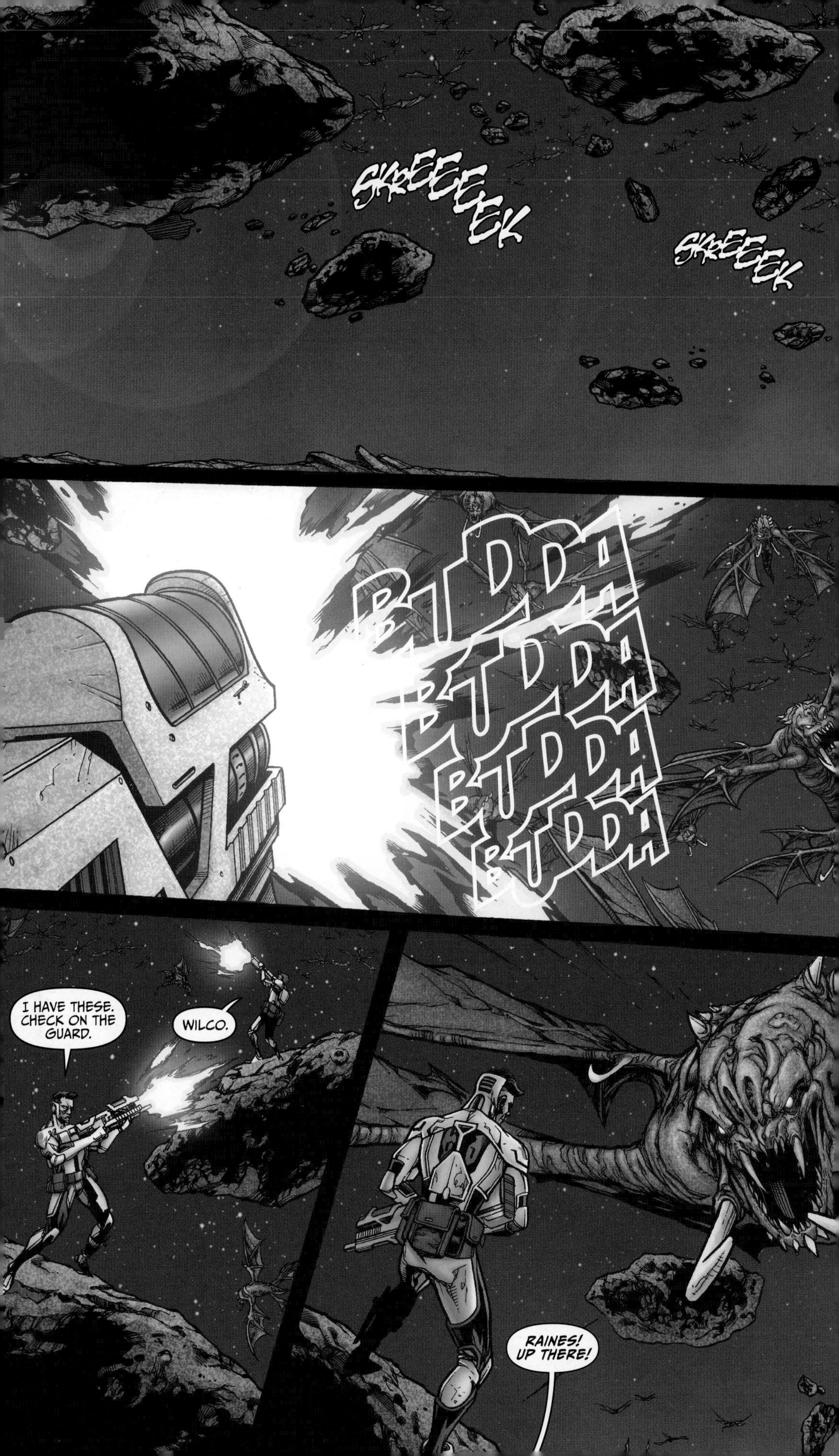
SKREEEEEK
SKREEEEK
BUDDA
BUDDA
BUDDA
BUDDA
I HAVE THESE. CHECK ON THE GUARD.
WILCO.
RAINES! UP THERE!

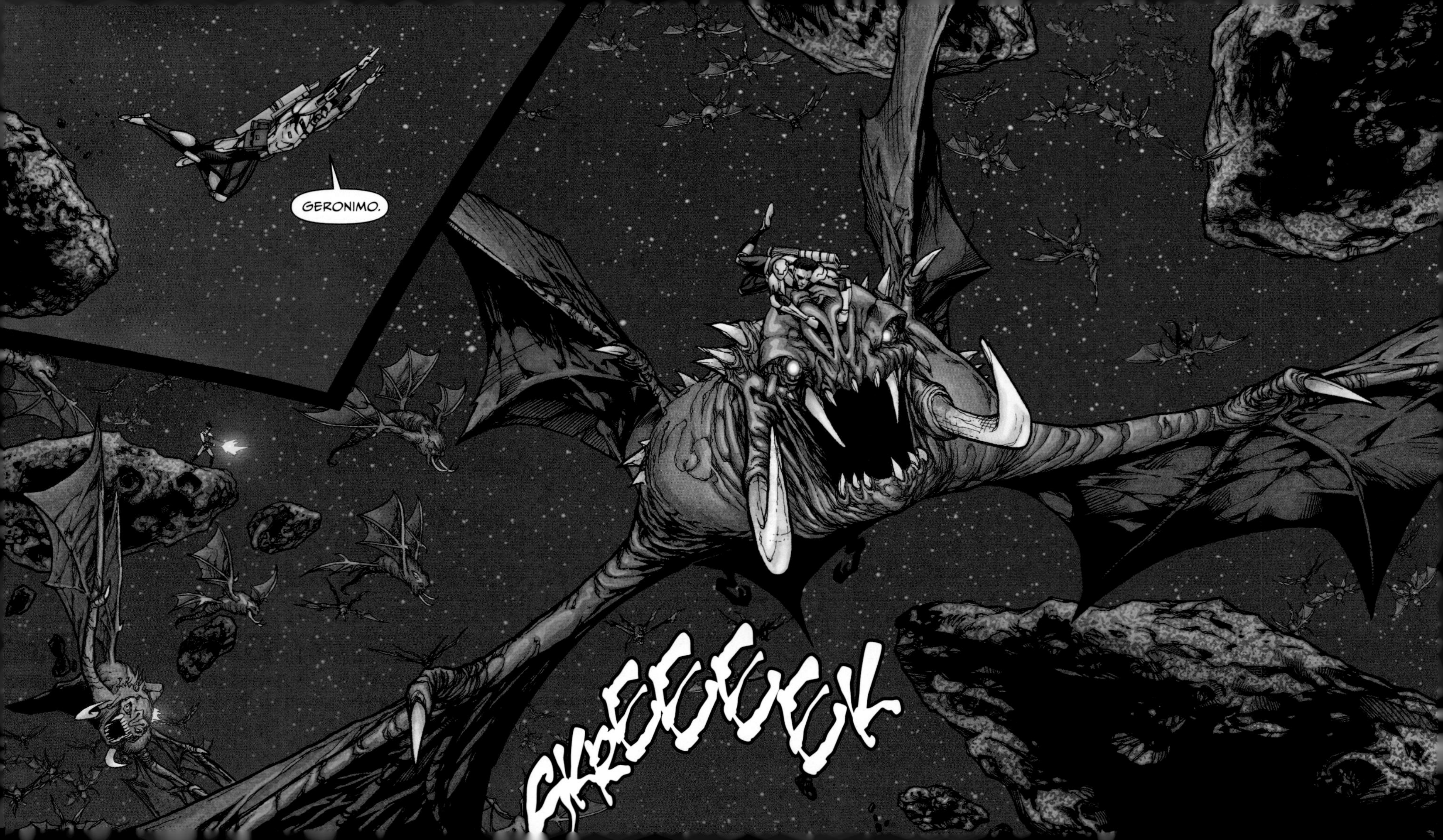
GERONIMO.
SKREEEEEEEK

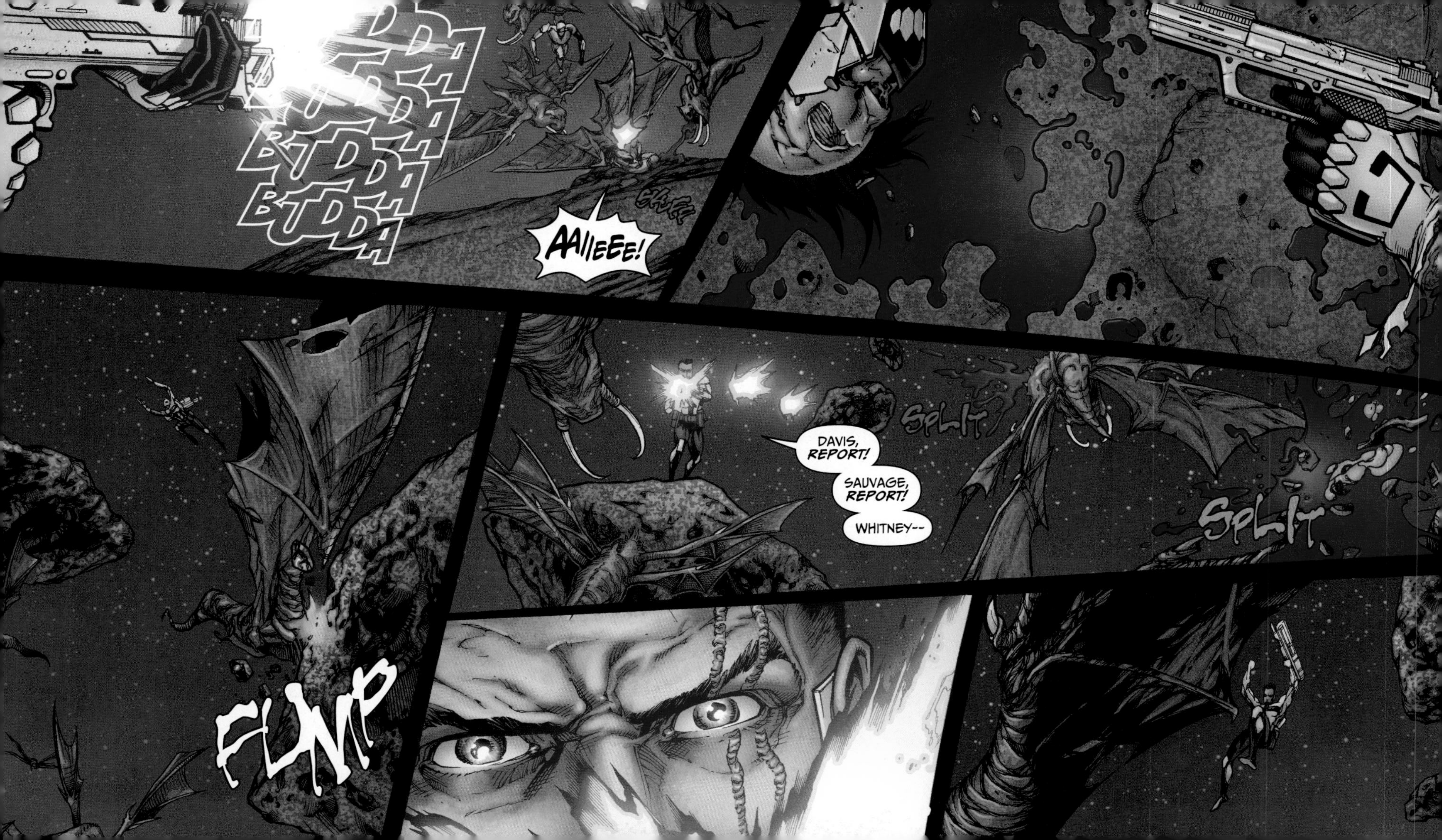
BUDDA BUDDA BUDDA BUDDA
AAIIEEE!
DAVIS, REPORT!
SAUVAGE, REPORT!
WHITNEY--
SPLIT
SPLIT
FLUMP

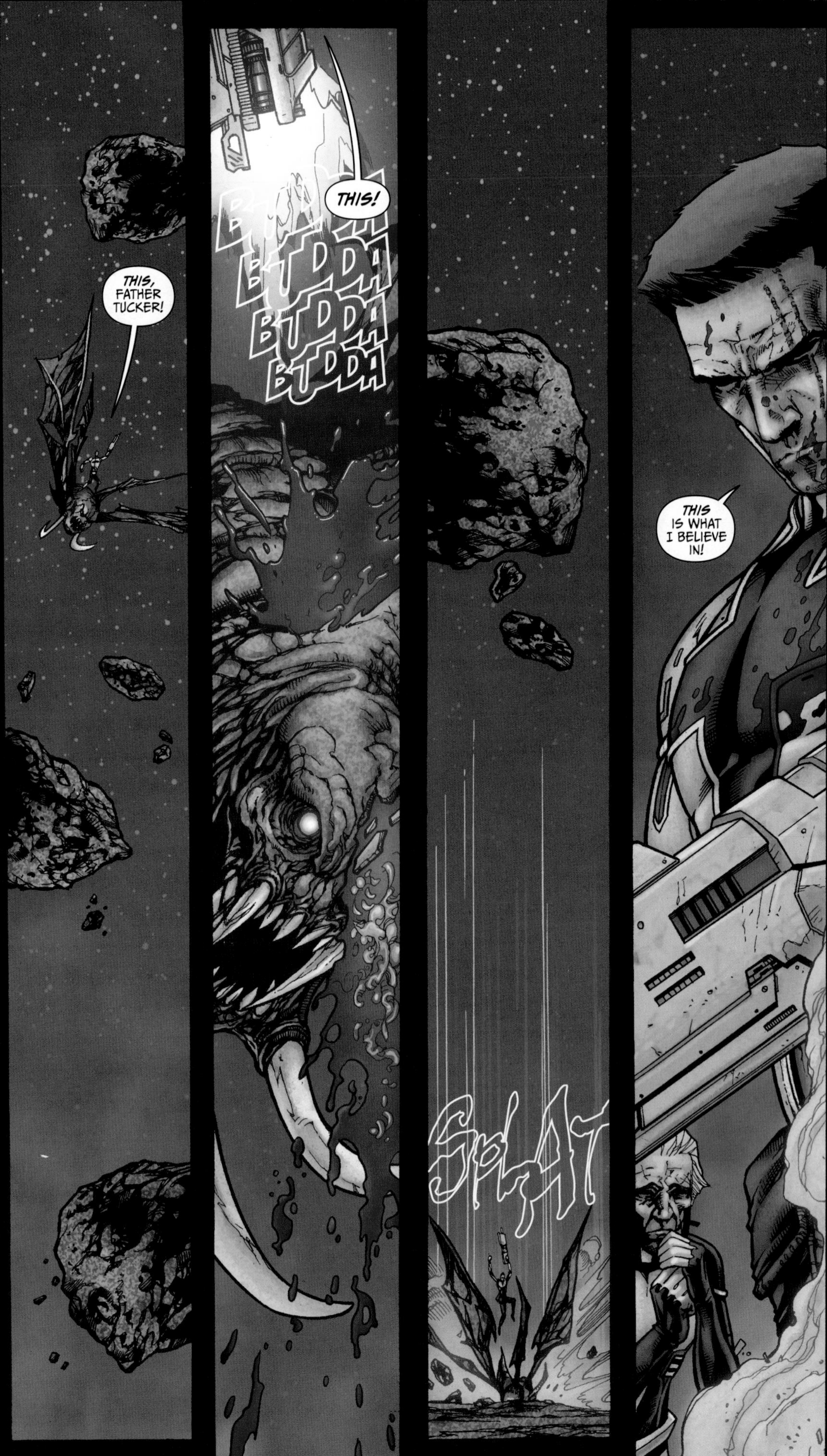
THIS, FATHER TUCKER!
THIS!
BUDDA BUDDA BUDDA BUDDA
SPLAT
THIS IS WHAT I BELIEVE IN!

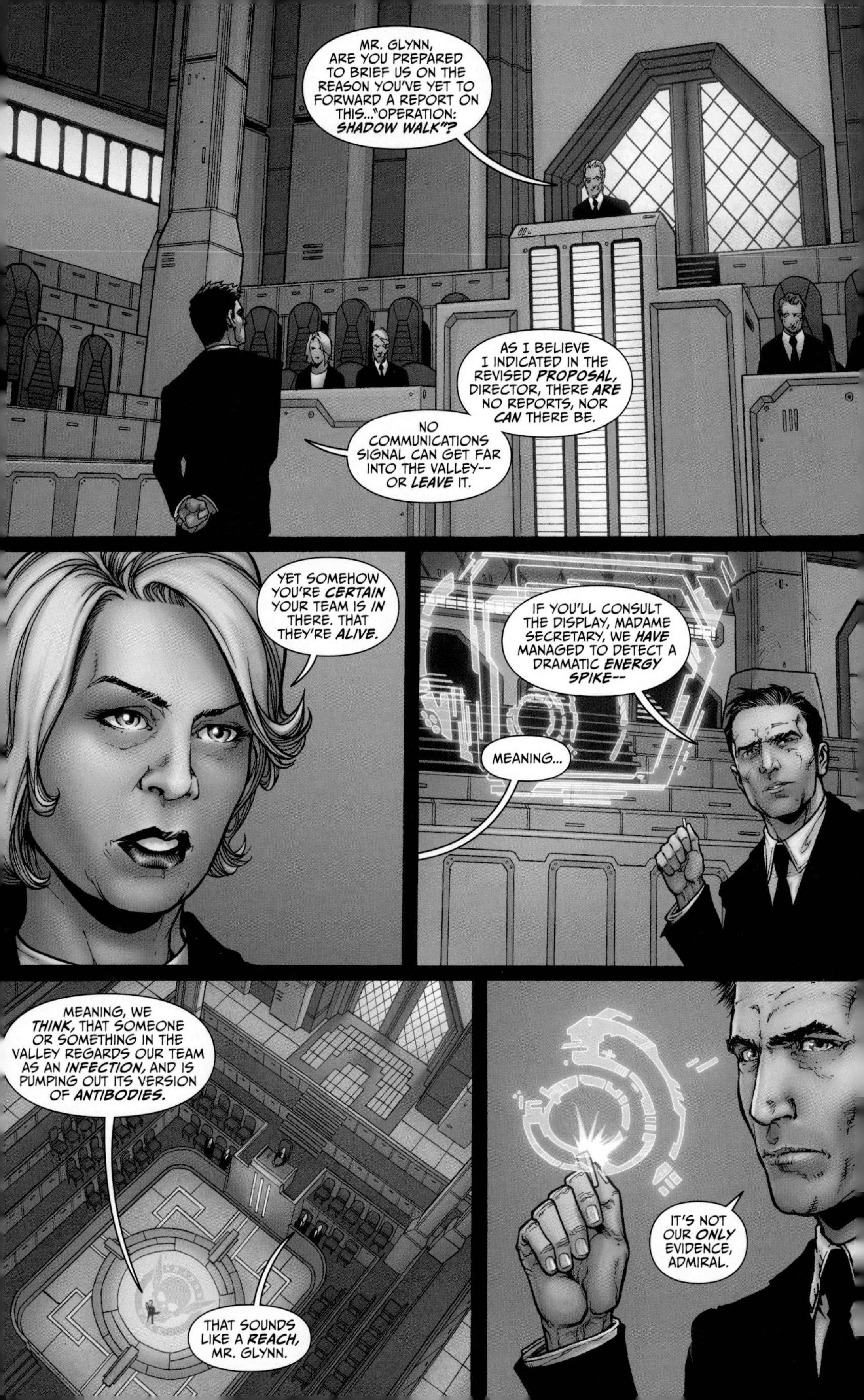
MR. GLYNN, ARE YOU PREPARED TO BRIEF US ON THE REASON YOU'VE YET TO FORWARD A REPORT ON THIS..."OPERATION: SHADOW WALK"?
AS I BELIEVE I INDICATED IN THE REVISED PROPOSAL, DIRECTOR, THERE ARE NO REPORTS, NOR CAN THERE BE.
NO COMMUNICATIONS SIGNAL CAN GET FAR INTO THE VALLEY-- OR LEAVE IT.
YET SOMEHOW YOU'RE CERTAIN YOUR TEAM IS IN THERE. THAT THEY'RE ALIVE.
IF YOU'LL CONSULT THE DISPLAY, MADAME SECRETARY, WE HAVE MANAGED TO DETECT A DRAMATIC ENERGY SPIKE--
MEANING...
MEANING, WE THINK, THAT SOMEONE OR SOMETHING IN THE VALLEY REGARDS OUR TEAM AS AN INFECTION, AND IS PUMPING OUT ITS VERSION OF ANTIBODIES.
THAT SOUNDS LIKE A REACH, MR. GLYNN.
IT'S NOT OUR ONLY EVIDENCE, ADMIRAL.

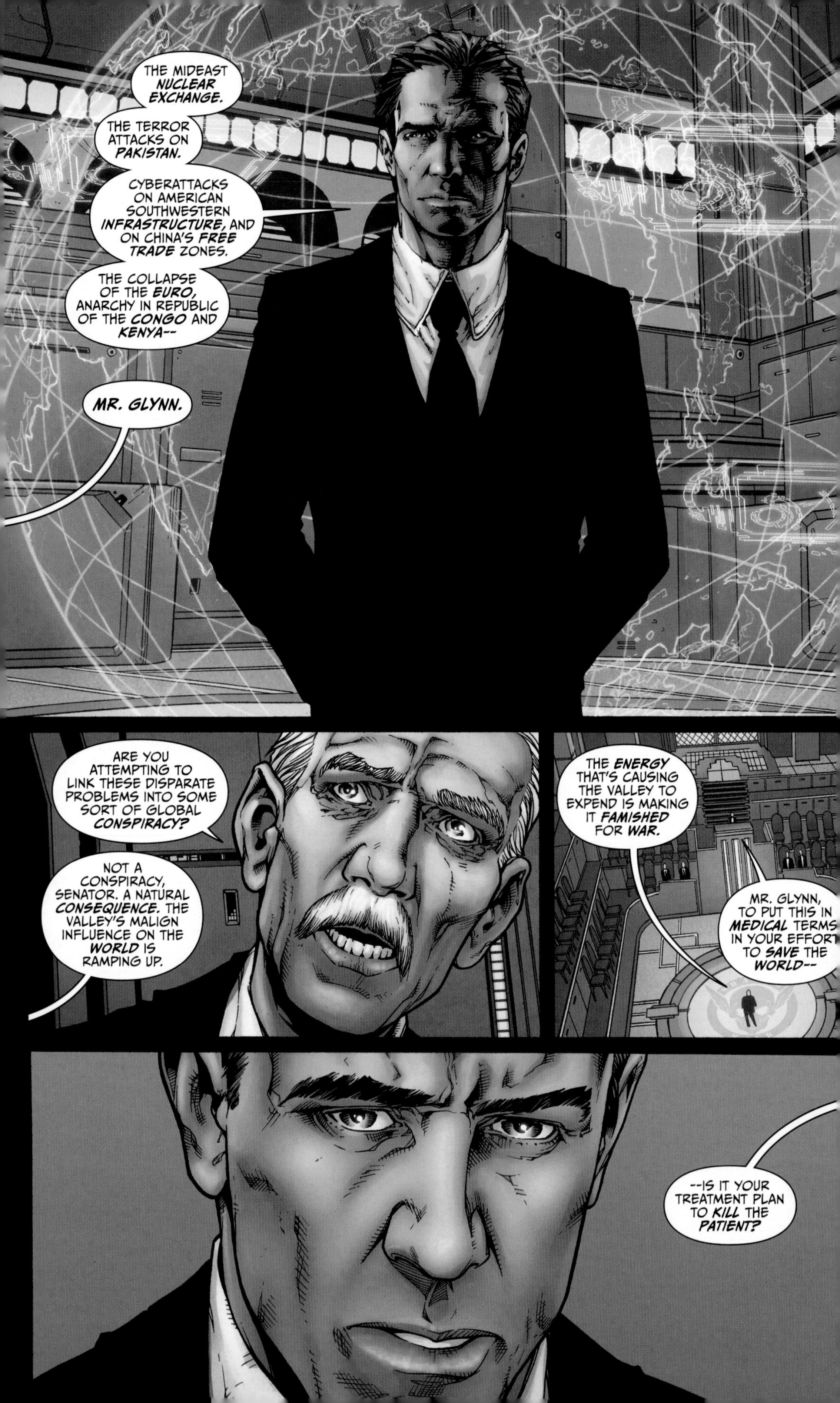

THE MIDEAST NUCLEAR EXCHANGE.
THE TERROR ATTACKS ON PAKISTAN.
CYBERATTACKS ON AMERICAN SOUTHWESTERN INFRASTRUCTURE, AND ON CHINA'S FREE TRADE ZONES.
THE COLLAPSE OF THE EURO, ANARCHY IN REPUBLIC OF THE CONGO AND KENYA--
MR. GLYNN.
ARE YOU ATTEMPTING TO LINK THESE DISPARATE PROBLEMS INTO SOME SORT OF GLOBAL CONSPIRACY?
NOT A CONSPIRACY, SENATOR. A NATURAL CONSEQUENCE. THE VALLEY'S MALIGN INFLUENCE ON THE WORLD IS RAMPING UP.
THE ENERGY THAT'S CAUSING THE VALLEY TO EXPEND IS MAKING IT FAMISHED FOR WAR.
MR. GLYNN, TO PUT THIS IN MEDICAL TERMS IN YOUR EFFORT TO SAVE THE WORLD--
--IS IT YOUR TREATMENT PLAN TO KILL THE PATIENT?

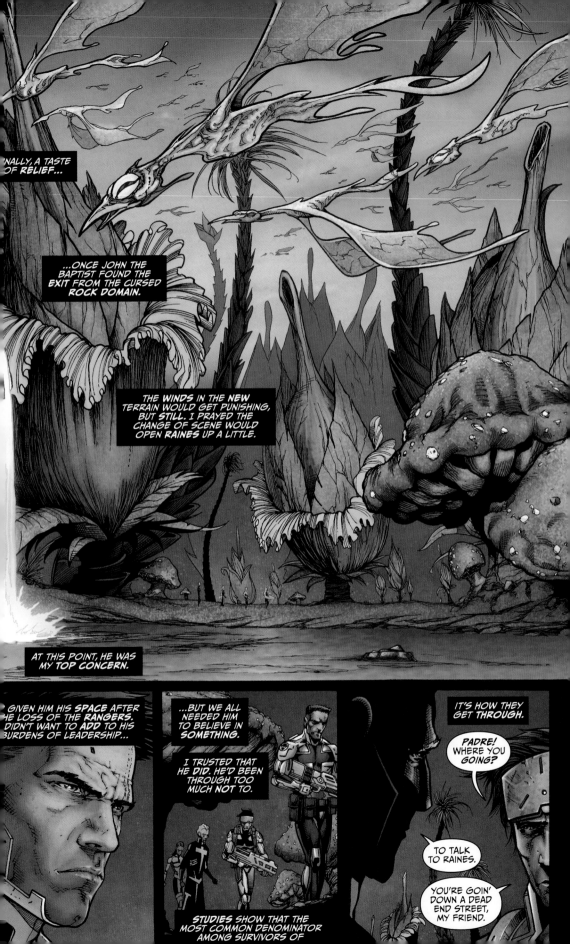

...NALLY, A TASTE OF RELIEF...

...ONCE JOHN THE BAPTIST FOUND THE EXIT FROM THE CURSED ROCK DOMAIN.

THE WINDS IN THE NEW TERRAIN WOULD GET PUNISHING, BUT STILL. I PRAYED THE CHANGE OF SCENE WOULD OPEN RAINES UP A LITTLE.

AT THIS POINT, HE WAS MY TOP CONCERN.

GIVEN HIM HIS SPACE AFTER THE LOSS OF THE RANGERS. DIDN'T WANT TO ADD TO HIS BURDENS OF LEADERSHIP...

...BUT WE ALL NEEDED HIM TO BELIEVE IN SOMETHING.

I TRUSTED THAT HE DID. HE'D BEEN THROUGH TOO MUCH NOT TO.

STUDIES SHOW THAT THE MOST COMMON DENOMINATOR AMONG SURVIVORS OF

IT'S HOW THEY GET THROUGH.

PADRE! WHERE YOU GOING?

TO TALK TO RAINES.

YOU'RE GOIN' DOWN A DEAD END STREET, MY FRIEND.

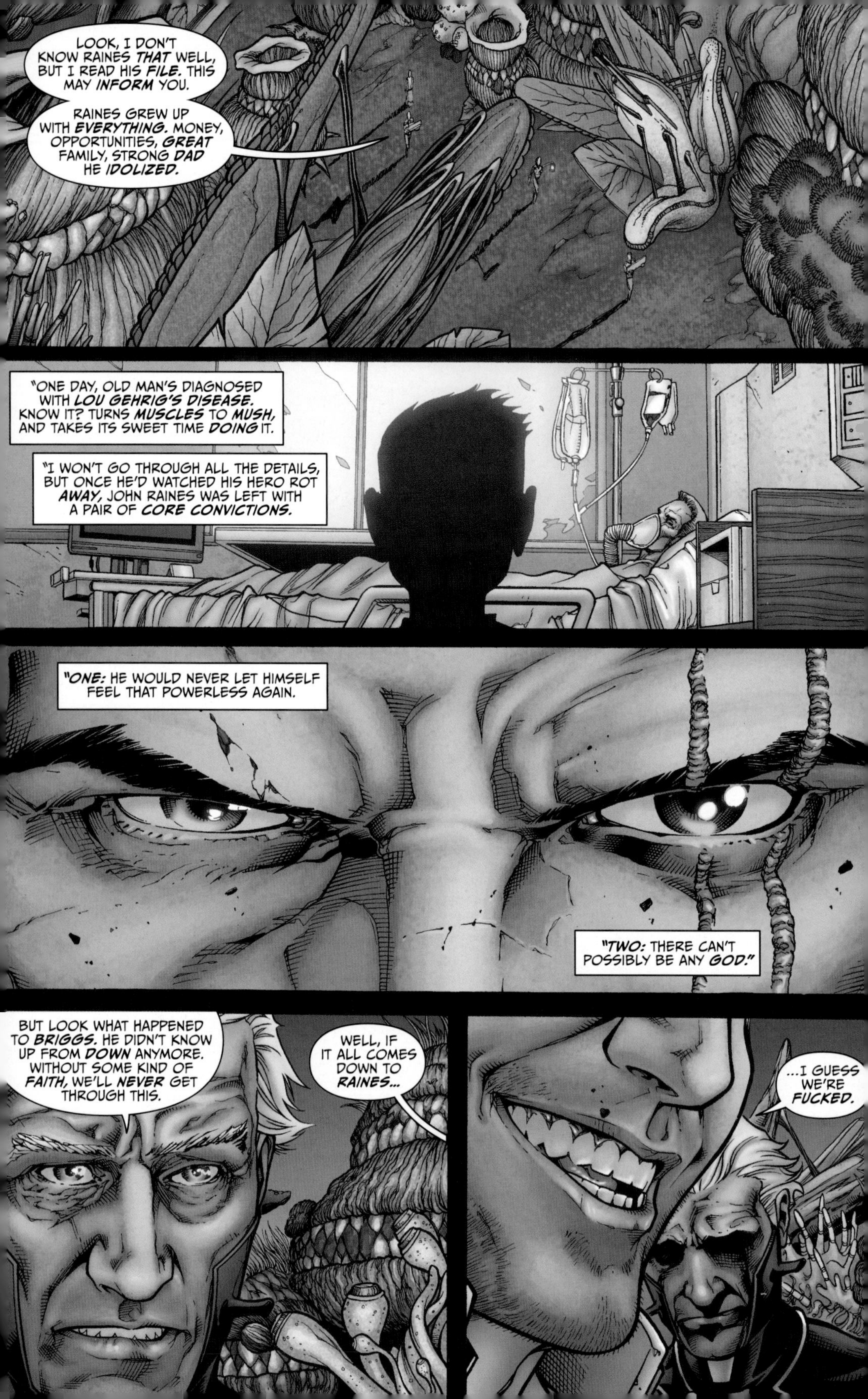
LOOK, I DON'T KNOW RAINES THAT WELL, BUT I READ HIS FILE. THIS MAY INFORM YOU.
RAINES GREW UP WITH EVERYTHING. MONEY, OPPORTUNITIES, GREAT FAMILY, STRONG DAD HE IDOLIZED.
"ONE DAY, OLD MAN'S DIAGNOSED WITH LOU GEHRIG'S DISEASE. KNOW IT? TURNS MUSCLES TO MUSH, AND TAKES ITS SWEET TIME DOING IT.
"I WON'T GO THROUGH ALL THE DETAILS, BUT ONCE HE'D WATCHED HIS HERO ROT AWAY, JOHN RAINES WAS LEFT WITH A PAIR OF CORE CONVICTIONS.
"ONE: HE WOULD NEVER LET HIMSELF FEEL THAT POWERLESS AGAIN.
"TWO: THERE CAN'T POSSIBLY BE ANY GOD."
BUT LOOK WHAT HAPPENED TO BRIGGS. HE DIDN'T KNOW UP FROM DOWN ANYMORE. WITHOUT SOME KIND OF FAITH, WE'LL NEVER GET THROUGH THIS.
WELL, IF IT ALL COMES DOWN TO RAINES...
...I GUESS WE'RE FUCKED.

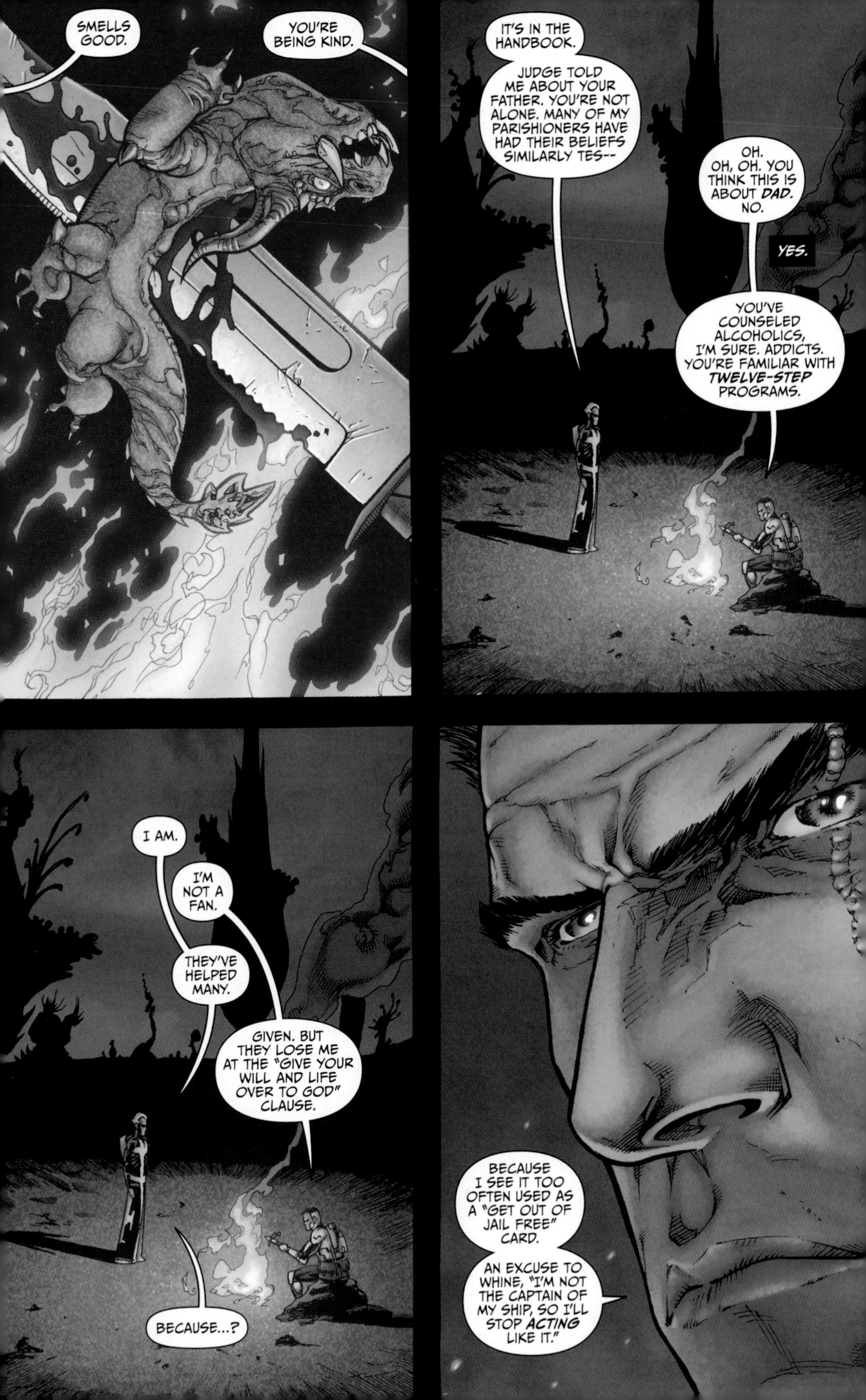
SMELLS GOOD.
YOU'RE BEING KIND.
IT'S IN THE HANDBOOK.
JUDGE TOLD ME ABOUT YOUR FATHER. YOU'RE NOT ALONE. MANY OF MY PARISHIONERS HAVE HAD THEIR BELIEFS SIMILARLY TES--
OH. OH, OH. YOU THINK THIS IS ABOUT DAD. NO.
YES.
YOU'VE COUNSELED ALCOHOLICS, I'M SURE. ADDICTS. YOU'RE FAMILIAR WITH TWELVE-STEP PROGRAMS.
I AM.
I'M NOT A FAN.
THEY'VE HELPED MANY.
GIVEN. BUT THEY LOSE ME AT THE "GIVE YOUR WILL AND LIFE OVER TO GOD" CLAUSE.
BECAUSE...?
BECAUSE I SEE IT TOO OFTEN USED AS A "GET OUT OF JAIL FREE" CARD.
AN EXCUSE TO WHINE, "I'M NOT THE CAPTAIN OF MY SHIP, SO I'LL STOP ACTING LIKE IT."

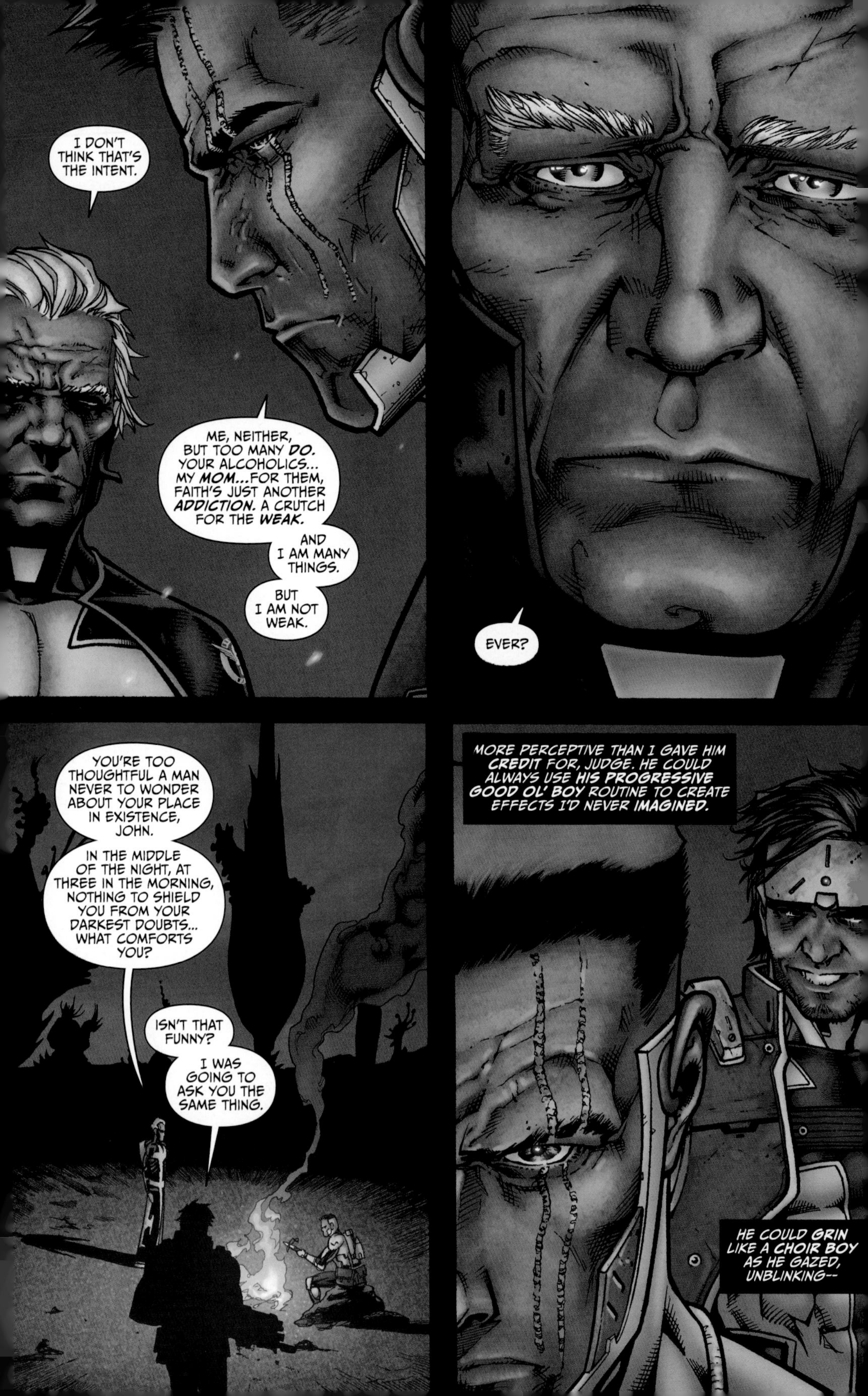
I DON'T THINK THAT'S THE INTENT.
ME, NEITHER, BUT TOO MANY DO. YOUR ALCOHOLICS... MY MOM...FOR THEM, FAITH'S JUST ANOTHER ADDICTION. A CRUTCH FOR THE WEAK.
AND I AM MANY THINGS.
BUT I AM NOT WEAK.
EVER?
YOU'RE TOO THOUGHTFUL A MAN NEVER TO WONDER ABOUT YOUR PLACE IN EXISTENCE, JOHN.
IN THE MIDDLE OF THE NIGHT, AT THREE IN THE MORNING, NOTHING TO SHIELD YOU FROM YOUR DARKEST DOUBTS... WHAT COMFORTS YOU?
ISN'T THAT FUNNY?
I WAS GOING TO ASK YOU THE SAME THING.
MORE PERCEPTIVE THAN I GAVE HIM CREDIT FOR, JUDGE. HE COULD ALWAYS USE HIS PROGRESSIVE GOOD OL' BOY ROUTINE TO CREATE EFFECTS I'D NEVER IMAGINED.
HE COULD GRIN LIKE A CHOIR BOY AS HE GAZED, UNBLINKING--

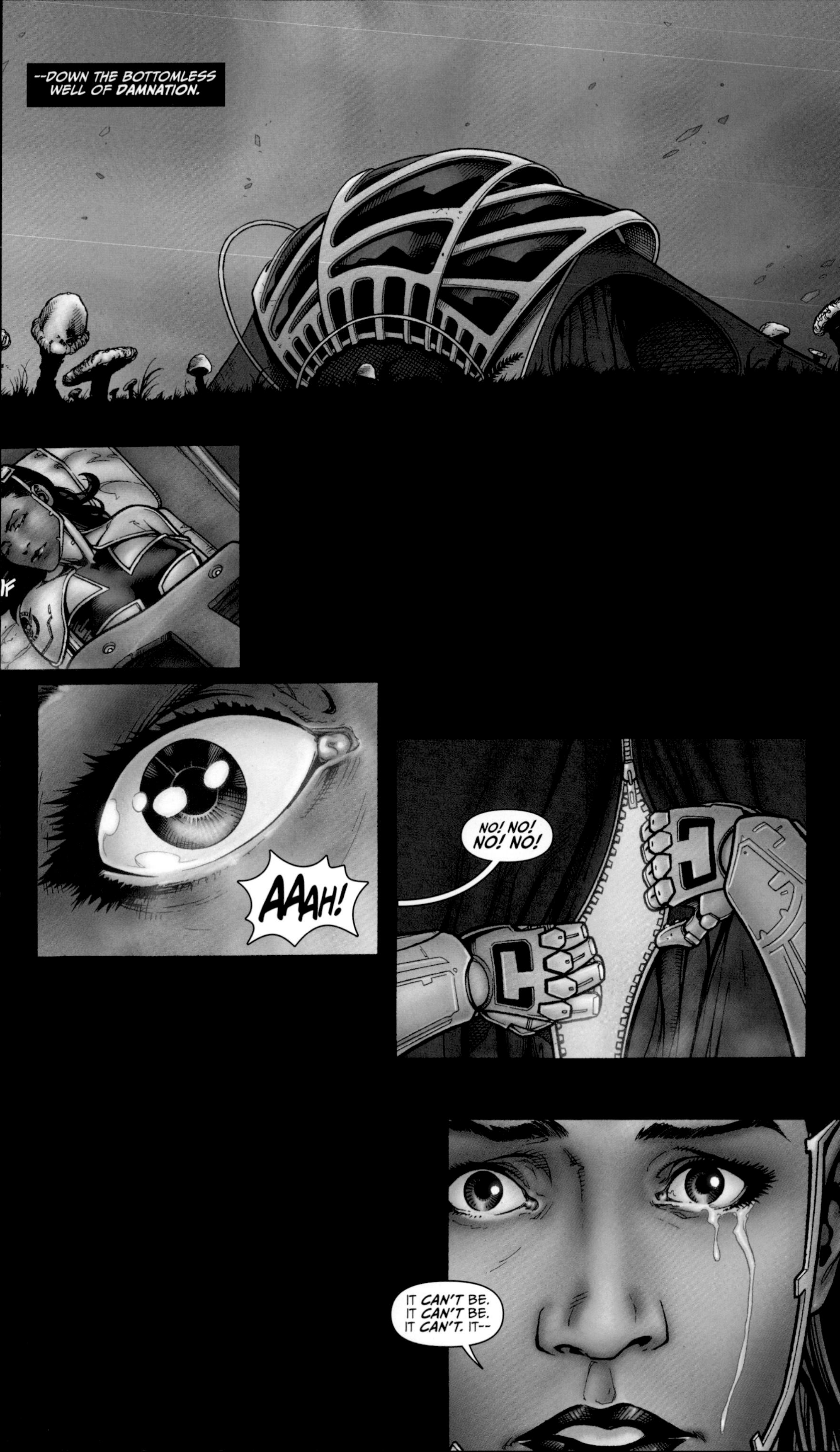
--DOWN THE BOTTOMLESS WELL OF DAMNATION.
AAAH!
NO! NO! NO! NO!
IT CAN'T BE. IT CAN'T BE. IT CAN'T. IT--

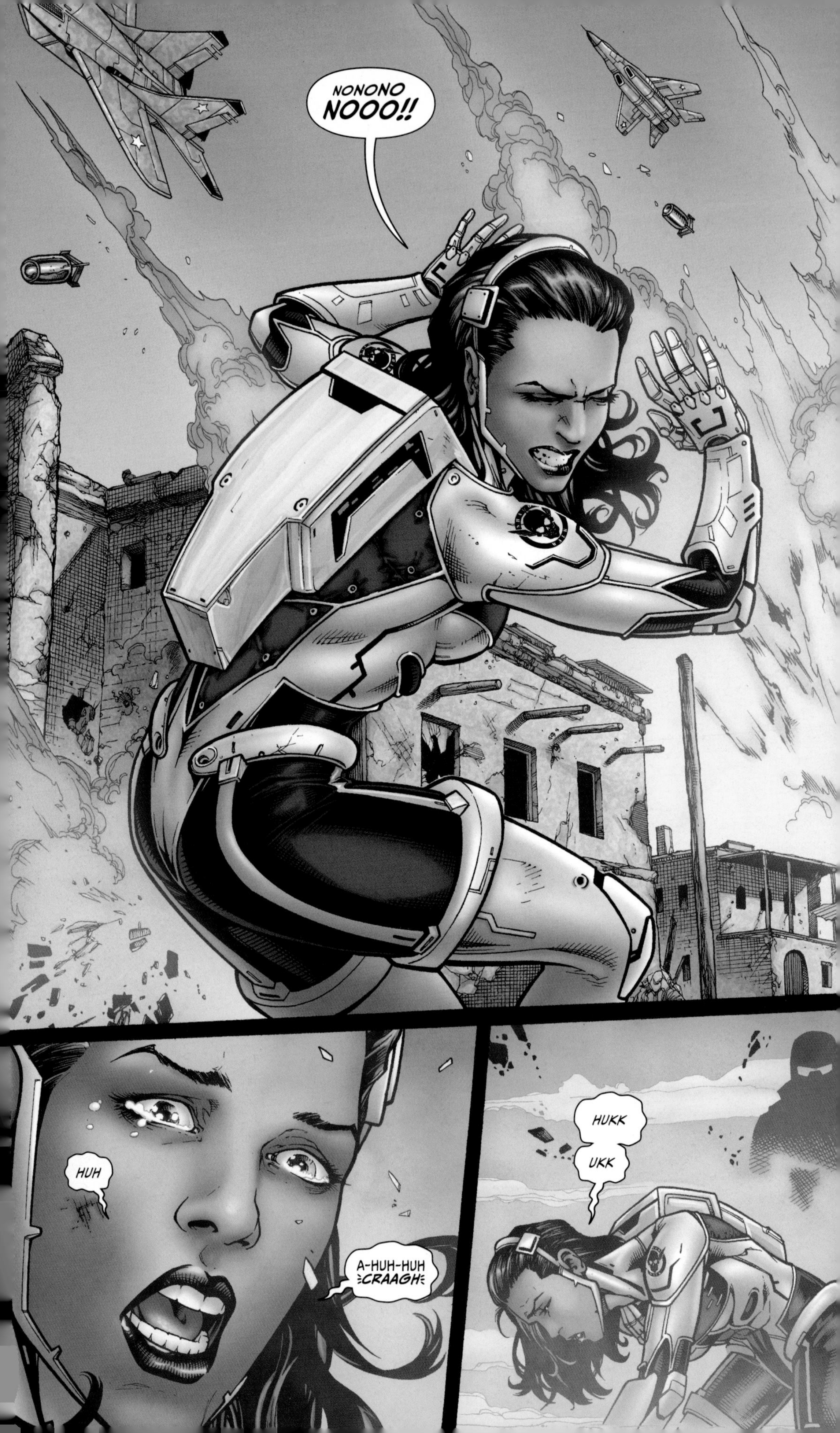
NONONO NOOO!!
HUH
A-HUH-HUH CRAAGH
HUKK
UKK

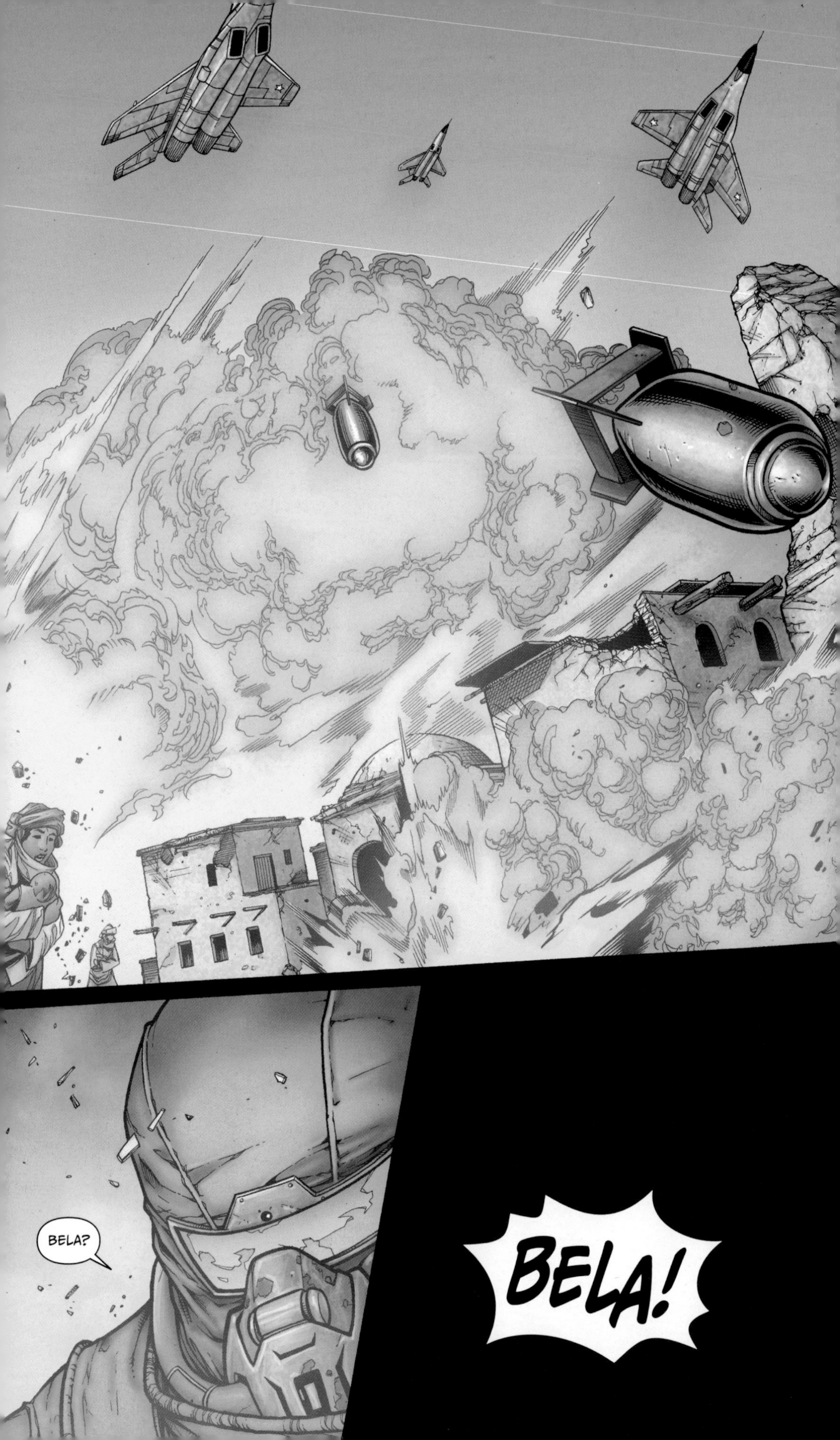
BELA?
BELA!

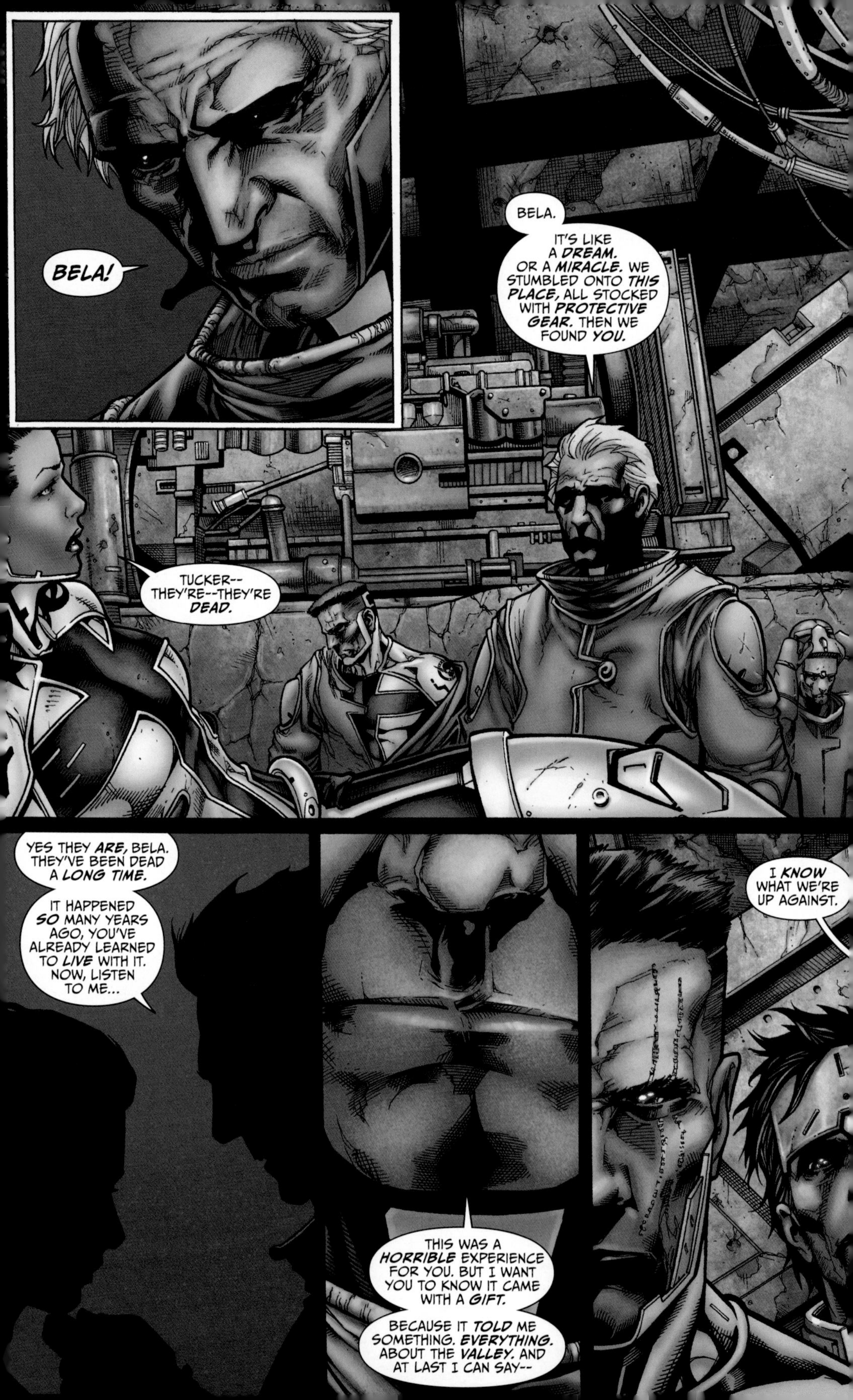
BELA!
BELA.
IT'S LIKE A DREAM. OR A MIRACLE. WE STUMBLED ONTO THIS PLACE, ALL STOCKED WITH PROTECTIVE GEAR. THEN WE FOUND YOU.
TUCKER-- THEY'RE--THEY'RE DEAD.
YES THEY ARE, BELA. THEY'VE BEEN DEAD A LONG TIME.
IT HAPPENED SO MANY YEARS AGO, YOU'VE ALREADY LEARNED TO LIVE WITH IT. NOW, LISTEN TO ME...
THIS WAS A HORRIBLE EXPERIENCE FOR YOU. BUT I WANT YOU TO KNOW IT CAME WITH A GIFT.
BECAUSE IT TOLD ME SOMETHING. EVERYTHING. ABOUT THE VALLEY. AND AT LAST I CAN SAY--
I KNOW WHAT WE'RE UP AGAINST.

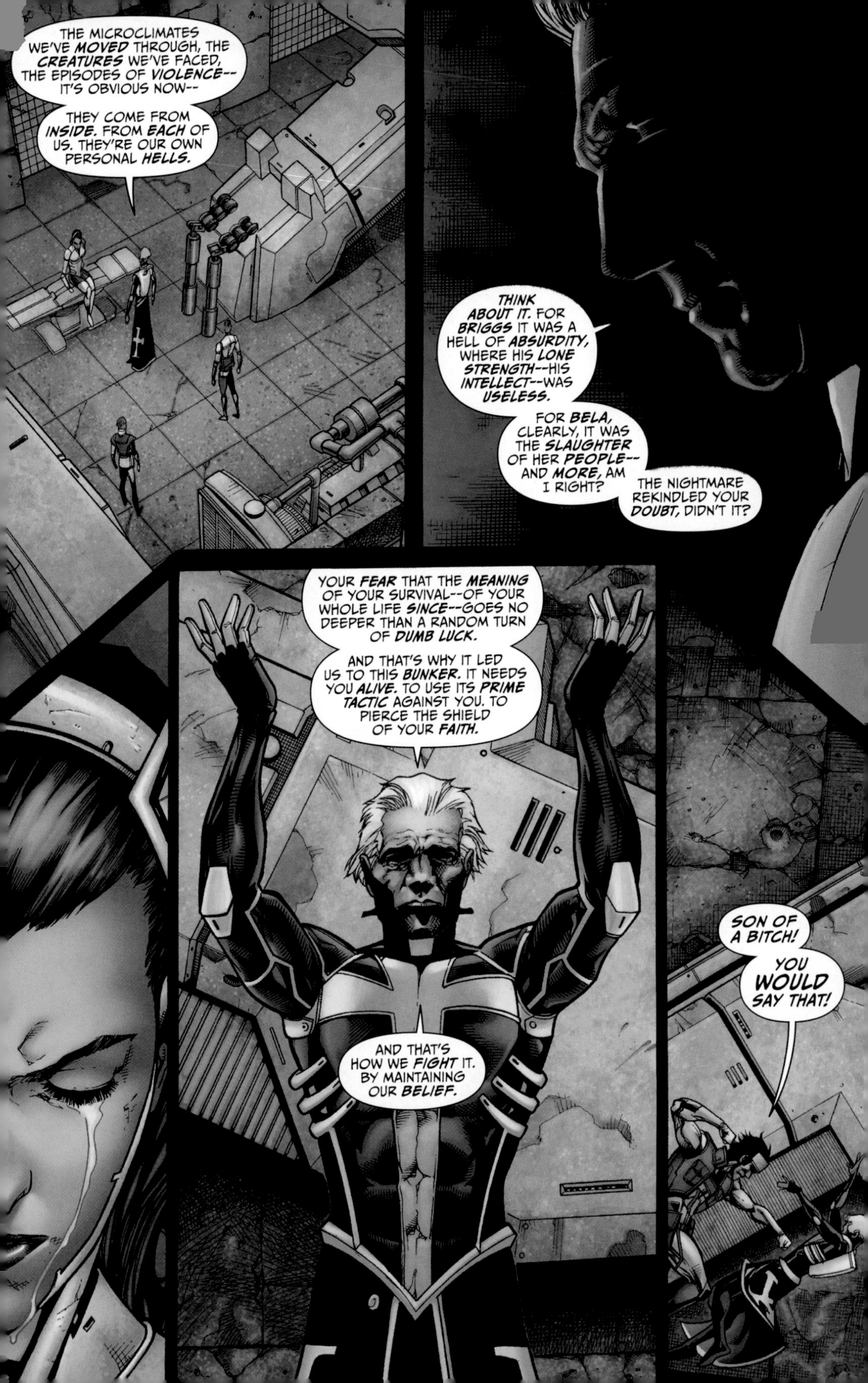
THE MICROCLIMATES WE'VE MOVED THROUGH, THE CREATURES WE'VE FACED, THE EPISODES OF VIOLENCE-- IT'S OBVIOUS NOW--
THEY COME FROM INSIDE. FROM EACH OF US. THEY'RE OUR OWN PERSONAL HELLS.
THINK ABOUT IT. FOR BRIGGS IT WAS A HELL OF ABSURDITY, WHERE HIS LONE STRENGTH--HIS INTELLECT--WAS USELESS.
FOR BELA, CLEARLY, IT WAS THE SLAUGHTER OF HER PEOPLE-- AND MORE, AM I RIGHT?
THE NIGHTMARE REKINDLED YOUR DOUBT, DIDN'T IT?
YOUR FEAR THAT THE MEANING OF YOUR SURVIVAL--OF YOUR WHOLE LIFE SINCE--GOES NO DEEPER THAN A RANDOM TURN OF DUMB LUCK.
AND THAT'S WHY IT LED US TO THIS BUNKER. IT NEEDS YOU ALIVE. TO USE ITS PRIME TACTIC AGAINST YOU. TO PIERCE THE SHIELD OF YOUR FAITH.
AND THAT'S HOW WE FIGHT IT. BY MAINTAINING OUR BELIEF.
SON OF A BITCH!
YOU WOULD SAY THAT!

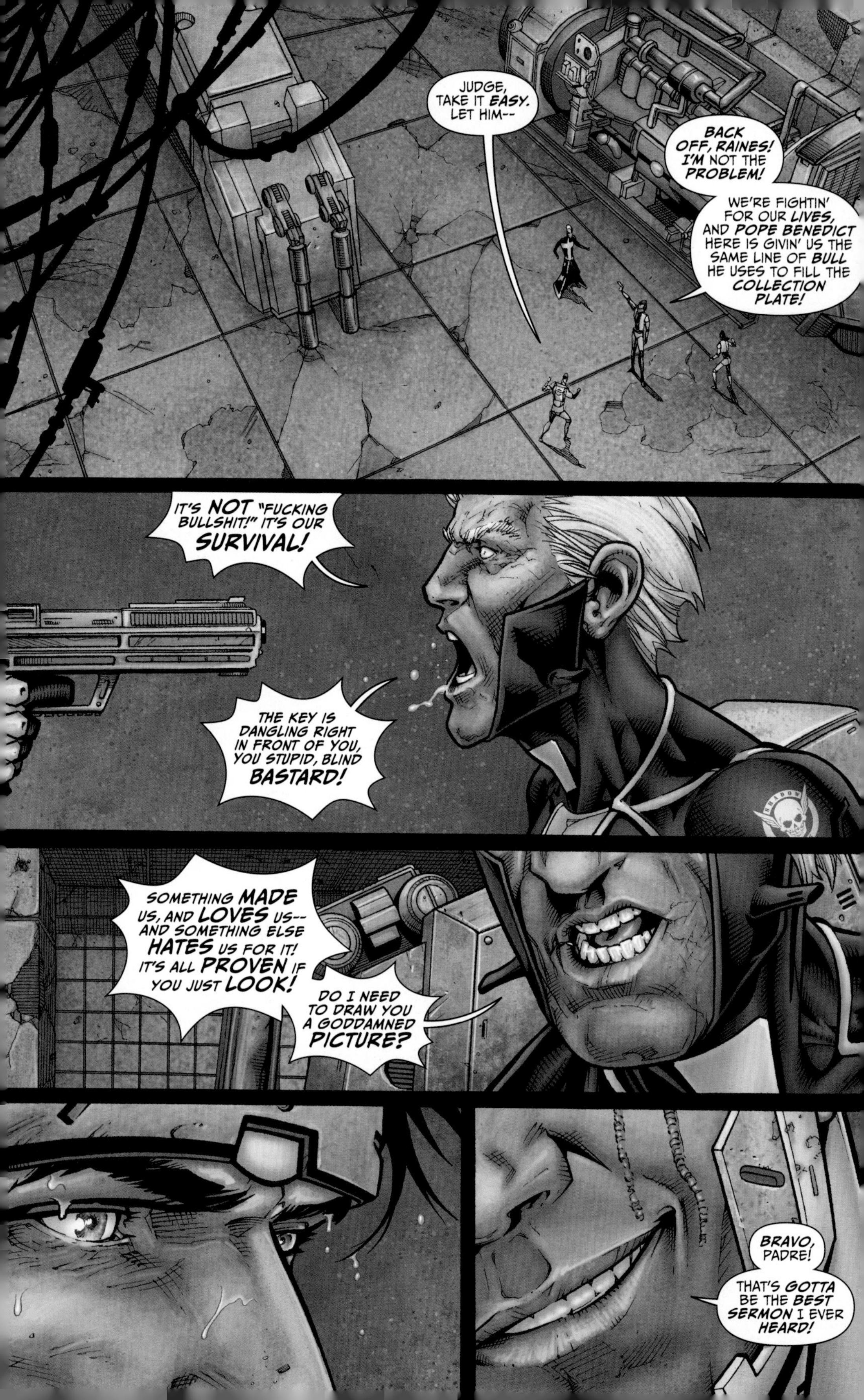
JUDGE, TAKE IT EASY. LET HIM--
BACK OFF, RAINES! I'M NOT THE PROBLEM!
WE'RE FIGHTIN' FOR OUR LIVES, AND POPE BENEDICT HERE IS GIVIN' US THE SAME LINE OF BULL HE USES TO FILL THE COLLECTION PLATE!
IT'S NOT "FUCKING BULLSHIT!" IT'S OUR SURVIVAL!
THE KEY IS DANGLING RIGHT IN FRONT OF YOU, YOU STUPID, BLIND BASTARD!
SOMETHING MADE US, AND LOVES US-- AND SOMETHING ELSE HATES US FOR IT! IT'S ALL PROVEN IF YOU JUST LOOK!
DO I NEED TO DRAW YOU A GODDAMNED PICTURE?
BRAVO, PADRE!
THAT'S GOTTA BE THE BEST SERMON I EVER HEARD!

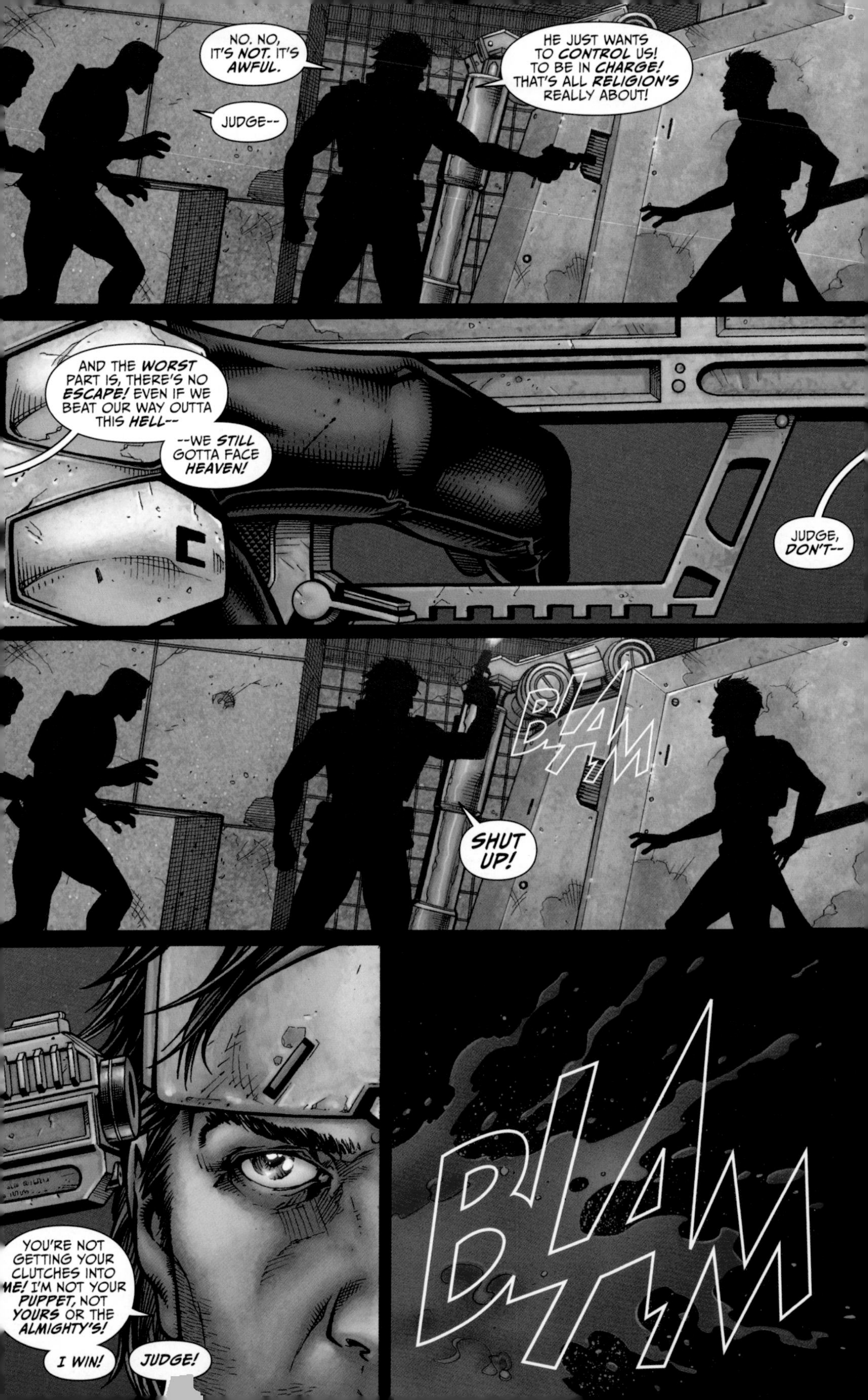
NO. NO, IT'S NOT. IT'S AWFUL.
JUDGE--
HE JUST WANTS TO CONTROL US! TO BE IN CHARGE! THAT'S ALL RELIGION'S REALLY ABOUT!
AND THE WORST PART IS, THERE'S NO ESCAPE! EVEN IF WE BEAT OUR WAY OUTTA THIS HELL--
--WE STILL GOTTA FACE HEAVEN!
JUDGE, DON'T--
BLAM
SHUT UP!
YOU'RE NOT GETTING YOUR CLUTCHES INTO ME! I'M NOT YOUR PUPPET, NOT YOURS OR THE ALMIGHTY'S!
I WIN!
JUDGE!
BLAM

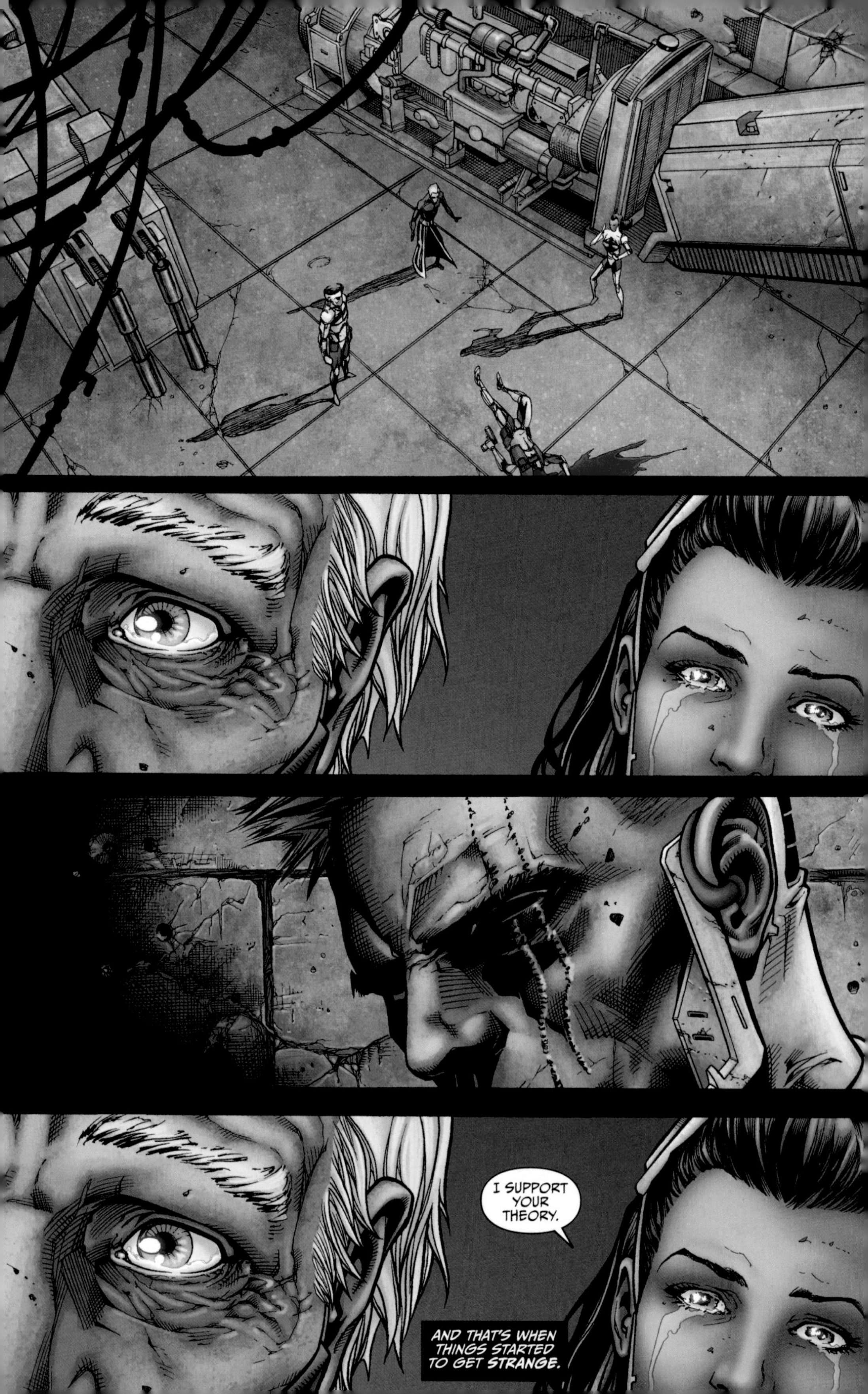
I SUPPORT YOUR THEORY.
AND THAT'S WHEN THINGS STARTED TO GET STRANGE.

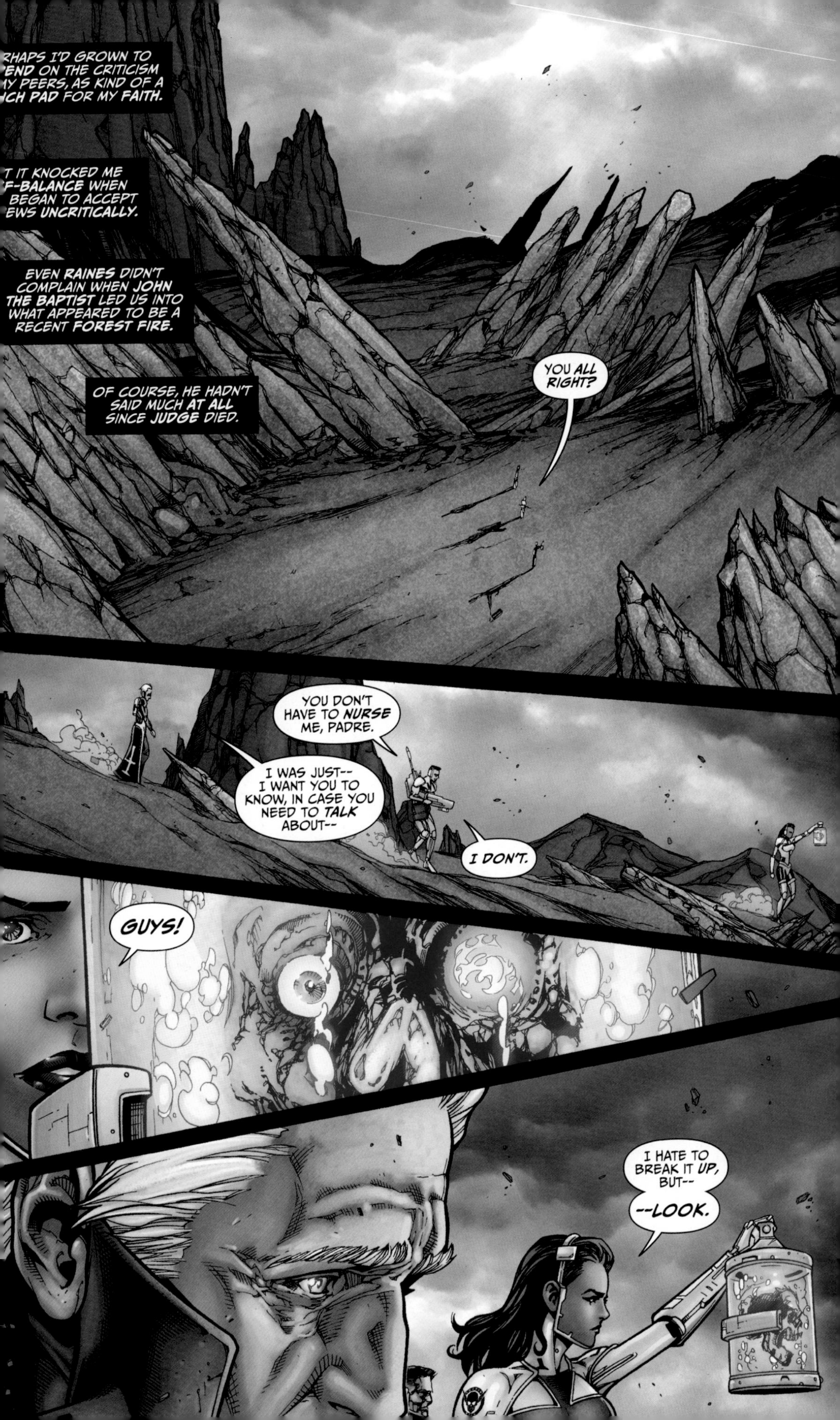
RHAPS I'D GROWN TO
'END ON THE CRITICISM
MY PEERS, AS KIND OF A
ICH PAD FOR MY FAITH.
T IT KNOCKED ME
F-BALANCE WHEN
BEGAN TO ACCEPT
EWS UNCRITICALLY.
EVEN RAINES DIDN'T COMPLAIN WHEN JOHN THE BAPTIST LED US INTO WHAT APPEARED TO BE A RECENT FOREST FIRE.
OF COURSE, HE HADN'T SAID MUCH AT ALL SINCE JUDGE DIED.
YOU ALL RIGHT?
YOU DON'T HAVE TO NURSE ME, PADRE.
I WAS JUST-- I WANT YOU TO KNOW, IN CASE YOU NEED TO TALK ABOUT--
I DON'T.
GUYS!
I HATE TO BREAK IT UP, BUT--
--LOOK.

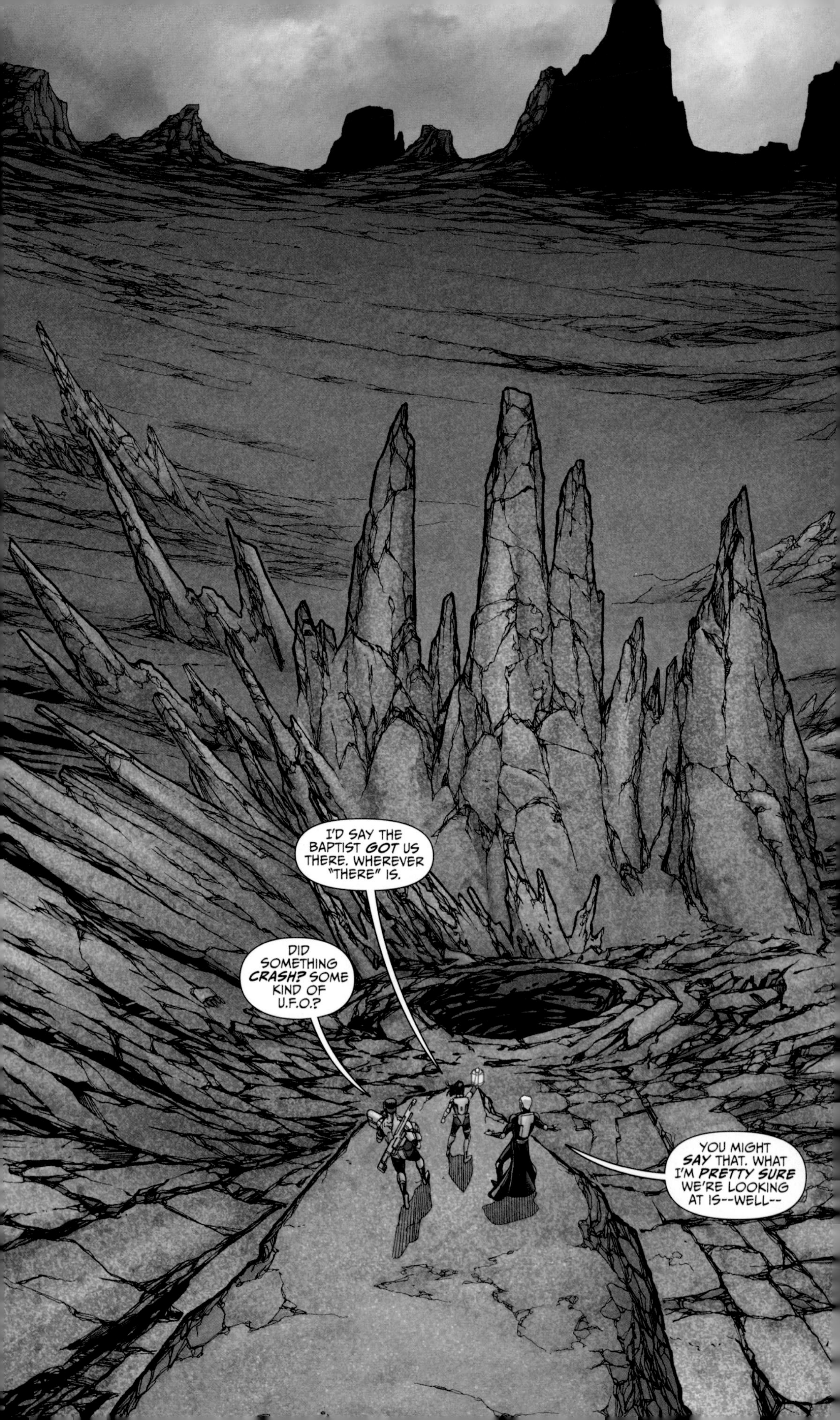
DID SOMETHING CRASH? SOME KIND OF U.F.O.?
I'D SAY THE BAPTIST GOT US THERE. WHEREVER "THERE" IS.
YOU MIGHT SAY THAT. WHAT I'M PRETTY SURE WE'RE LOOKING AT IS--WELL--

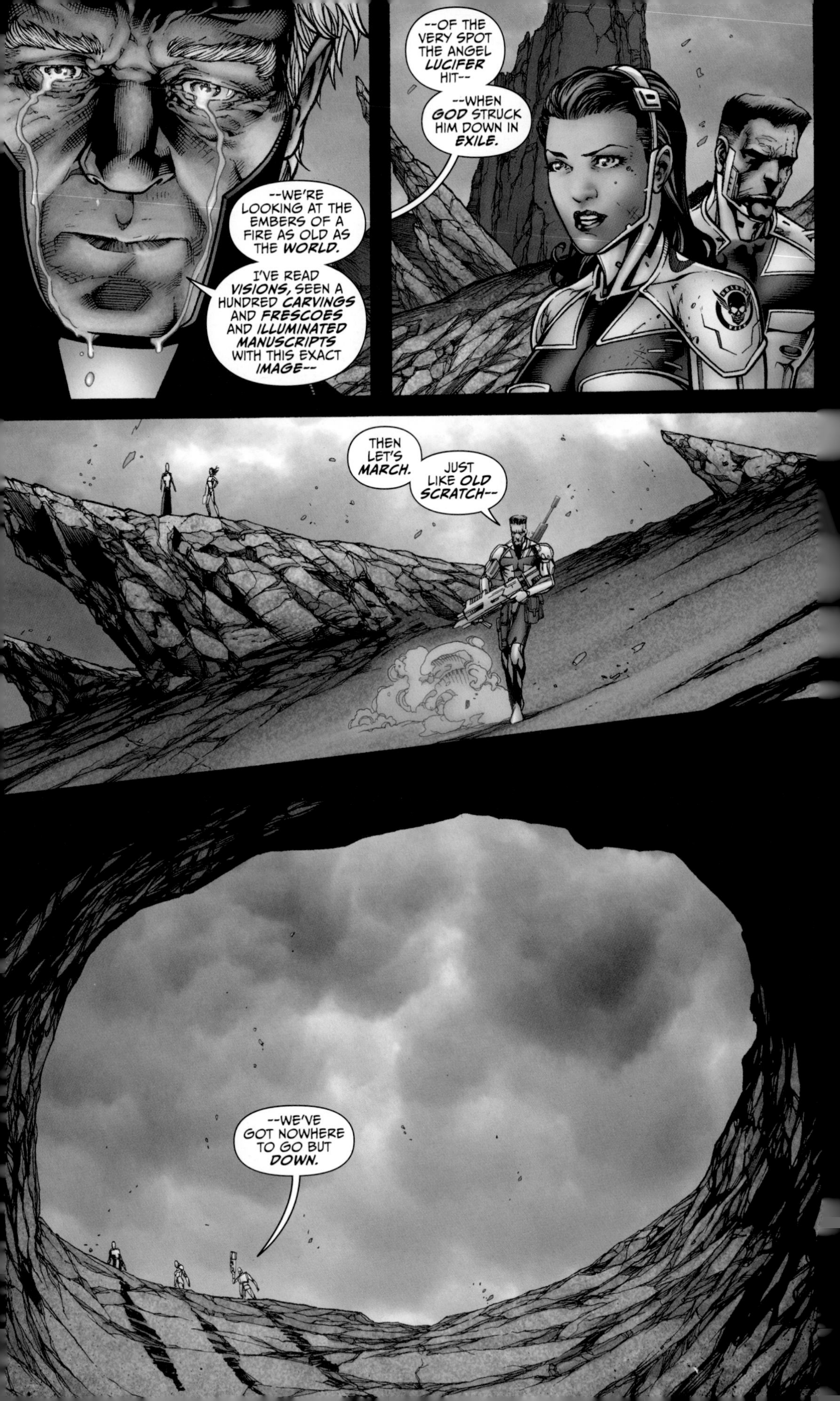
--WE'RE LOOKING AT THE EMBERS OF A FIRE AS OLD AS THE WORLD.
I'VE READ VISIONS, SEEN A HUNDRED CARVINGS AND FRESCOES AND ILLUMINATED MANUSCRIPTS WITH THIS EXACT IMAGE--
--OF THE VERY SPOT THE ANGEL LUCIFER HIT--
--WHEN GOD STRUCK HIM DOWN IN EXILE.
THEN LET'S MARCH.
JUST LIKE OLD SCRATCH--
--WE'VE GOT NOWHERE TO GO BUT DOWN.

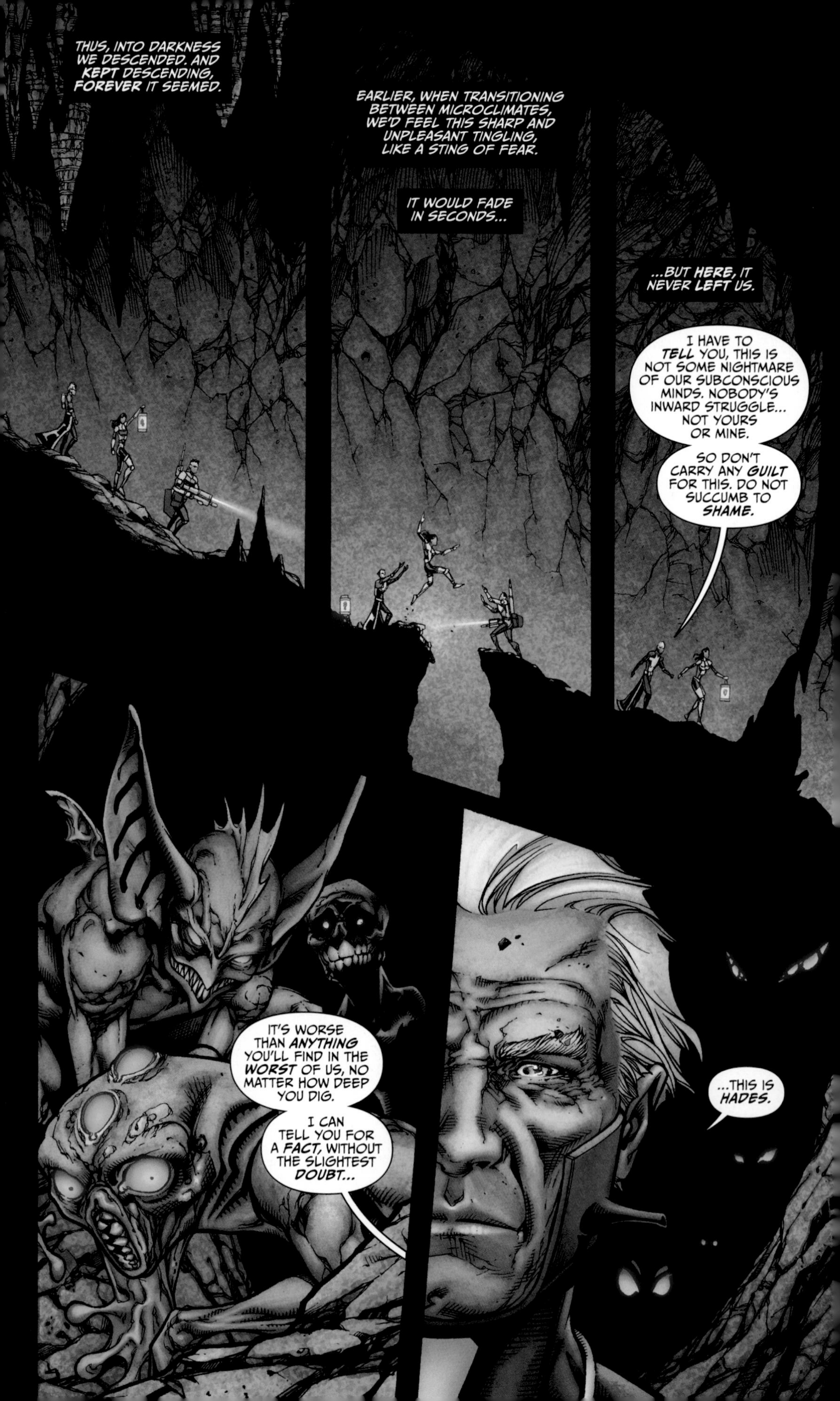
THUS, INTO DARKNESS WE DESCENDED. AND KEPT DESCENDING, FOREVER IT SEEMED.
EARLIER, WHEN TRANSITIONING BETWEEN MICROCLIMATES, WE'D FEEL THIS SHARP AND UNPLEASANT TINGLING, LIKE A STING OF FEAR.
IT WOULD FADE IN SECONDS...
...BUT HERE, IT NEVER LEFT US.
I HAVE TO TELL YOU, THIS IS NOT SOME NIGHTMARE OF OUR SUBCONSCIOUS MINDS. NOBODY'S INWARD STRUGGLE... NOT YOURS OR MINE.
SO DON'T CARRY ANY GUILT FOR THIS. DO NOT SUCCUMB TO SHAME.
IT'S WORSE THAN ANYTHING YOU'LL FIND IN THE WORST OF US, NO MATTER HOW DEEP YOU DIG.
I CAN TELL YOU FOR A FACT, WITHOUT THE SLIGHTEST DOUBT...
...THIS IS HADES.

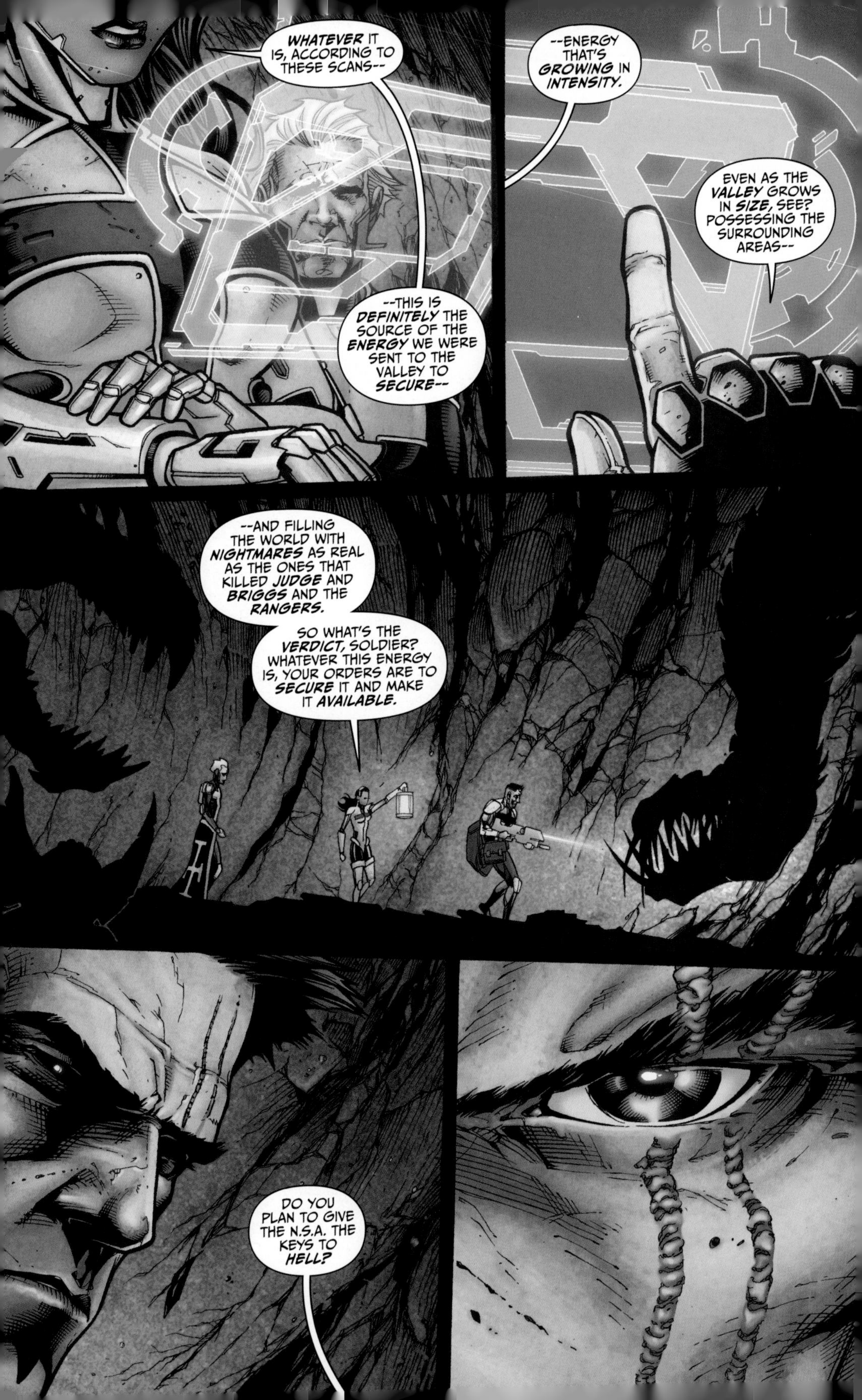
WHATEVER IT IS, ACCORDING TO THESE SCANS--
--THIS IS DEFINITELY THE SOURCE OF THE ENERGY WE WERE SENT TO THE VALLEY TO SECURE--
--ENERGY THAT'S GROWING IN INTENSITY.
EVEN AS THE VALLEY GROWS IN SIZE, SEE? POSSESSING THE SURROUNDING AREAS--
--AND FILLING THE WORLD WITH NIGHTMARES AS REAL AS THE ONES THAT KILLED JUDGE AND BRIGGS AND THE RANGERS.
SO WHAT'S THE VERDICT, SOLDIER? WHATEVER THIS ENERGY IS, YOUR ORDERS ARE TO SECURE IT AND MAKE IT AVAILABLE.
DO YOU PLAN TO GIVE THE N.S.A. THE KEYS TO HELL?

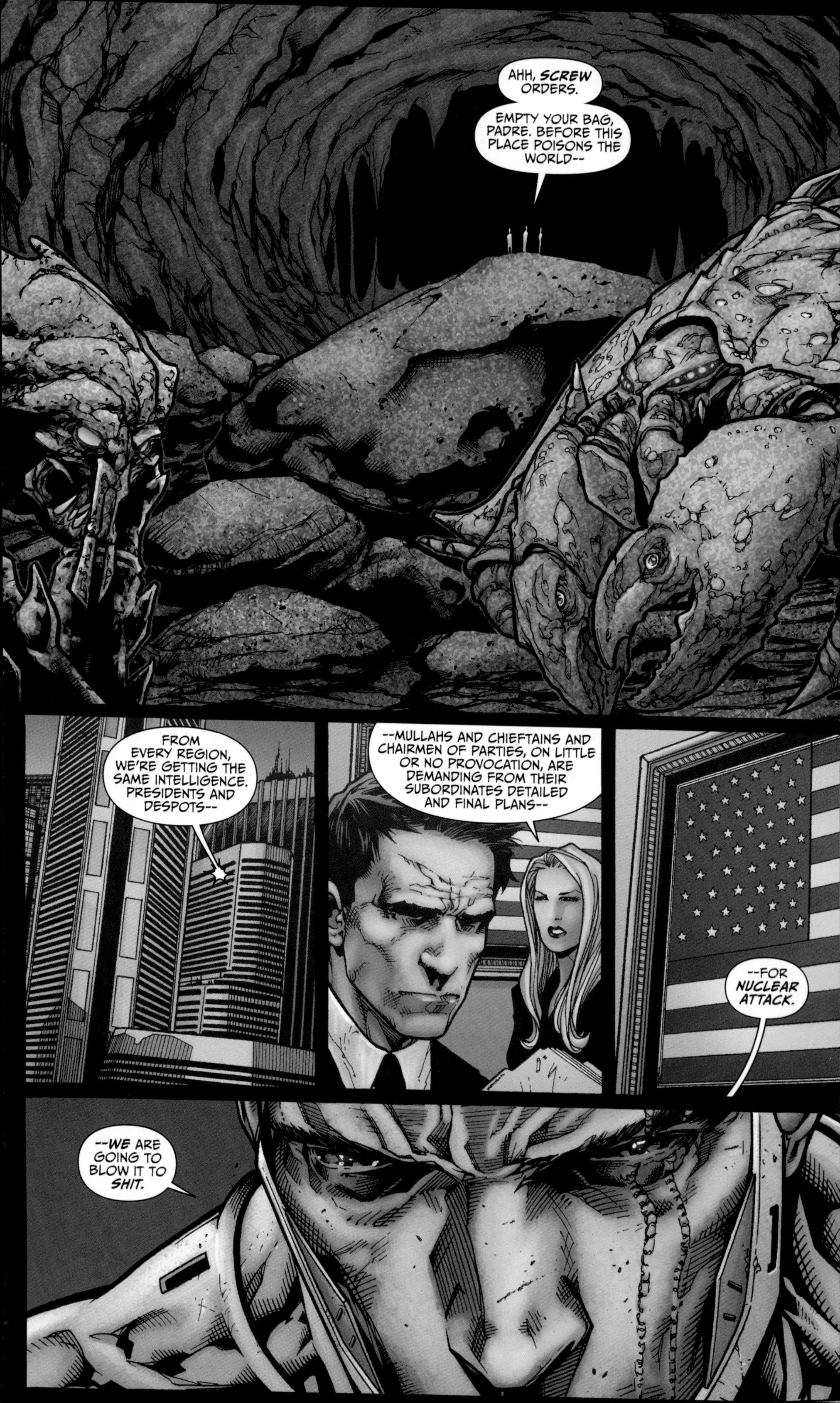
AHH, SCREW ORDERS.
EMPTY YOUR BAG, PADRE. BEFORE THIS PLACE POISONS THE WORLD--
FROM EVERY REGION, WE'RE GETTING THE SAME INTELLIGENCE. PRESIDENTS AND DESPOTS--
--MULLAHS AND CHIEFTAINS AND CHAIRMEN OF PARTIES, ON LITTLE OR NO PROVOCATION, ARE DEMANDING FROM THEIR SUBORDINATES DETAILED AND FINAL PLANS--
--FOR NUCLEAR ATTACK.
--WE ARE GOING TO BLOW IT TO SHIT.

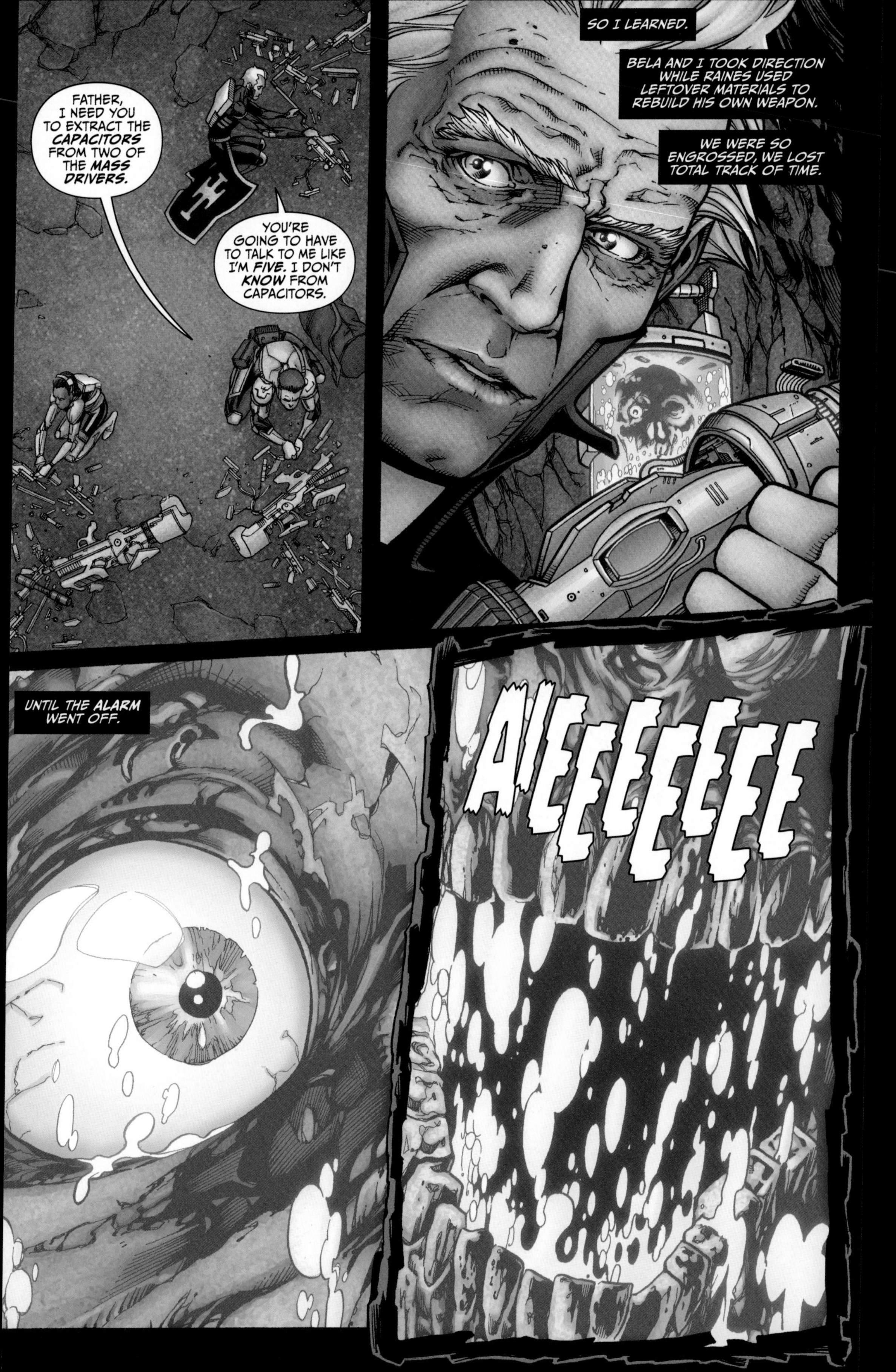
FATHER, I NEED YOU TO EXTRACT THE CAPACITORS FROM TWO OF THE MASS DRIVERS.
YOU'RE GOING TO HAVE TO TALK TO ME LIKE I'M FIVE. I DON'T KNOW FROM CAPACITORS.
SO I LEARNED.
BELA AND I TOOK DIRECTION WHILE RAINES USED LEFTOVER MATERIALS TO REBUILD HIS OWN WEAPON.
WE WERE SO ENGROSSED, WE LOST TOTAL TRACK OF TIME.
UNTIL THE ALARM WENT OFF.
AIEEEEEEEE

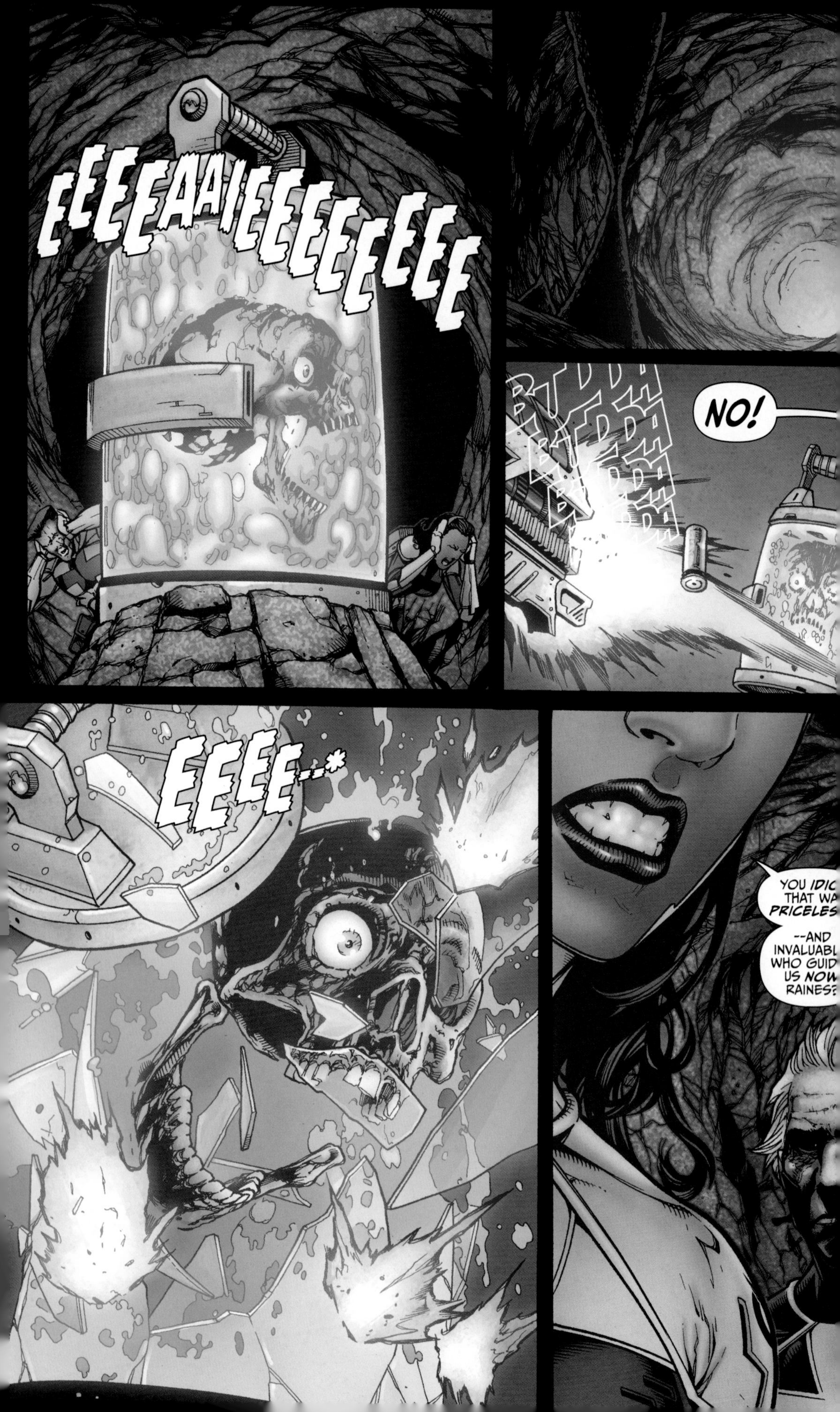
EEEEAAIEEEEEEEE
NO!
EEEE--*
YOU IDIC THAT WA PRICELES
--AND INVALUABL WHO GUID US NOW RAINES?

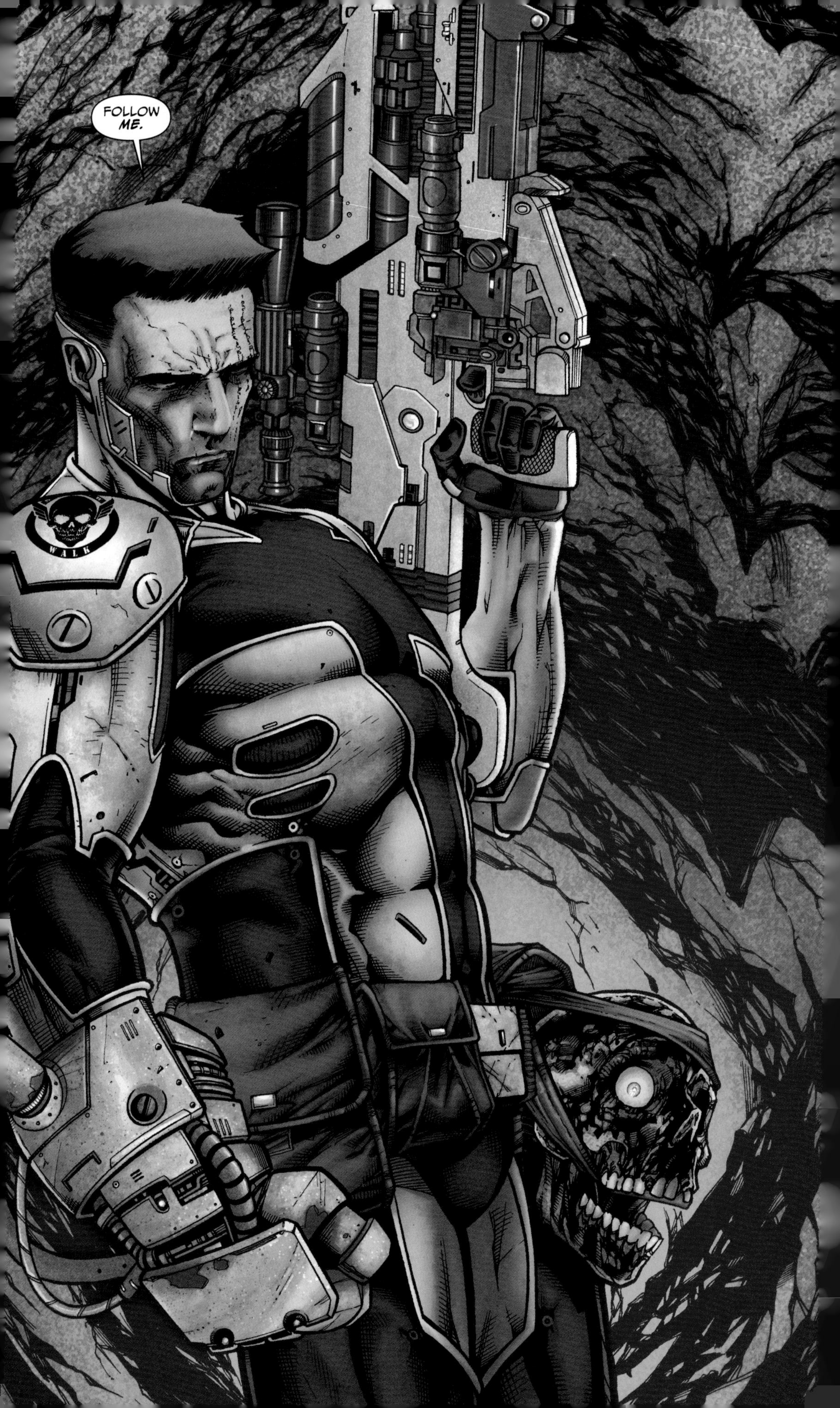
FOLLOW ME.
W A L K

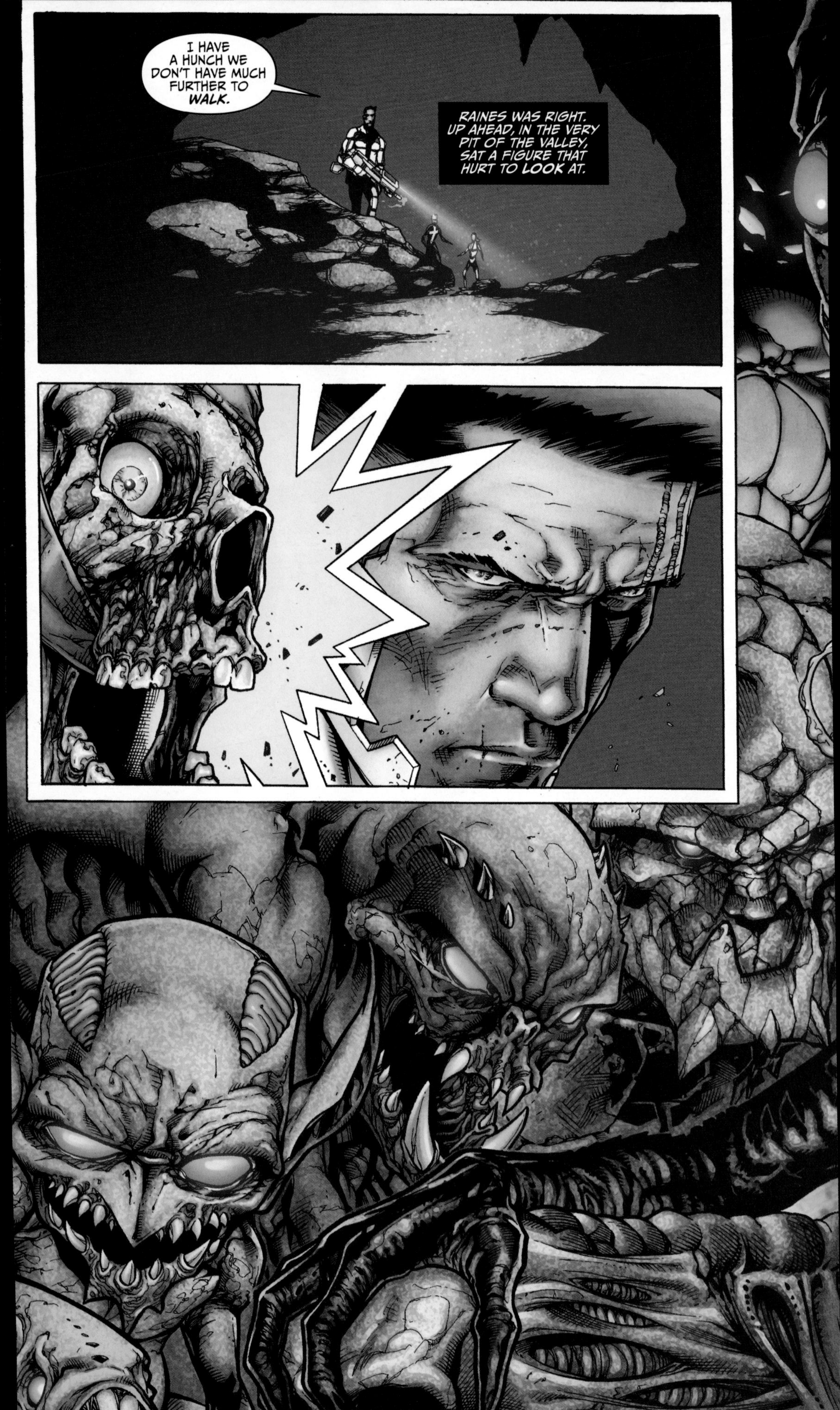
I HAVE A HUNCH WE DON'T HAVE MUCH FURTHER TO WALK.
RAINES WAS RIGHT. UP AHEAD, IN THE VERY PIT OF THE VALLEY, SAT A FIGURE THAT HURT TO LOOK AT.

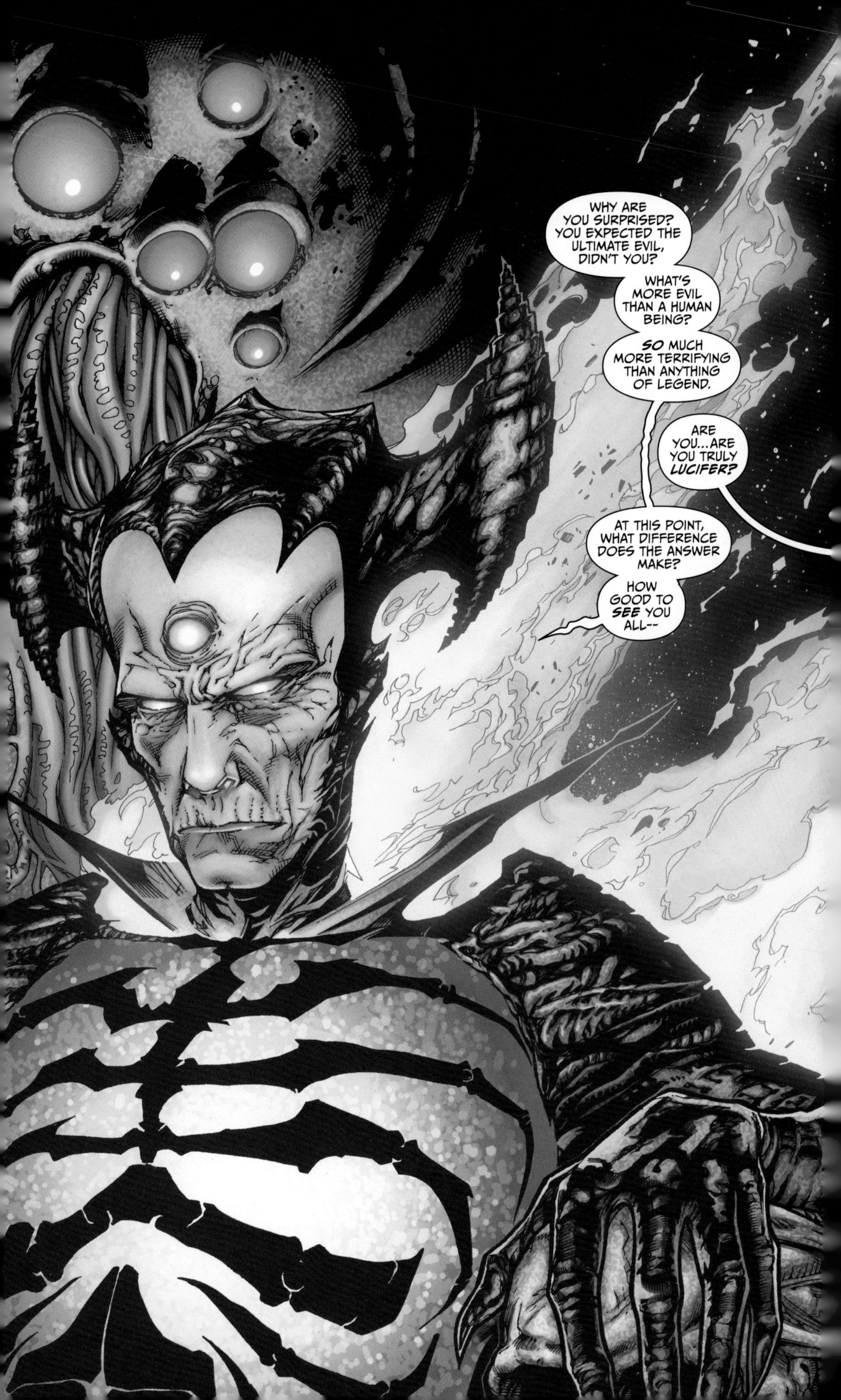

WHY ARE YOU SURPRISED? YOU EXPECTED THE ULTIMATE EVIL, DIDN'T YOU?
WHAT'S MORE EVIL THAN A HUMAN BEING?
SO MUCH MORE TERRIFYING THAN ANYTHING OF LEGEND.
ARE YOU...ARE YOU TRULY *LUCIFER?*
AT THIS POINT, WHAT DIFFERENCE DOES THE ANSWER MAKE?
HOW GOOD TO *SEE* YOU ALL--

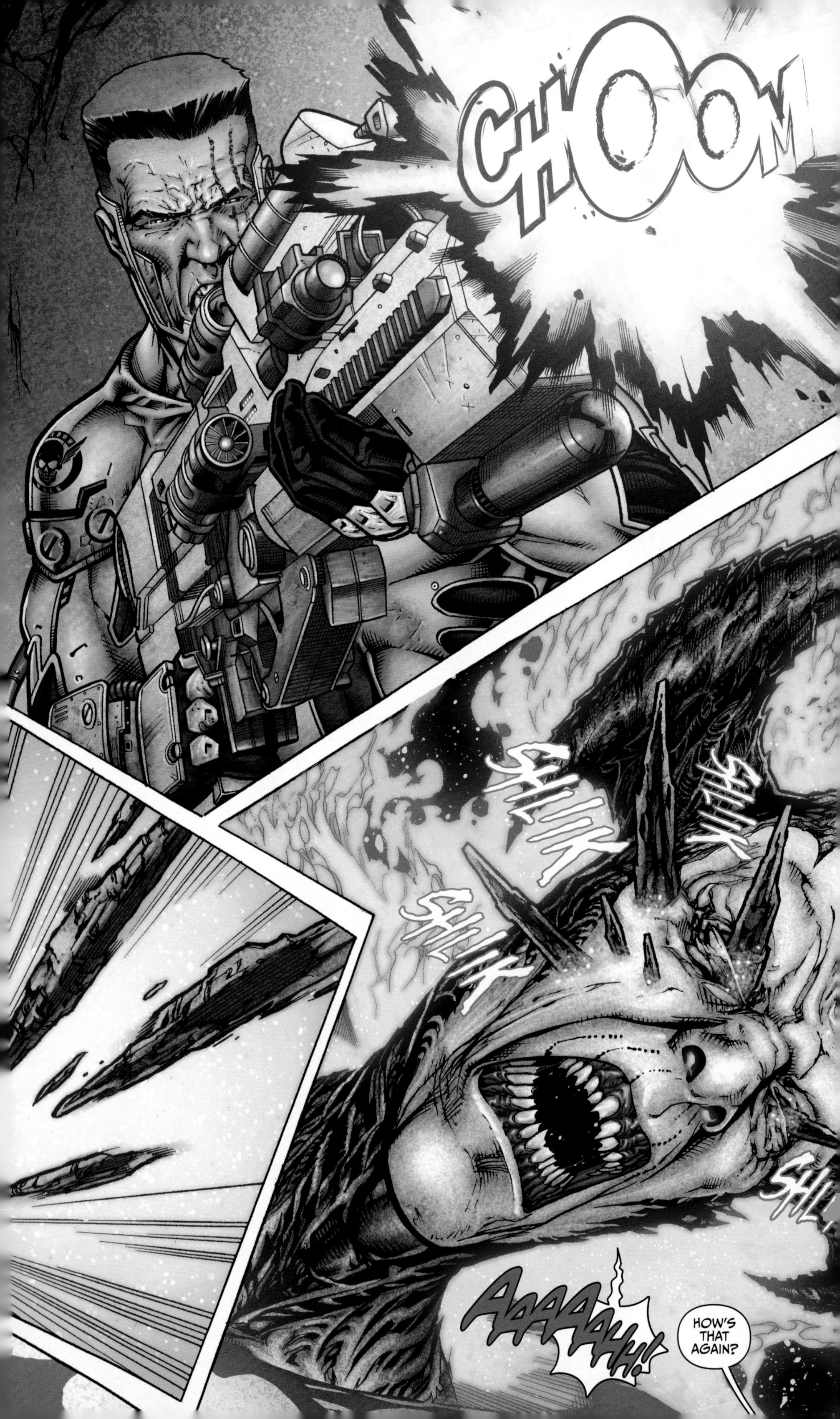
CHOOM
SHLIK
SHLIK
SHLIK
AAAAAHH!
HOW'S THAT AGAIN?

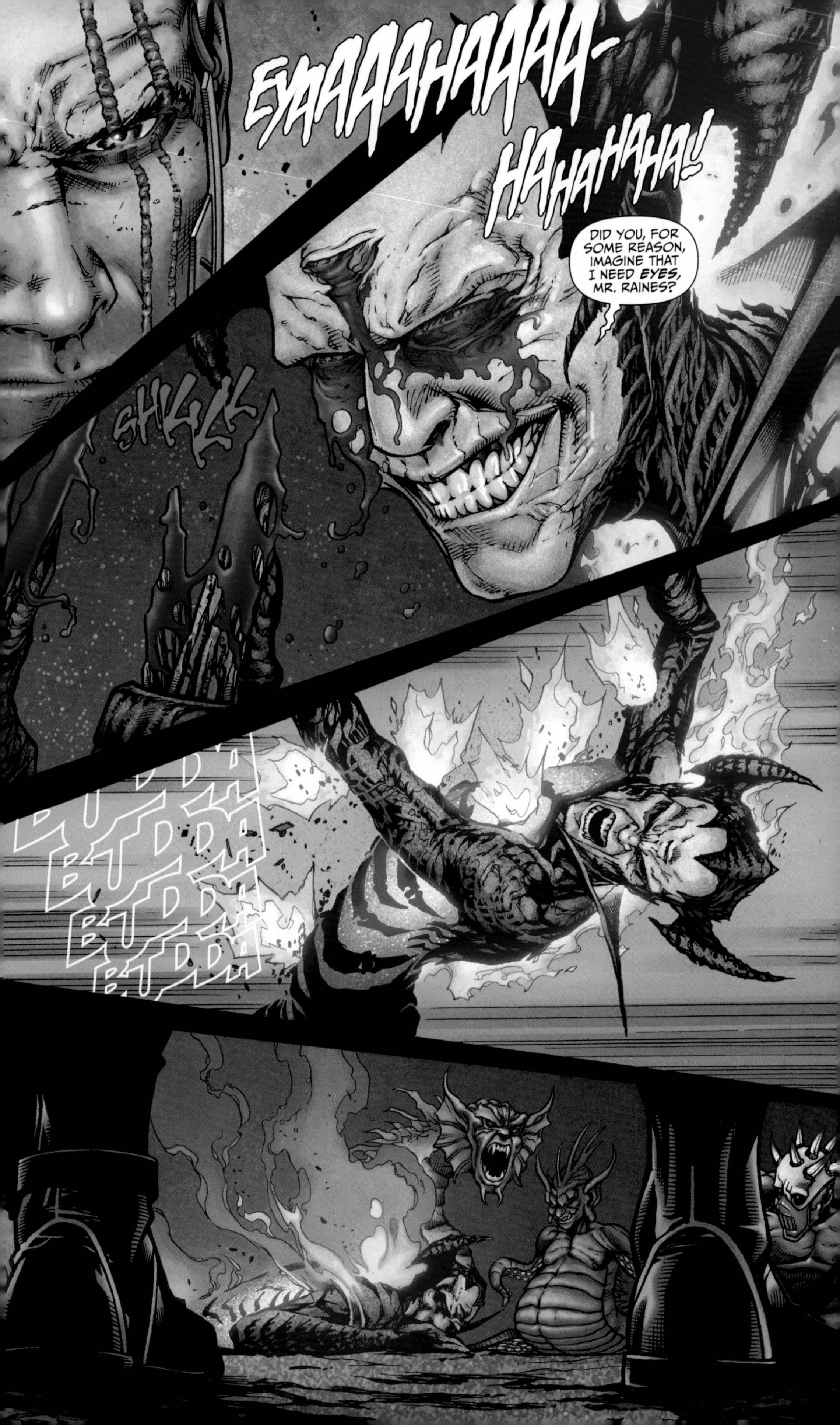

EYAAAAHAAAAA-
HAHAHAHA!
DID YOU, FOR SOME REASON, IMAGINE THAT I NEED EYES, MR. RAINES?
SHLLK
BUDDA BUDDA BUDDA BUDDA

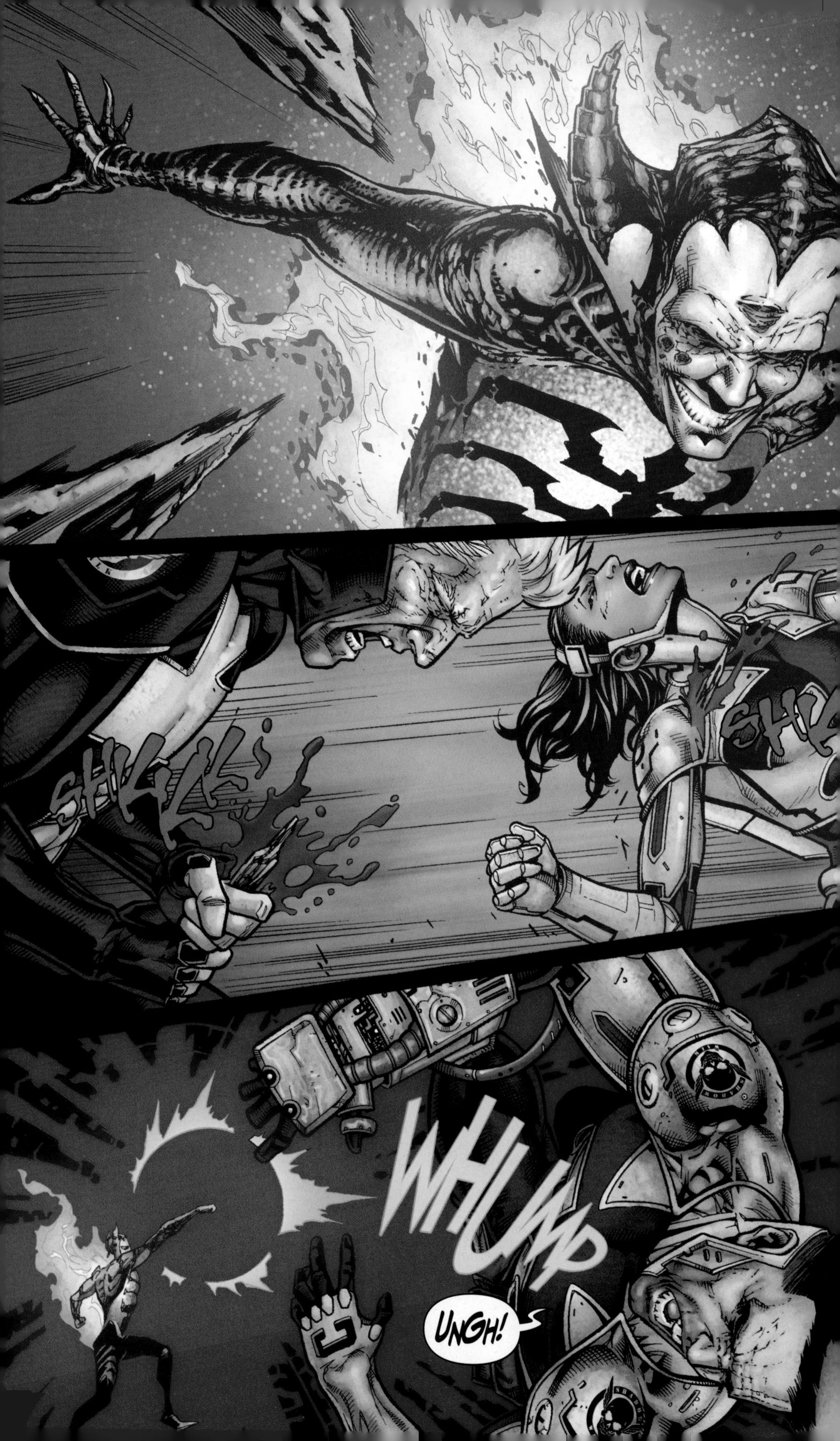
SHKK!
SHK
WHUMP
UNGH!

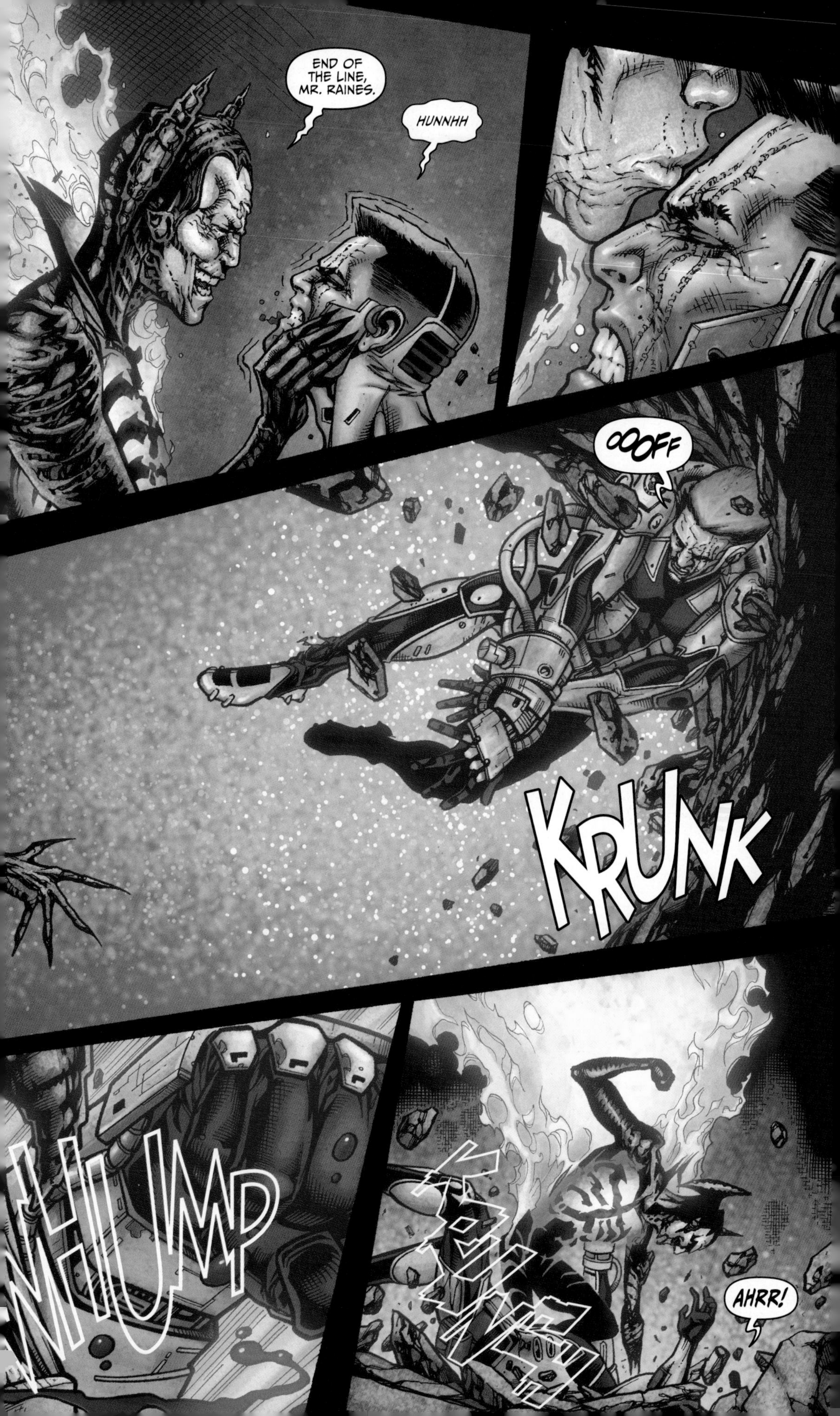
END OF THE LINE, MR. RAINES.
HUNNHH
OOOFF
KRUNK
WHUMP
AHRR!

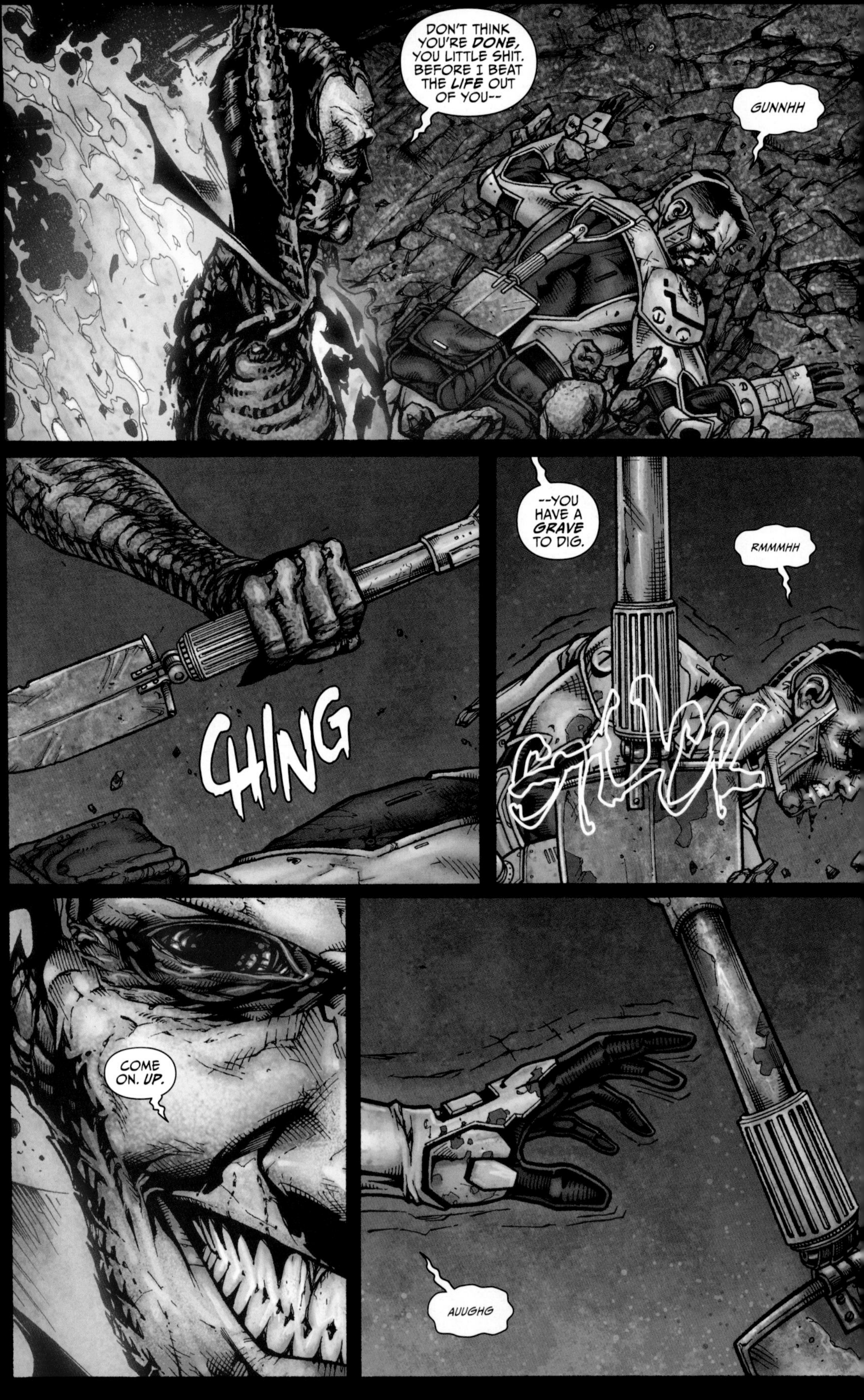
DON'T THINK YOU'RE *DONE,* YOU LITTLE SHIT. BEFORE I BEAT THE *LIFE* OUT OF YOU--
GUNNHH
CHING
--YOU HAVE A *GRAVE* TO DIG.
RMMMHH
SHUCK
COME ON. *UP.*
AUUGHG

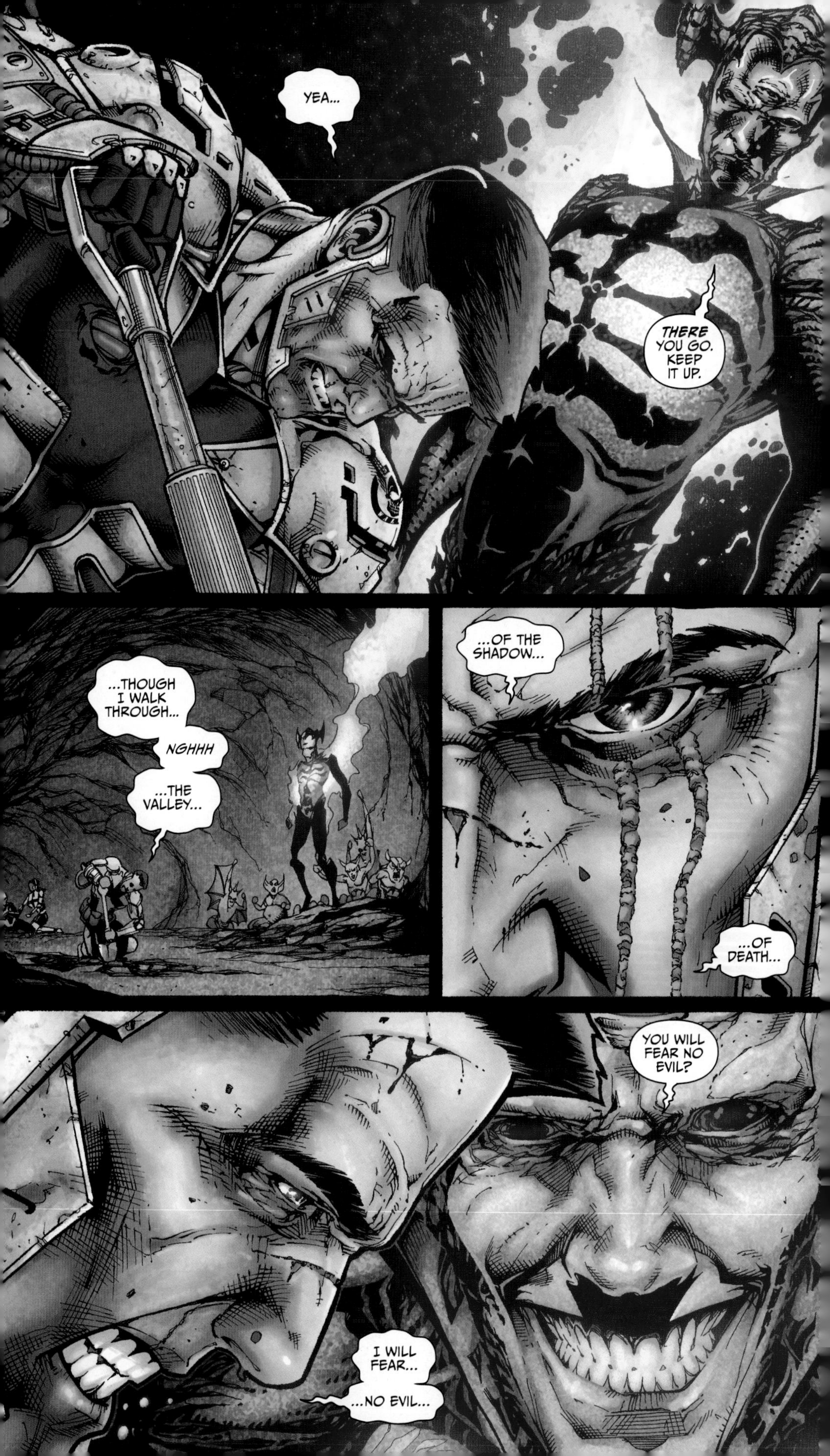
YEA...
THERE YOU GO. KEEP IT UP.
...THOUGH I WALK THROUGH...
NGHHH
...THE VALLEY...
...OF THE SHADOW...
...OF DEATH...
YOU WILL FEAR NO EVIL?
I WILL FEAR...
...NO EVIL...

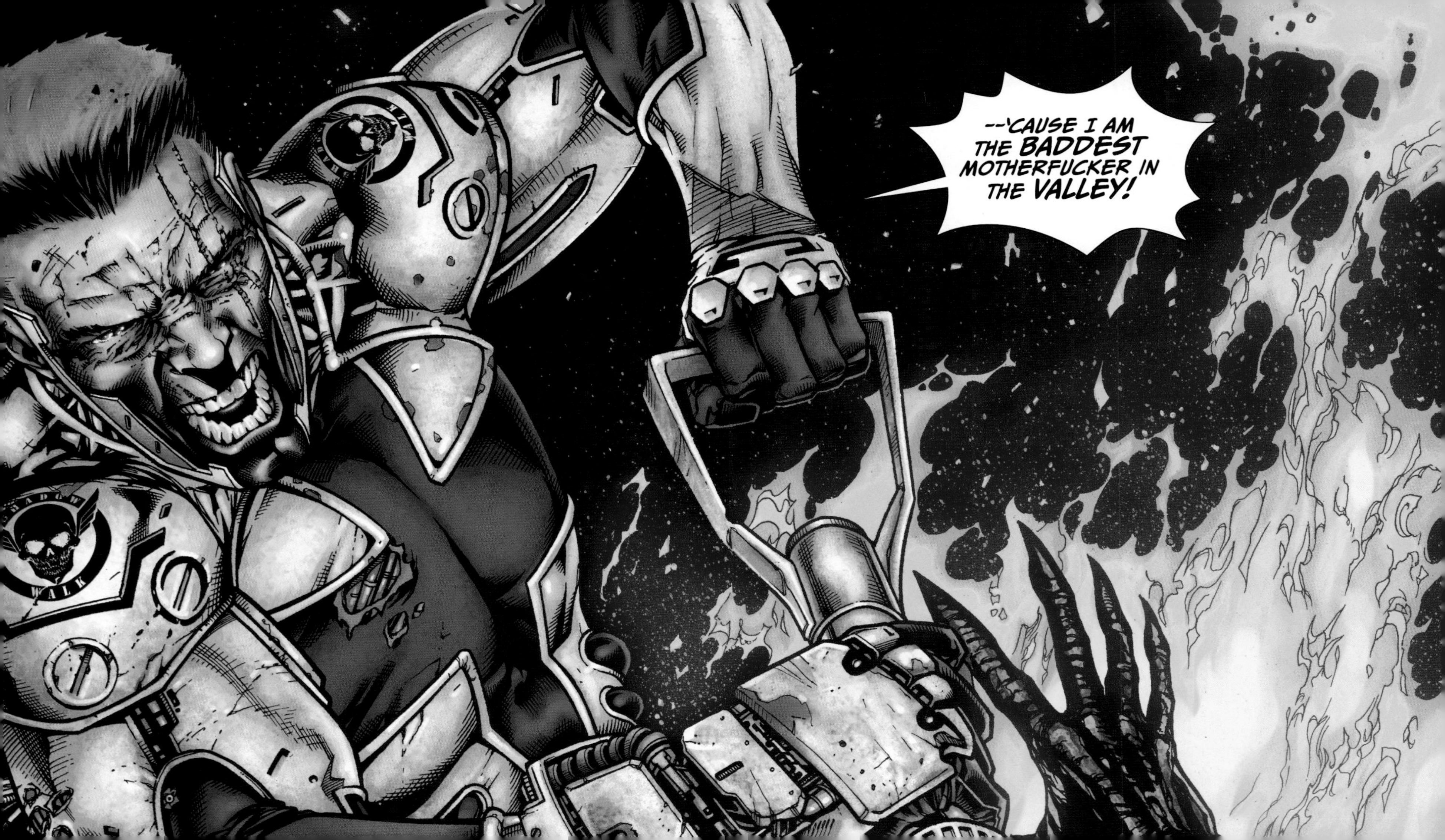
--'CAUSE I AM THE BADDEST MOTHERFUCKER IN THE VALLEY!
SHADOW WALK

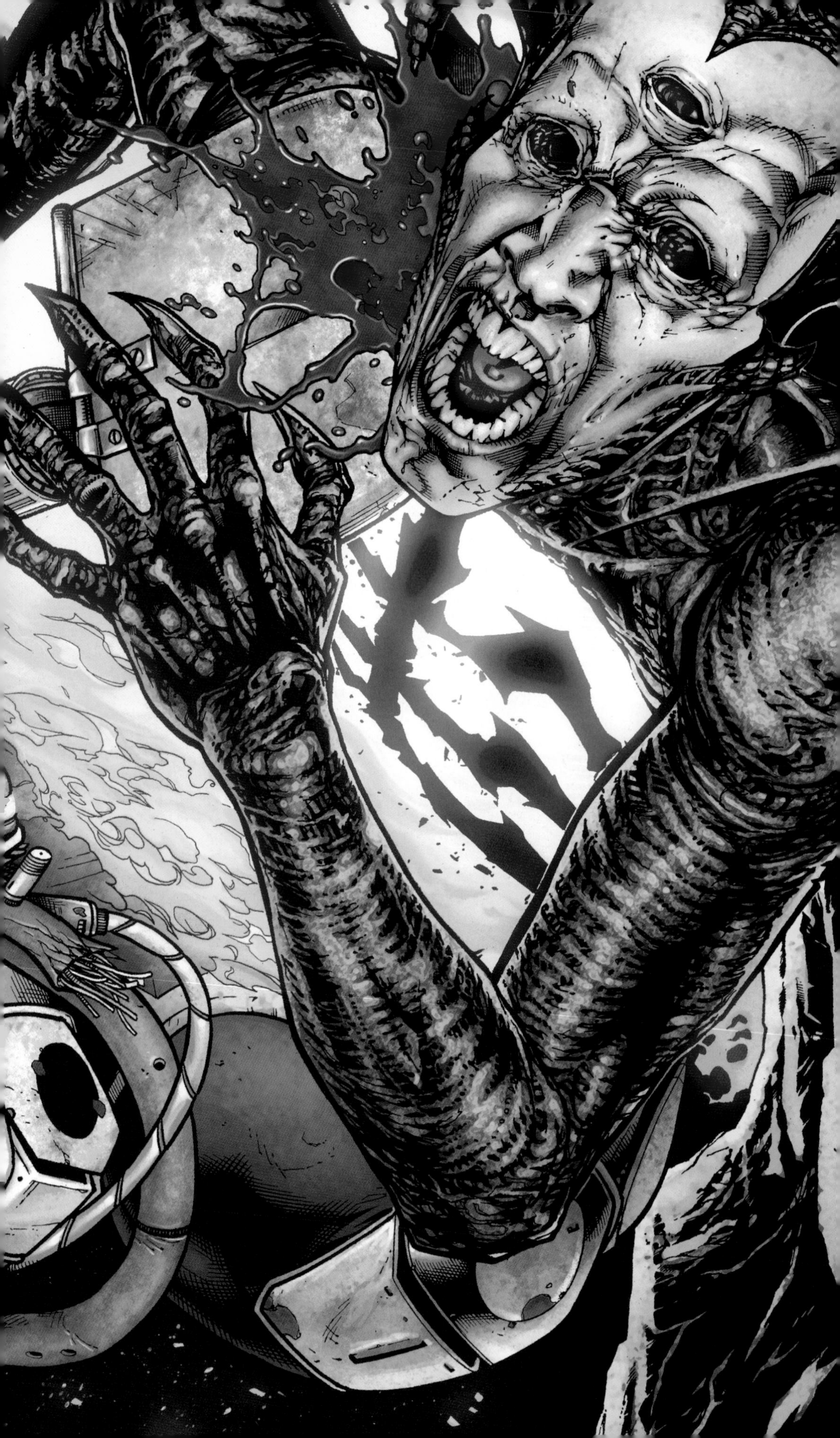

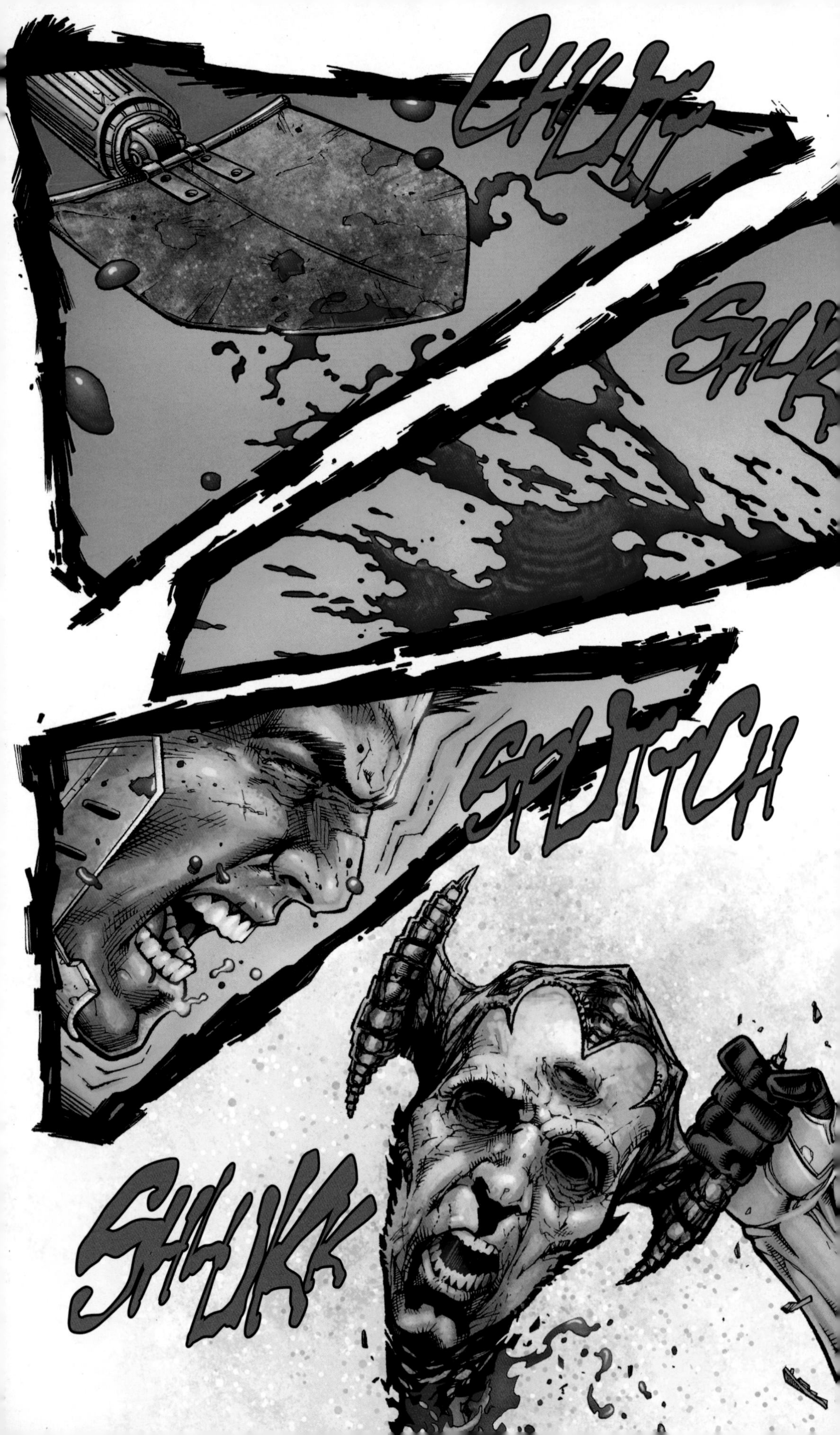
CHUK
SHUK
SPLUTCH
SHUKK

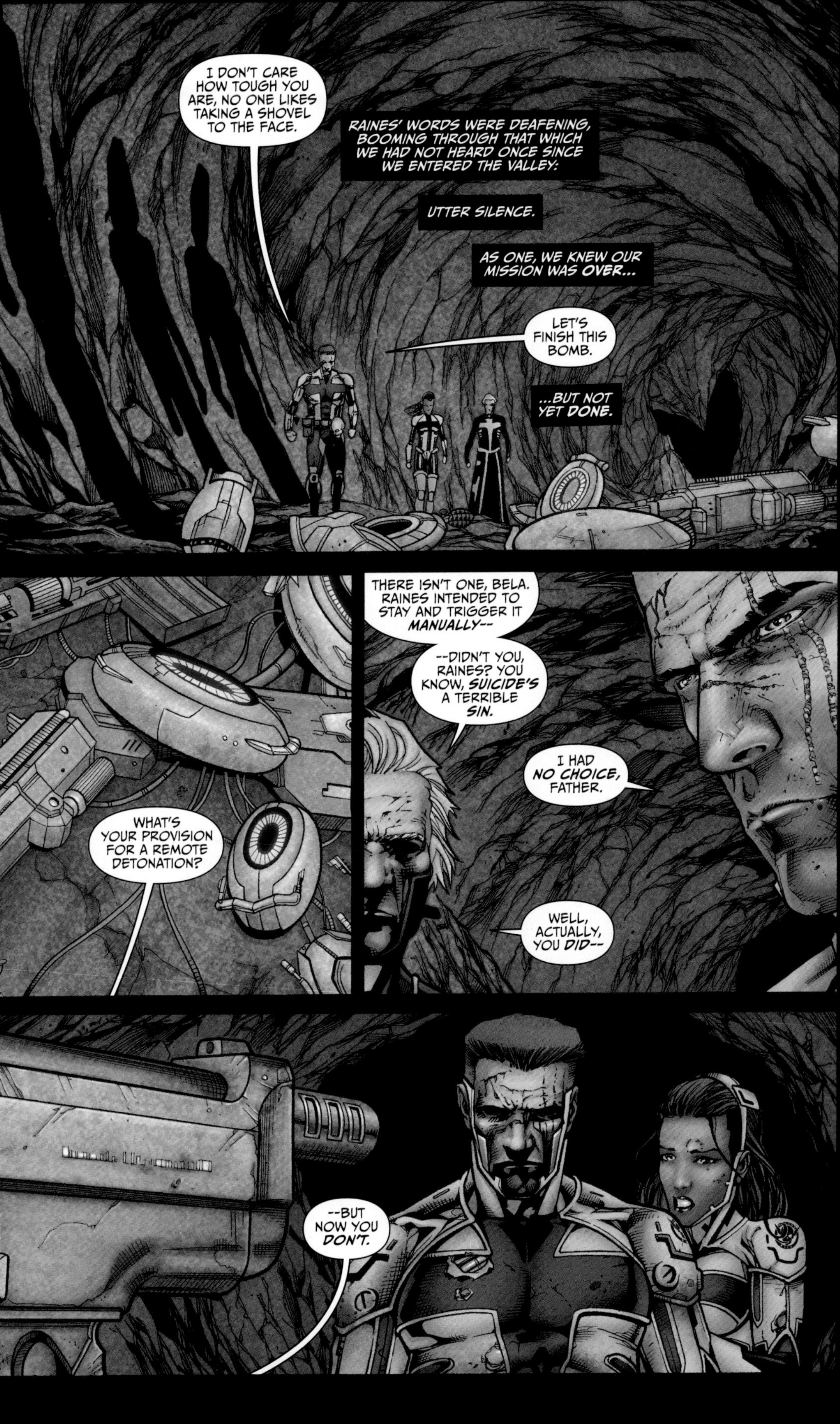
I DON'T CARE HOW TOUGH YOU ARE, NO ONE LIKES TAKING A SHOVEL TO THE FACE.
RAINES' WORDS WERE DEAFENING, BOOMING THROUGH THAT WHICH WE HAD NOT HEARD ONCE SINCE WE ENTERED THE VALLEY:
UTTER SILENCE.
AS ONE, WE KNEW OUR MISSION WAS OVER...
LET'S FINISH THIS BOMB.
...BUT NOT YET DONE.
WHAT'S YOUR PROVISION FOR A REMOTE DETONATION?
THERE ISN'T ONE, BELA. RAINES INTENDED TO STAY AND TRIGGER IT MANUALLY--
--DIDN'T YOU, RAINES? YOU KNOW, SUICIDE'S A TERRIBLE SIN.
I HAD NO CHOICE, FATHER.
WELL, ACTUALLY, YOU DID--
--BUT NOW YOU DON'T.

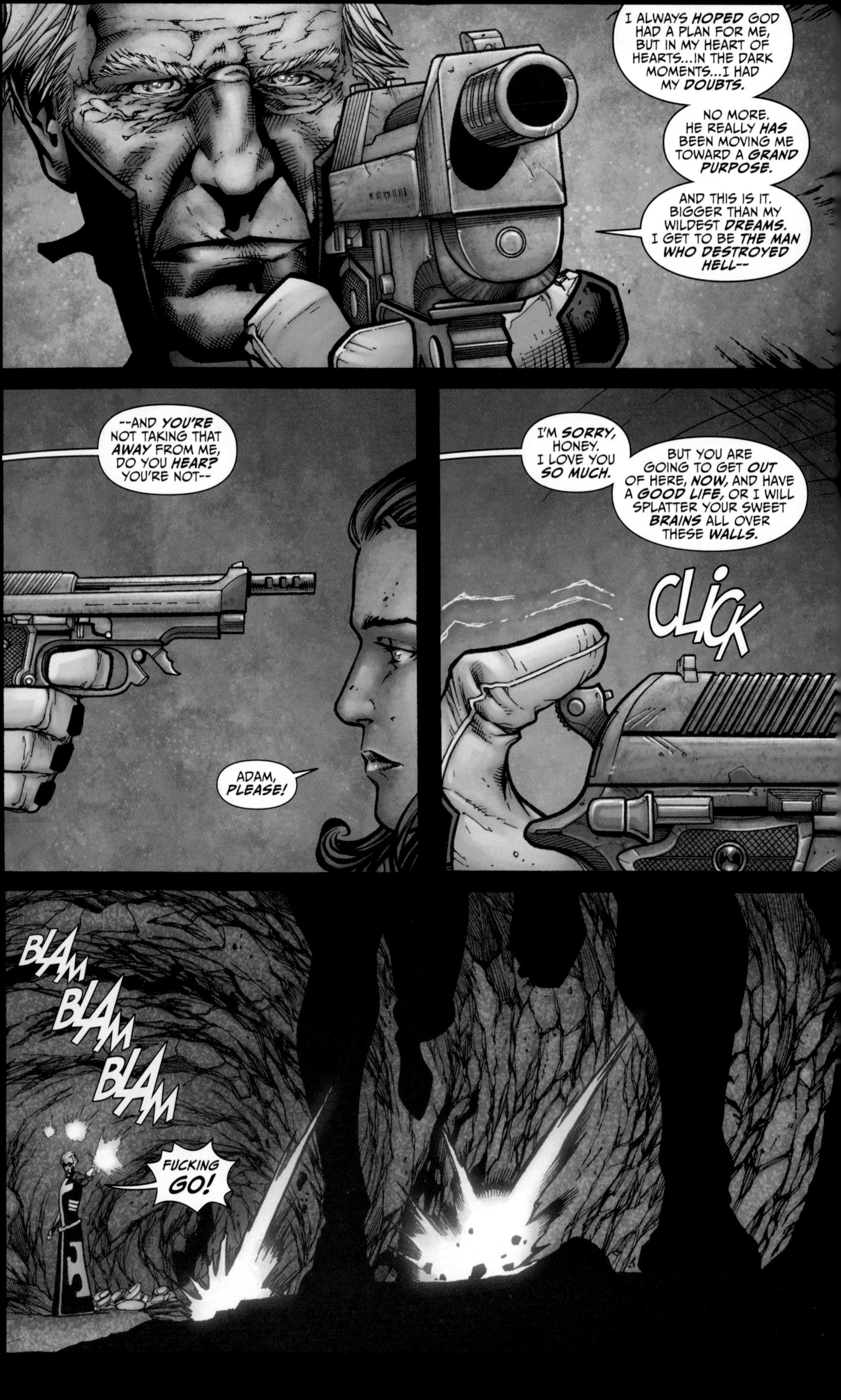

I ALWAYS HOPED GOD HAD A PLAN FOR ME, BUT IN MY HEART OF HEARTS...IN THE DARK MOMENTS...I HAD MY DOUBTS.
NO MORE. HE REALLY HAS BEEN MOVING ME TOWARD A GRAND PURPOSE.
AND THIS IS IT. BIGGER THAN MY WILDEST DREAMS. I GET TO BE THE MAN WHO DESTROYED HELL--
--AND YOU'RE NOT TAKING THAT AWAY FROM ME, DO YOU HEAR? YOU'RE NOT--
ADAM, PLEASE!
I'M SORRY, HONEY. I LOVE YOU SO MUCH.
BUT YOU ARE GOING TO GET OUT OF HERE, NOW, AND HAVE A GOOD LIFE, OR I WILL SPLATTER YOUR SWEET BRAINS ALL OVER THESE WALLS.
CLICK
BLAM BLAM BLAM
FUCKING GO!

ADAM!

YOU **HEARD** HIM! WE GET AS FAR AWAY AS WE CAN, AS **FAST** AS WE CAN!

NO!

COME ON. THERE'S NOTHING WE CAN DO FOR HIM.

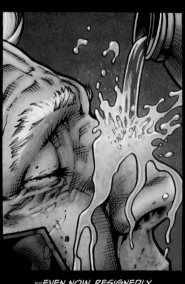

MY LORD GOD--

--EVEN NOW, RESIGNEDLY AND WILLINGLY--

--I ACCEPT THY HAND, WITH ALL ITS ANXIETIES--

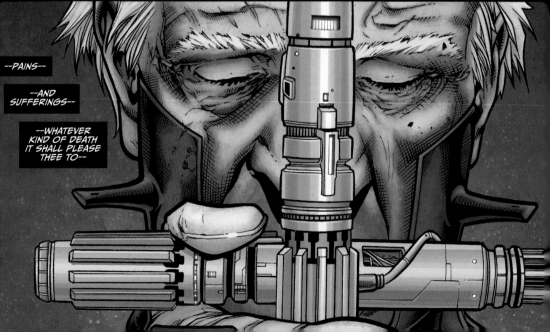

--PAINS--

--AND SUFFERINGS--

--WHATEVER KIND OF DEATH IT SHALL PLEASE THEE TO--

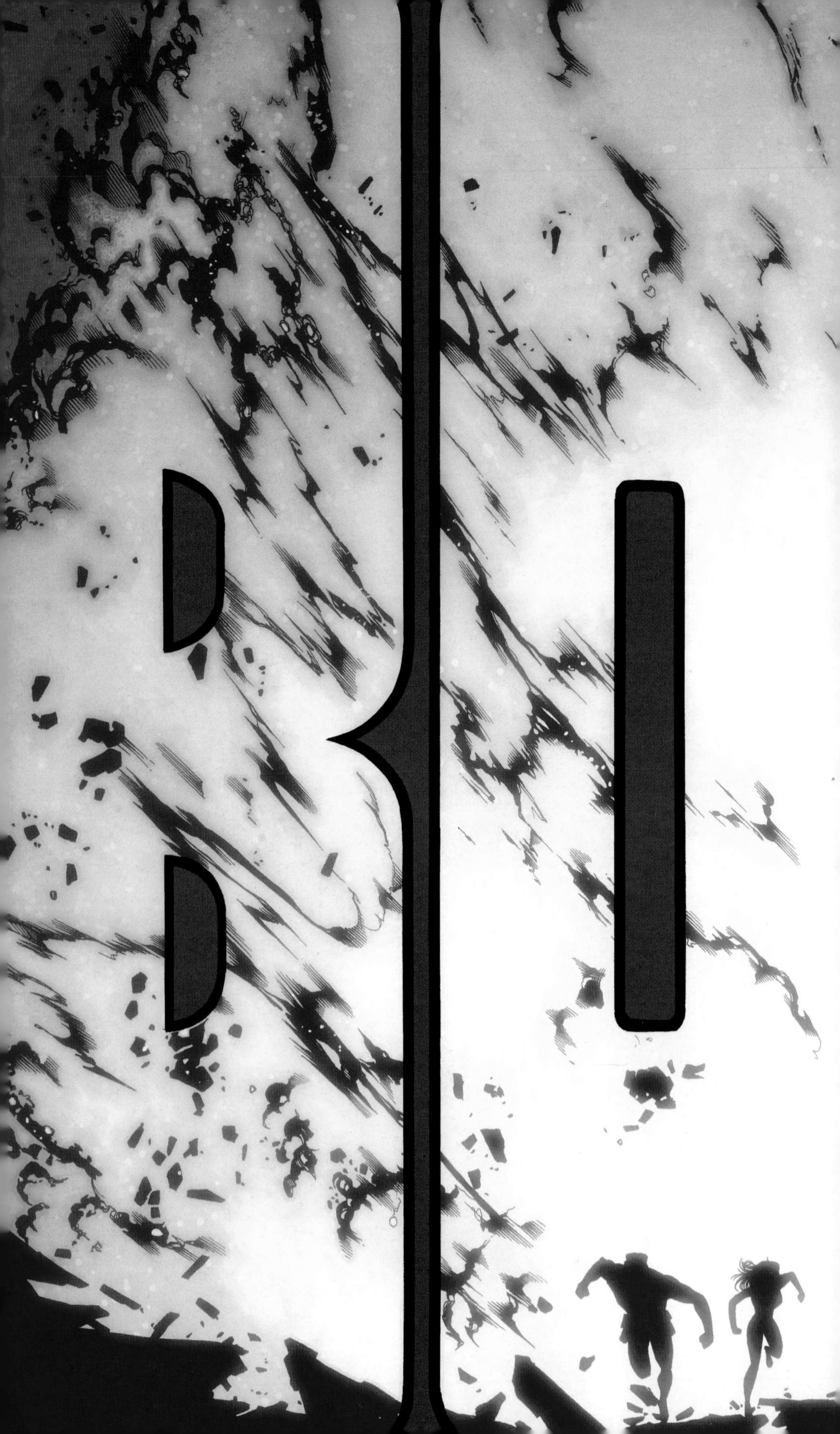

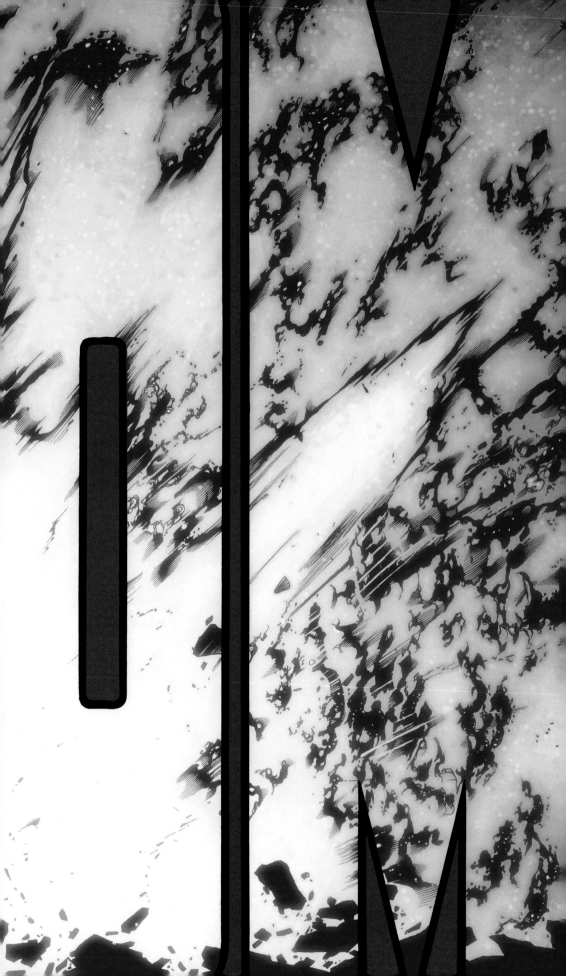

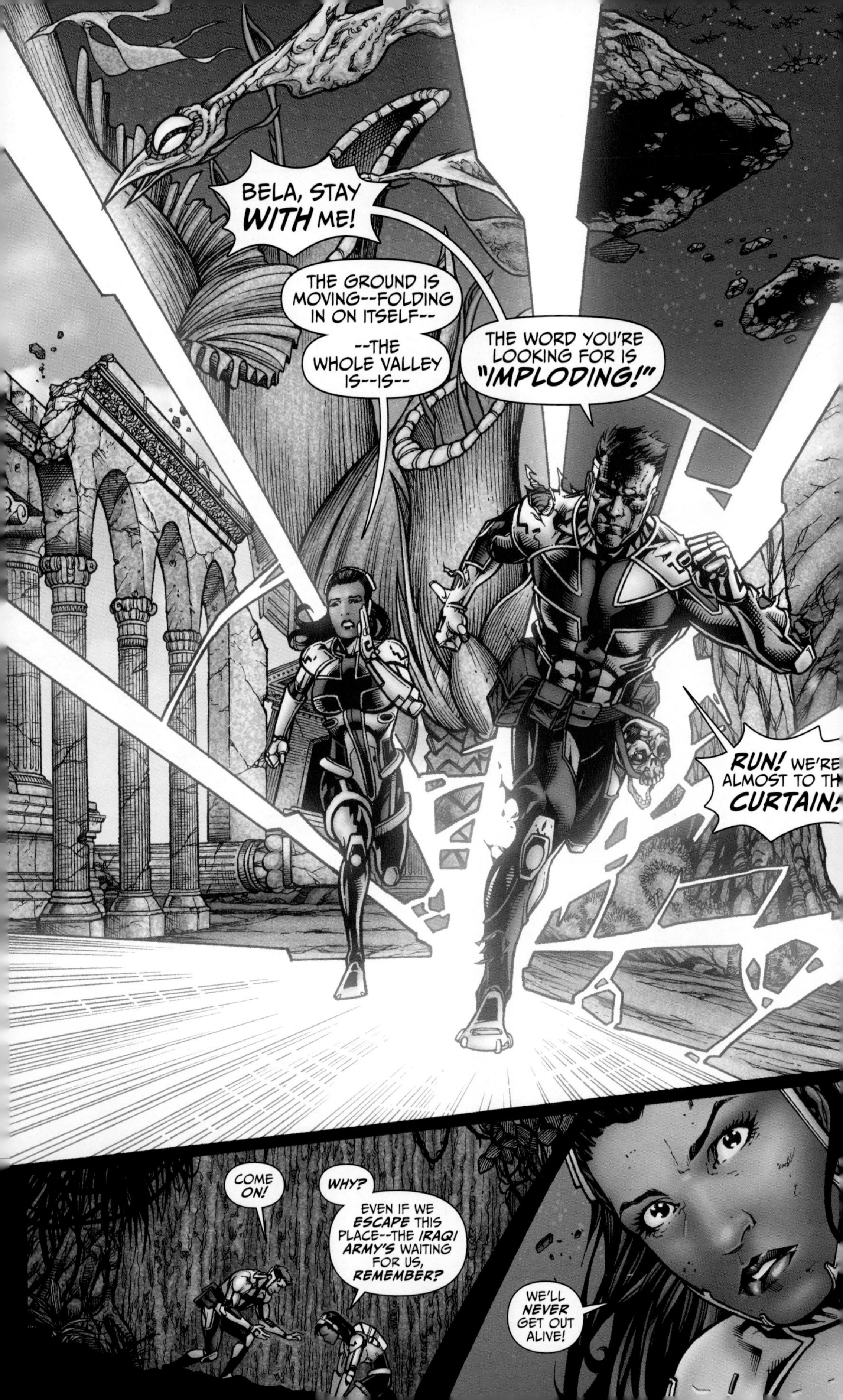
BELA, STAY WITH ME!
THE GROUND IS MOVING--FOLDING IN ON ITSELF--
--THE WHOLE VALLEY IS--IS--
THE WORD YOU'RE LOOKING FOR IS "IMPLODING!"
RUN! WE'RE ALMOST TO TH CURTAIN!
COME ON!
WHY?
EVEN IF WE ESCAPE THIS PLACE--THE IRAQI ARMY'S WAITING FOR US, REMEMBER?
WE'LL NEVER GET OUT ALIVE!

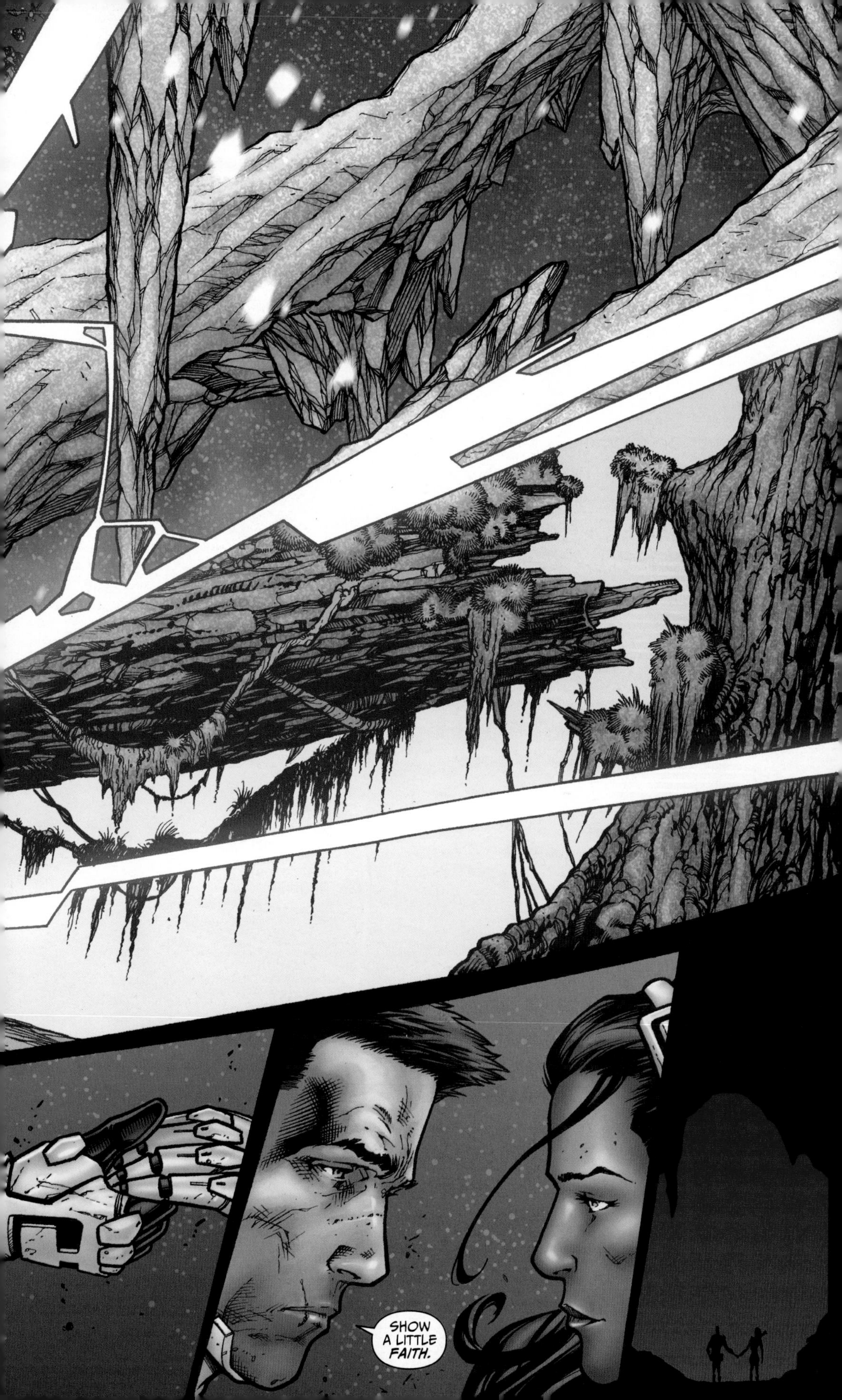
SHOW A LITTLE FAITH.

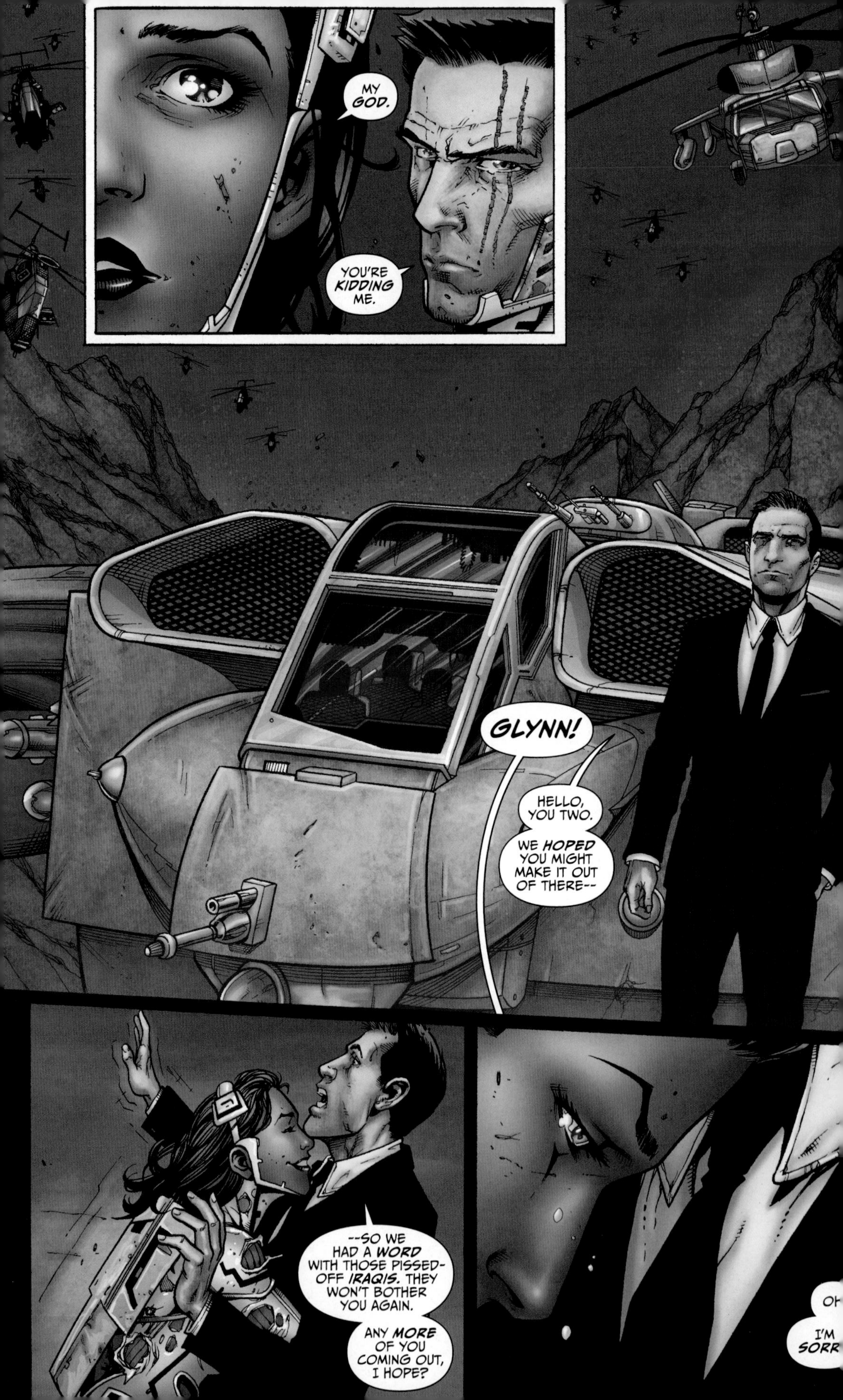
MY GOD.
YOU'RE KIDDING ME.
GLYNN!
HELLO, YOU TWO.
WE HOPED YOU MIGHT MAKE IT OUT OF THERE--
--SO WE HAD A WORD WITH THOSE PISSED-OFF IRAQIS. THEY WON'T BOTHER YOU AGAIN.
ANY MORE OF YOU COMING OUT, I HOPE?
I'M

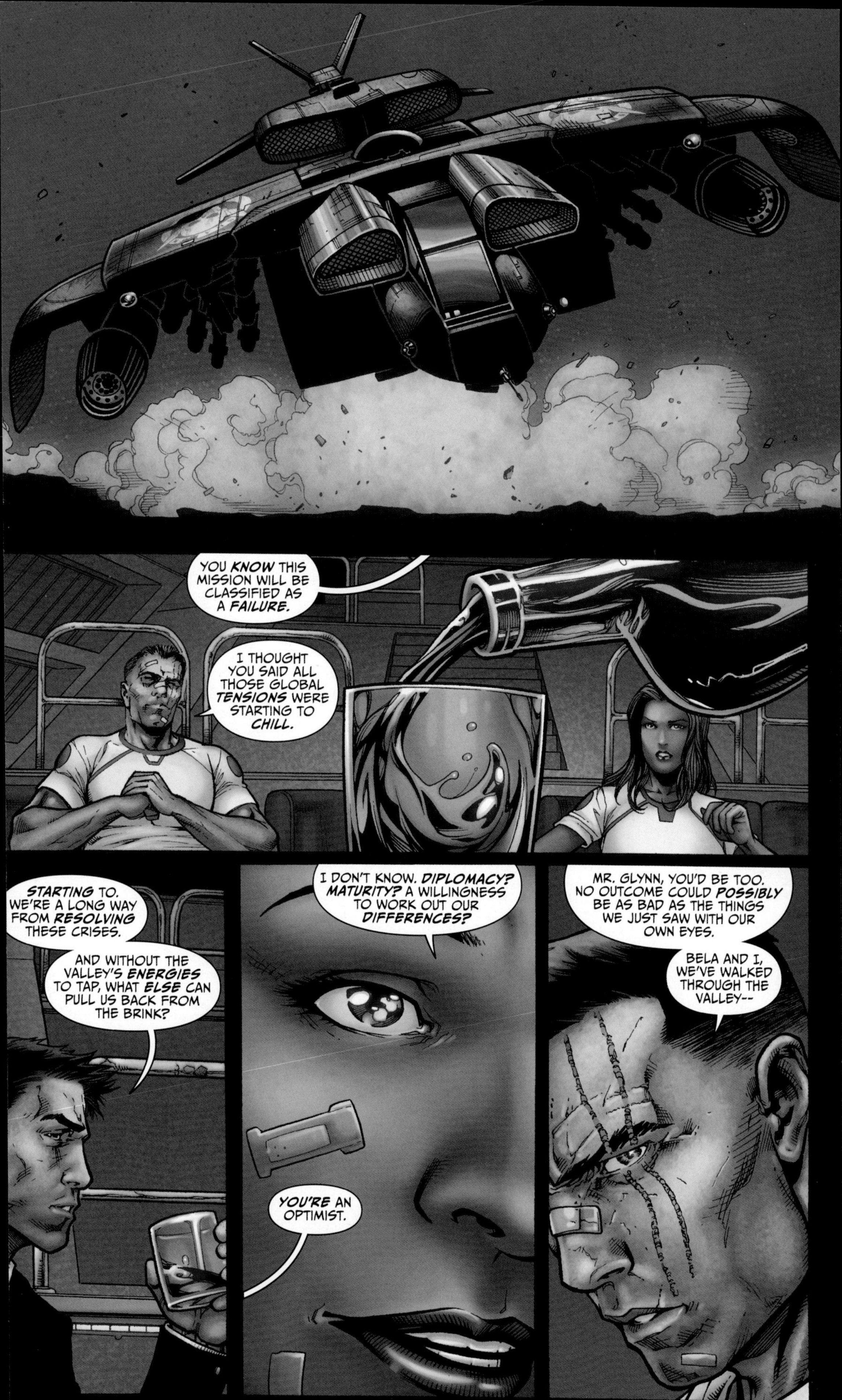
YOU KNOW THIS MISSION WILL BE CLASSIFIED AS A FAILURE.
I THOUGHT YOU SAID ALL THOSE GLOBAL TENSIONS WERE STARTING TO CHILL.
STARTING TO. WE'RE A LONG WAY FROM RESOLVING THESE CRISES.
AND WITHOUT THE VALLEY'S ENERGIES TO TAP, WHAT ELSE CAN PULL US BACK FROM THE BRINK?
I DON'T KNOW. DIPLOMACY? MATURITY? A WILLINGNESS TO WORK OUT OUR DIFFERENCES?
YOU'RE AN OPTIMIST.
MR. GLYNN, YOU'D BE TOO. NO OUTCOME COULD POSSIBLY BE AS BAD AS THE THINGS WE JUST SAW WITH OUR OWN EYES.
BELA AND I, WE'VE WALKED THROUGH THE VALLEY--

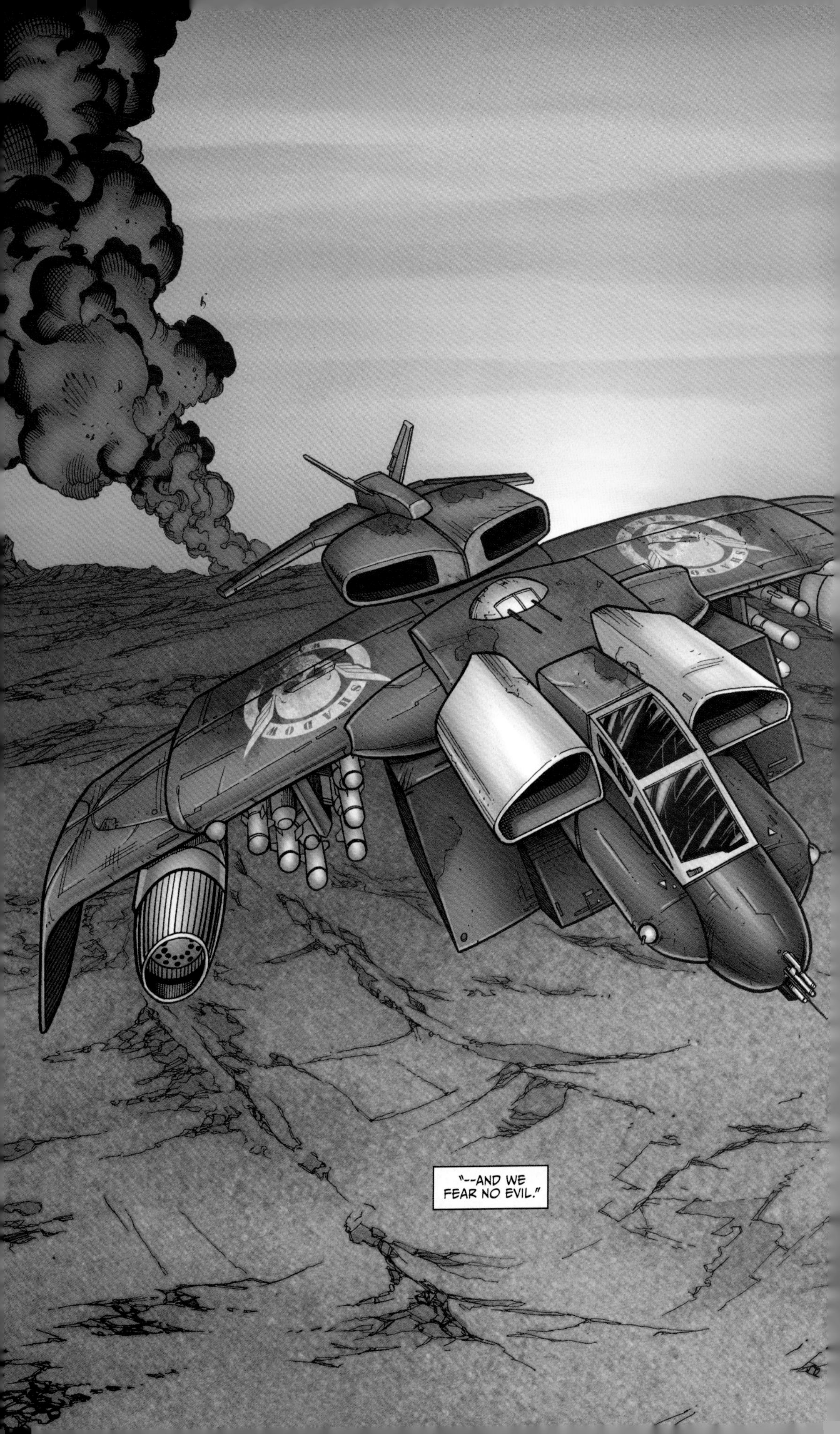
"--AND WE
FEAR NO EVIL."